You Create It Yourself

Journals & Letters on a Bowing Pilgrimage

by

Heng Sure Ph.D.
and
Heng Ch'au Ph.D.

Volume Four

Buddhist Text Translation Society
Dharma Realm Buddhist University
Dharma Realm Buddhist Association
Burlingame, California U.S.A.

You Create It Yourself
Journals & Letters on a Bowing Pilgrimage. Volume Four.

Published and translated by:

Buddhist Text Translation Society
1777 Murchison Drive, Burlingame, CA 94010-4504

© 2007   **Buddhist Text Translation Society**
         Dharma Realm Buddhist University
         Dharma Realm Buddhist Association

First edition 2007

16 15 14 13 12 11 10 09 08 07   12 11 10 9 8 7 6 5 4 3 2

ISBN 978-0-88139-909-7

Printed in Malaysia.

Note: Contents previously published under the title "With One Heart Bowing to the City of Ten Thousand Buddhas"

Addresses of the Dharma Realm Buddhist Association branches are listed at the back of this book.

   Library of Congress Cataloging-in-Publication Data

Heng Sure, 1949-
  You create it yourself / Heng Sure and Heng Ch'au.
    p. cm. -- (Journals & letters on a bowing pilgrimage ; v. 4)
  ISBN 978-0-88139-909-7 (hard cover : alk. paper)
  1. Spiritual life--Buddhism. 2. Heng Sure, 1949- 3. Heng Ch'au. 4.
Buddhist pilgrims and pilgrimages--California. I. Heng Ch'au. II.
Title. III. Series.

  BQ5625.H469 2007
  294.3'43509794--dc22

2007002697

Contents

Preface

Three steps, one bow – three steps along the side of the highway, then a bow to the ground, so that knees, elbows, hands, and forehead touch the earth, then rise, join the palms together, and take three more steps, then begin another bow. Hour after hour, day after day, for two and a half years, this was how they made their pilgrimage. In China, devout Buddhists sometimes undertake the arduous and prayerful practice of three steps, one bow, for the last few hundred yards of a journey to a sacred site. But this was California, and these two pilgrim-monks were young Americans. Dressed in their robes and sashes, carrying no money, armed with nothing but discipline and reverence, they walked and bowed 800 miles along the narrow shoulder of the Pacific Coast Highway. Progressing a mile a day, they bowed from downtown Los Angeles north along the coast, through Santa Barbara and along the Big Sur, through San Francisco and across the Golden Gate, then 100 miles farther north to the City of Ten Thousand Buddhas, a newly founded religious and educational center in Mendocino County. As they bowed, their prayer was that the world would be free of disaster, calamity, and war.

The silent monk in the lead was Heng Sure. Originally from Toledo, Ohio, he had found his way in 1974 to Gold Mountain Buddhist Monastery in San Francisco. There on a side street of the Mission District, an eminent Chinese monk, the Venerable Master

Hsuan Hua, was living in obscurity as he carried out his pioneering work of transplanting the Buddhist monastic tradition to the West. Moved by Master Hua's virtue and wisdom, Heng Sure joined other young Americans in taking a monastic name and the full ordination of a Buddhist monk.

During his subsequent studies, Heng Sure read of a bowing pilgrimage made in the 1880's by the Venerable Hsu Yun ("Empty Cloud"), who was the most distinguished Chinese monastic of his generation. Master Yun had bowed every third step across the breadth of China; it had taken him five years. Heng Sure knew that Master Yun had been patriarch of the Wei Yang Lineage of the Chan School, and he knew that his own abbot and teacher, Master Hua, was the current patriarch, having received the lineage transmission from Master Yun in 1949. Inspired by this close connection, Heng Sure asked Master Hua if he could undertake his own pilgrimage of three steps, one bow. Master Hua approved, but said, "Wait."

Heng Sure had to wait a year. What he needed, Master Hua said, was the right companion and protector. It was to be Heng Chau. Originally from Appleton, Wisconsin, Heng Chau had come to Berkeley to study martial arts, and he had become an adept in several traditions. When his tai-chi teacher finally told him, "Chan is higher than any martial art," Heng Chau crossed the Bay to study at Gold Mountain Monastery. He soon heard about Heng Sure's vow, and he asked if he could bow with him. Within a week Heng Chau took novice precepts and made a formal vow to bow beside Heng Sure, as well as handle the logistics of cooking, cleaning, setting up camp, and talking with strangers.

Thus the pilgrimage began. Master Hua saw them off as they left Gold Wheel Monastery in Los Angeles on 7 May 1977. To Heng Chau, the martial artist, he said, "You can't use your martial arts on the pilgrimage. Heng Sure's vow is to seek an end to calamities, disasters and war; so how can you yourselves be involved in violence? If either of you fights – or even indulges in anger – you will no longer be my disciples." For protection from the dangers of the

road, Master Hua instructed them to practice instead the four uncon-
ditional attitudes of the Bodhisattva: kindness, compassion, joy, and
equanimity. It was by no means the last time that the two bowing
monks would need their teacher's advice.

On the road, the two pilgrims followed their monastic discipline
strictly – eating one vegetarian meal a day; never going indoors,
sleeping sitting up in the old 1956 Plymouth station wagon that
served as their shelter. In the evenings after a day of bowing they
studied the Avatamsaka Sutra (Flower Adornment Sutra) by the light
of an oil lamp. They translated passages into English and attempted
to put into practice the principles of the text in their day-to-day
experiences on the road, as their teacher had encouraged them to do.
The monks guarded their concentration by avoiding newspapers, by
leaving the car radio silent, and by keeping to a strict meditation
schedule. Heng Sure held a vow of silence for the entire journey, and
it became Heng Chau's job to talk with the many people who stopped
along the highway with questions. Occasionally the visitors were
hostile, and some threatened violence, but the greater number were
curious, and often the curious became the monks' protectors,
bringing them food and supplies until the monks had bowed their
way out of range.

Everything important that happened on the highway – the
mistakes and the growth, the trials and remarkable encounters, the
dangers and the insights, the hard work with the body and in the mind
– the pilgrims reported in letters to Master Hua. He would answer in
person by visiting them from time to time, giving them indispensable
spiritual guidance, admonishment, humor, and timely instructions –
both lofty and mundane. These letters are the contents of this volume.
They were not written with the thought that they would be published.
Rather, they were a medium in which the two monks attempted to
speak to their teacher as openly and sincerely as possible about their
experience on the road. As such, the letters preserve an unadorned
account of an authentic spiritual journey.

The Venerable Master Hsuan Hua

A Brief Portrait

"I have had many names," he once said, "and all of them are false." In his youth in Manchuria, he was known as "the Filial Son Bai"; as a young monk he was An Tzu ("Peace and Kindness"); later, in Hong Kong, he was Tu Lun ("Wheel of Rescue"); finally, in America, he was Hsuan Hua, which might be translated as "one who proclaims the principles of transformation." To his thousands of disciples across the world, he was always also "Shr Fu" – "Teacher."

Born in 1918 into a peasant family in a small village on the Manchurian plain, Master Hua was the youngest of ten children. He attended school for only two years, during which he studied the Chinese Classics and committed much of them to memory. As a young teenager, he opened a free school for both children and adults. He also began then one of his lifelong spiritual practices: reverential bowing. Outdoors, in all weathers, he would make over 800 prostrations daily, as a profound gesture of his respect for all that is good and sacred in the universe.

He was nineteen when his mother died, and for three years he honored her memory by sitting in meditation in a hut beside her grave. It was during this time that he made a resolve to go to America to teach the principles of wisdom. As a first step, at the end of the period of mourning, he entered San Yuan Monastery, took as his teacher Master Chang Chih, and subsequently received the full ordination of a Buddhist monk at Pu To Mountain. For ten years he devoted himself to study of the Buddhist scriptural tradition and to mastery of both the Esoteric and the Chan Schools of Chinese Buddhism. He had also read and contemplated the scriptures of Christianity, Taoism, and Islam. Thus, by the age of thirty, he had already established through his own experience the four major imperatives of his later ministry in America: the primacy of the monastic tradition; the essential role of moral education; the need for Buddhists to ground themselves in traditional spiritual practice and authentic scripture; and, just as essential, the importance and the power of ecumenical respect and understanding.

In 1948, Master Hua traveled south to meet the Venerable Hsu Yun, who was then already 108 years old and China's most distinguished spiritual teacher. From him Master Hua received the patriarchal transmission in the Wei Yang Lineage of the Chan School. Master Hua subsequently left China for Hong Kong. He spent a dozen years there, first in seclusion, then later as a teacher at three monasteries which he founded.

Finally, in 1962, he went to the United States, at the invitation of several of his Hong Kong disciples who had settled in San Francisco. By 1968, Master Hua had established the Buddhist Lecture Hall in a loft in San Francisco's Chinatown, and there he began giving nightly lectures, in Chinese, to an audience of young Americans. His texts were the major scriptures of the Mahayana. In 1969, he astonished the monastic community of Taiwan by sending there, for final ordination, two American women and three American men, all five of them fully trained as novices, fluent in Chinese and conversant with Buddhist scripture. During subsequent years, the Master trained and oversaw the ordination of hundreds of monks and nuns who came to California from every part of the world to study with him. These monastic disciples now teach in the 28 temples, monasteries and convents that the Master founded in the United States, Canada, and several Asian countries.

Although he understood English well and spoke it when it was necessary, Master Hua almost always lectured in Chinese. His aim was to encourage Westerners to learn Chinese, so that they could become translators, not merely of his lectures, but of the major scriptural texts of the Buddhist Mahayana. His intent was realized. So far, the Buddhist Text Translation Society, which he founded, has issued over 130 volumes of translation of the major Sutras, together with a similar number of commentaries, instructions, and stories from the Master's teaching.

As an educator, Master Hua was tireless. From 1968 to the mid 1980's he gave as many as a dozen lectures a week, and he traveled extensively on speaking tours. At the City of Ten Thousand Buddhas in Talmage, California, he established formal training programs for monastics and for laity; elementary and secondary schools for boys and for girls; and Dharma Realm Buddhist University, together with the University's branch, the Institute for World Religions, in Berkeley.

Throughout his life the Master taught that the basis of spiritual practice is moral practice. Of his monastic disciples he required strict purity, and he encouraged his lay disciples to adhere to the five precepts of the Buddhist laity. Especially in his later years, Confucian texts were often the subject of his lectures, and he held to the Confucian teaching that the first business of education is moral education. He identified six rules of conduct as the basis of communal life at the City of Ten Thousand Buddhas; the six rules prohibit contention, covetousness, self-seeking, selfishness, profiting at the expense of the community, and false speech. He asked that the children in the schools he had founded recite these prohibitions every morning before class. In general, although he admired the independent-mindedness of Westerners, he believed that they lacked ethical balance and needed that stabilizing sense of public morality which is characteristic of the East.

The Venerable Master insisted on ecumenical respect, and he delighted in inter-faith dialogue. He stressed commonalities in religious traditions – above all their emphasis on proper conduct, on compassion, and on wisdom. He was also a pioneer in building bridges between different Buddhist national traditions. He often brought monks from Theravada countries to California to share the duties of transmitting the precepts of ordination. He invited Catholic priests to celebrate the mass in the Buddha-Hall at the City of Ten Thousand Buddhas, and he developed a late-in-life friendship with Paul Cardinal Yu-Bin, the exiled leader of the Catholic Church in China and Taiwan. He once told the Cardinal: "You can be a Buddhist among the Catholics, and I'll be a Catholic among Buddhists." To the Master, the essential teachings of all religions could be summed up in a single word: wisdom.

* * *

Bowing between winter storms near Morro Bay

Devoted laypeople come out to join the
bowing monks throughout the pilgrimage

You Create It Yourself

* * * * * * * *

February 1978

Heng Chau • February 20, 1978
An untapped natural resource

John Blades, a tour guide from nearby Hearst San Simeon State Historical Monument, stopped early this A.M. on his motorcycle.

"I just wanted to find out what kind of people you are. What you're doing takes real character and patience, and I've found these are the best kind of people to be around," he said. John took off his motorcycle helmet and continued.

"My job is pretty good because the people I work with are open-minded, a 'bunch of crazies.' We keep each other outgoing and active. I was pretty introverted when I got out of high school, but Air Force, college, and a few other experiences changed that soon. I'm really interested in what you're doing. I haven't found my true groove yet."

> "They perfect the Bodhisattvas' path. They constantly extend their hands in preparation for vast giving. Their steps are peaceful as they travel about – heroic, courageous, without fear."
>
> Avatamsaka Sutra
> Ten Transferences Chapter

The world is full of people like John whose hands are "constantly extended for vast giving;" people who want to do something worthwhile and of benefit to humankind. They want to expand the limits of their own potential and give heroically to the cause of peace.

But there's so little available. John went into the Air Force, not because he wanted to be soldier, but out of a desire to explore himself and the world. He wanted to reach out and travel. There's a bulging reservoir of courage and compassion in the young people of the world, an untapped natural resource waiting for the "right groove" to come along.

Why not turn all the bombers, military cargo, jets, and battleships into "people ships" that could fly Medical-Disaster Relief Corps of trained young people anywhere in the world for any emergency? Or create an Environmental Corps who are trained to work in all aspects of clean air, water, and food. There could be a Senior Citizen Brigade, specializing in facilitating natural ways to cope with problems of housing, health care, dying, and loneliness. Or a Children's Corps that provided crisis intervention for families, well trained to deal with child abuse, delinquencies, learning disabilities, etc. The potential is endless.

Heng Sure
Good that you didn't take a shortcut

Voices In My Ear. Bad Advisor Defeated!

A little yinny voice in my ear wanted to break up my practices last night. "Stop sitting. You're really tired." (I was.) "Don't force it. You need sleep. You were in lotus for evening recitation, that's enough. You've got a good sate, why hurt yourself?"

I didn't like the sound of that voice. So I kept my legs in place for the scheduled minimum – one hour of concentrated sitting *no matter what*. Had to do the 42 Hands and Eyes twice because invasion by bugs prevented usual recitation of Hands at noon. No problem.

Voice spoke again: "Just do the Hands, then quit. That's enough." I came really close to stopping but a thought of the

Master's kindness towards me gave me strength. I said to myself, "Hang in there, Kuo Chen. Only a little longer and you can be true. No falseness! Repay your debt."

Great fire and pain raged in my body as the little voice wheedled on. I couldn't cut it out – so I chose not to listen to it. Just as the pain got really unbearable I heard in my other ear a verse from the evening Sutra lecture.

"I will take on limitless sufferings on behalf of living beings. I will use my body to ransom them from pain and cause them to be happy and peaceful."

Avatamsaka Sutra
Ten Transferences Chapter

How could I not sit still? Rriiinng! Period over. As I got into my sleeping bag, I heard another voice – the Master's – say, "If the causal ground is not true, the result is confused." Good that you didn't take a shortcut, Kuo Chen. You've got to go through all the work ahead, not around it. Amitabha.

Heng Chau • February 21, 1978
Straight and wholesome

Cold ocean fog from dawn to dusk. It's like bowing in empty space. Suddenly there's a sound as a blur of colored metal comes flying by and disappears into the silent, cotton-thick cloud all around us. The conditioned and temporary nature of all things stands out. Everything appears and disappears before our eyes.

Man: What has attracted your attention mostly so far on this trip?

Monk: The bowing.

Man: Have you seen some unusual things and had strange experiences?

Monk: Everything's made from the mind.

Man: *All* made from the mind, really!?

Monk: When our minds are thinking strange and unusual thoughts, then we see unusual things and have strange experiences. When our minds are straight and wholesome, then what we experience is straight and wholesome.

Man: But don't you notice a lot of other things? I mean isn't your attention drawn to what's around you?

Monk: The whole idea is to 'return the light and illumine within.' Sure, we notice things and get distracted, but this is the cause of confusion. Our work is to hold our minds to a single condition so we aren't so muddled and blown around by everything. Then the world's a little more peaceful.

Man: That's really interesting. I never thought about it before.

> "His mind is not chaotic or scattered. It is neither turbid or base. His mind has only a single condition: it is wholesome, still and fixed... His mind is good at dwelling peace."
>
> Avatamsaka Sutra
> Ten Transferences Chapter

> "Form itself is emptiness; emptiness itself is form."
>
> Prajna Paramita Sutra

Heng Sure
The highest form of martial arts

The Dharma Protector Speakers.

"Here we are in the middle of the Sutra – it's all around us and we can't see it. Our teacher does everything to get us to wake up and we still stumble on, unaware of the totality of states. It's all there within the Sutra, the entirety of the mind. But the only way to reach it is by practicing perfect virtue.

"Ch'an is the highest form of martial arts. You don't make any mistakes. Self-defense is needed only when you've made a mistake and you have to fight your karma.

"Martial arts make you feel good, but I feel best after a good, hard period of Ch'an. Plus when you get good, you can be comfortable and totally free. You'll never see miles on martial artists the way you will on a Ch'an person."

"The Bodhisattva considers and contemplates all sounds… He is skillful in his awareness of the marks of sounds… He knows that all sounds do not exist, in fact, they cannot be gotten at."

Avatamsaka Sutra
Ten Practices Chapter

Heng Sure • February 22, 1978
A Buddhist Flora

Dear Shr Fu,
Back to the Nature.

Best wishes from Three Steps, One Bow to the Venerable Abbot and the Great Assembly. We are in Harmony. Harmony, California, population 18. Halfway between Cayucos and Cambria. Every day the hills get greener, the sky looks bluer, the people get fewer, the morning fog grows thicker. The landscape includes long snakes and long-haired cattle on winter forage. A passing biology major from Cal Poly confirms that what Heng Chau saw on Sunday *was* a mountain lion.

On the advice of a Dharma-protector we have begun to eat the green weeds that grow beside the road. Gathering wild food is a good dharma. It's free, like the Buddha-nature. Before we discover that the Buddhas of all time and space come from the mind, we run all over the Dharma Realm looking for the Path. Then we hear it's been inside our true mind all along – all we have to do is uncover it. Ah! Wild food is the same. The fields look full of weeds until someone says, "Hey! That weed you're standing on tastes like the finest supermarket greens, better, even, 'cause it's free and fresh and abundant." Ah! the field of weeds becomes a nutritious garden. The challenge now to the cultivator is to not think of his stomach every time he looks at the ground. Three Steps, One Bow has given us a new appreciation of much that we have overlooked or taken for granted. It deserves mentioning as an inexhaustible storehouse of food for pilgrims and mountain hermits of the future. We don't trip out into extended food-gathering – we can identify five or six varieties of plants that grow nearly everywhere. In five minutes we can pick a potful (watch *carefully* for insects – this is their world, too!), then wash and boil them for two minutes. Done. What's more, we have been looking for more bitter foods to dispel "fire-energy" that comes with meditation. Dandelions and mustard green have just enough natural bitterness to drop the fire without being too bitter to swallow.

Our lives grow more natural and more simple as we bow away the artificial views and habits we learned over the years. The natural and simple truth: all conditioned things will die. Our bodies are temporary unions of earth, air, fire, and water. No amount of natural food will keep the body healthy when it comes time to die. The back-to-nature movement is on the right track, but if it stops with roadside weeds and granola, it hasn't gone back far enough. Buddhist disciples are part of the truly important movement in the modern world – the "back-to-the-'true' nature" movement. The true self-nature does not perish; it is our birthright as living beings. By cultivating the Path that all Buddhas have walked, we return to the biggest Nature there is.

"The 'wind and light of our original ground' have a special and wonderfully delightful flavor that is quite inexhaustible. If we wish to try its taste we must simply purify our minds."

Water and Mirror Reflections
by Venerable Master Hua

You might say the Master is talking about the Bodhi plant – the one we most want to identify, eat, and share with all our Dharma friends. This plant is not in the edible-plant field-guides, because it's special – it grows on the mind-ground. Our teacher shows us where to look, how to recognize it, and how to harvest it. Here is the way it could be listed in *A Buddhist Flora*:

Species: Enlightenment.
Variety: wonderful.
Habitat: within the true heart of all living beings.
Distribution: throughout the Dharma Realm.
Season: eternal.
Description: see Flower Garland Sutra for references.
Wonderful beyond words.

More Car Stories.

Our Plymouth cave-on-wheels is not an ordinary car. We suspect it is a dragon, maybe a transformed disciple of the Master's who volunteered to work on Three Steps, One Bow. The car is always protecting our Dharma and speaking it for us, too. Some nights under the bright moon it just plain looks like a dragon with a beard and tail. It should have collapsed a dozen times by now, but it keeps right on rolling. Once during the heavy storms in early February, the car refused to start. We were parked right on the highway shoulder. The gas station man couldn't start the dragon – nothing worked. The car sat tight while we bowed in ankle-deep puddles. We had planned to drive into Morro Bay that morning to dry the gear out at a laundromat, but no dice – the car was wet. Suddenly a familiar blue bus appeared beside us with three golden figures strapped to the seats. It was Upasaka Kuo Tsai, who had come down to take us and the three Buddha images to L.A. Had we gone to the laundromat he never would have found us. "Well, let's give the car one more try." Vroom! It started like a champ and away we went. "Do you mean to say the car knew someone was coming and deliberately held you there for the rendezvous?" "Well, how else do you explain it?" There are all sorts of strange marvels in the world – countless, inexhaustible, measureless, and unfathomable – and they all proceed from the zero in the mind. How inconceivable! Amitabha!

Disciple Guo Chen (Heng Sure)
bows in respect

Heng Chau • February 22, 1978
There are no shortcuts or bargains

Quiet day of bowing in open country. Spring winds waving the tall grass and cleansing our minds.

Bowing thoughts…

Ch'an, Dhyana in Sanskrit, or Zen in Japanese, is the practice of "still contemplation." It's the furnace for smelting the pure gold from one's own self-nature. All the raw materials are already in our hands. Set your mind and will to it, maintain the pure precepts and one is certain to smash through the dark coverings and obtain the fruit of enlightenment.

All things naturally return to the source in their own way and time. When you find the path with true heart a thousand horses couldn't keep you away; if you're not ready, a thousand horses couldn't pull you across. We walk home by ourselves; others, even Buddhas, can only show the way.

> "Where was there ever a man of wisdom who got to see
> and hear the Buddha without cultivation of pure vows, and
> walking the same path the Buddha walked?"
>
> Avatamsaka Sutra – Verse in Praise in
> the Tushita Heaven Palace Chapter

So although all beings have the Buddha-nature, all are not Buddhas. We are "gems in the rough" that need to be rubbed, ground, and polished before we shine like a jewel. Without hard work we are just uncut stones, stuck in the mud, buried in the earth.

There are no shortcuts or bargains. Walking the Buddha's path is an inch for an inch. Heng Sure and I are learning about the truth of self-reliance: out here we get back exactly what we put out. There's no one to lean on and nothing to climb on for a free ride. That's just how it really is.

> "It is just like gold which, although it is found in metallic compounds, when properly smelted according to the method, separates from its impurities and becomes progressively more bright and pure. So too is the Bodhisattva dwelling on the Ground of Leaving Defilement like this."
>
> Avatamsaka Sutra
> Ten Grounds Chapter, Second Ground

Sincerely doing our work we should be mirrors, not sponges. When things arise, respond and reflect; when they are gone, be still and quiet. By not absorbing and clutching after things, we don't interfere with others. Standing on our own gives other people room to stand on their own and grow strong in their own light.

Stan, the retired man from Boise, Idaho, stopped with an offering and to say goodbye.

"The car and I are both getting too old to drive out much further, so we'll have to say goodbye," he said reaching out to shake hands. "It's been an honor knowing you."

Heng Sure
Like drilling wood to make a fire

> If one hears the Dharma as it is,
> That all Buddhas are born from it.
> Although he might pass through measureless suffering,
> He will not forsake the practices of enlightenment.
>
> Avatamsaka Sutra – Verses in Praise in
> the Tushita Heaven Palace Chapter

The Dharma reveals the myriad wonder of humankind's oldest body of wisdom. It speaks of the nature of the Universe and rings with the authority of a body of knowledge encompassing the entire cosmos.

Mt. Sumeru, the heavens, the ten Dharma realms, kalpas, the adornments of the Pure Land – we first heard these names from the Master as he lectured the Dharma from the High Seat. The Buddhist description of nature sounded quaint, at first, sometimes downright inconceivable. After spending a year in contemplation out in Nature, these concepts are no longer unclear notions. All along it was I who was fuzzy and narrow, not the Dharma. The Buddhist view of the universe is older than time.

Science gave me my half-baked understanding of the world. Our scientists simply don't know the truth. They apply little measuring devices and guess at the rest. Galileo was put under arrest for calling the Sun the center of the galaxy instead of the Earth. That was only three hundred years ago. The Avatamsaka Sutra was available for a millennium before that. Science is just now discovering "The Tao of Physics" as Capra calls it. The best new theories come close to the ancient Buddhist cosmology.

We are uninformed. The Dharma has opened a door to the universe in its original substance and nature. Our job is to learn its lessons about reality and explain it for everyone. The Buddhadharma is an inexhaustible storehouse of wonderful treasures!

This month it's time to make fire by drilling wood. Everywhere I turn I meet this analogy:

> Like drilling wood to make a fire,
> If one rests before the sparks appear,
> The fire, like the effort, will disappear.
> The lazy one is also thus.
>
> Avatamsaka Sutra – The Bodhisattvas
> Ask For Clarification Chapter

Effort should be used in every thought through all the day and night. I'll start with one step at a time. Ch'an sitting first. I can sit long, bear pain, and pass through the first barrier into the clear and painless state beyond. Most often, the alarm clock goes off at this point. The temptation to stop concentrating is strong. But if the wood drilling is going to start the fire, I need to make progress in Ch'an; I'll have to sit through the clock and on into the unknown silent spaces.

Maybe extending the sit by five minutes each week and making a time chart would be a useful expedient.

> "Sit long. If you can sit for three days and enter samadhi, do it."
>
> Master Hua

This will take some courage and patience with pain. Here's how it can work. First set my heart on it. *Want* to stay in full lotus for at least three hours each night. Where there's a will, there's a way.

Heng Chau • February 23, 1978
Tears are useless

A car full of people pulled on to the shoulder ahead of us. A woman got out, staggering and holding a bottle. She watched us bow. Everyone in the car became quiet. She dropped her bottle, walked up to us, fell down on her knees and started sobbing. She knelt beside us in the gravel and cried, repenting of being an alcoholic and wasting her life.

We didn't say anything but in our hearts we wanted to say, "It's okay. Don't waste a second. Tears are useless. Turn around, go towards the good and repay your parents' kindness. From today don't drink anymore, don't kill or steal, don't lie or be immoral. If you can avoid these then everything will soon get better and your life won't have been wasted. Be strong and dignified. Turn around and go back to your true, pure nature."

T'ao Yuan-ming's poem, "The Return," came to mind as the woman stood up and dried her tears.

> I am going home!
> My fields and gardens are choked with weeds.
> Why should I not return?
> My mind has been my body's slave.
> But why should I remain melancholy?
> Having awakened to the past,
> I need not reproach myself.
> I know that in the future I can make up for it.
> I know that I am not far from the path of confusion.
> But I'm now awake to the present as "right,"
>   and the past as "wrong."

Heng Chau • February 23, 1978
The Monk in the Grave did not come here in vain

Dear Shr Fu,

I wrote a short essay this a.m. about some things that have become clearer to me about Buddhism and America while doing Three Steps, One Bow.

Buddhism in America

Morro Bay, California

This country was settled by people from all over the world – every race and color imaginable. They all shared one thing: the United States, which stood for a chance to start over, an opportunity to change old habits and renew. They were all looking for a paradise they had lost. Leaving their homes and the familiar, they came in search of a pure land and to reclaim their natural innocence. Dreamers and idealists, these people were seekers of stillness and after ultimate peace and freedom. This is still true today and people are still coming to America for liberty and Eden.

But we haven't found it yet. Why? You might say one reason is we weren't looking in the right places. It's a lot like the story in the Dharma Flower Sutra about a wealthy man whose son was discontent and wanted to run away from home. But before he left, his parents, fearing he would become a drifter and penniless vagrant, secretly sewed a wish-fulfilling pearl in their son's clothing. The son left and sure enough became down-and-out. But he didn't realize that a priceless pearl was sewn in his clothing so he couldn't benefit from it.

Americans are a lot like the wealthy man's son. We are always unhappy at home and itching for freedom. So we have run outside:

pursued wealth and sought "more, better, and bigger" – cars, homes, and highs. Yet all this worldy accomplishment that has made this the richest country in the world has not produced paradise. Our material success has brought little freedom or security. We are as restless and uprooted as ever, maybe even more so than two hundred years ago. The harder and faster we search for the "pearl" outside, the further from home we go. "Off an inch in the beginning" we are "off a thousand miles in the end." Morro Bay is at "the end" in lots of ways and a good example of why Buddhism is taking root in Western soil.

Virginia and John McKenzie, of Morro Bay, and their four kids are a typical American family. College graduates, they made their home in South Pasadena and began to live the good and promising life. "But it wasn't just if you had a color T.V. that mattered," related Virginia, "it was *how many* color T.V.s you had that counted." Something was missing and more success over the years failed to correct it. "So we sold the T.V.s and the Cadillac, bought an old station wagon, and moved to the mountains." They lived there for three years and learned a lot. "I learned how to save rubber bands and felt like I was in kindergarten again." But the kids needed "school and scouts" so they moved to Morro Bay as a compromise – a city, but not polluted and upside down like L.A., they thought.

In a short time, the oil corporations and gas and electric companies set up huge plant facilities. The "developers" flowed in, parceling and building, until Morro Bay swelled in size and headaches. "The freeway is getting closer, and this 'nice, quiet community' has a serious drug problem with its children. We are very concerned." said Virginia, "Our kids are good kids, but when *it's right in* the schools…".

The McKenzie family read about the City of Ten Thousand Buddhas in a San Francisco paper and saw us bowing. They have spearheaded a campaign of support and are "just really happy for a chance to give." They send out gas, water, and food regularly. I explained briefly about how the Sangha are "fields of blessings," people give *through* us not *to* us. Giving is a way to plant good seeds and nourish what Buddhism represents: enlightenment, compassion, ending suffering, and ultimate wisdom. "That's neat!" said Virginia. "Like planting seeds, kind of. I don't understand a whole lot. All I think of when I give is up there (City of Ten Thousand Buddhas). I see all those fine faces, wonderful land, and good buildings and what they are being used for and I 'send it up' to help it grow." She gestures like a cheerleader. Of the five precepts, she said, "Boy, holding precepts would take a big weight off your back, wouldn't it?"

Cliff and Vicky are a young married couple who live in a high-rent, crowded condominium development community called Baywood in Morro Bay. They aren't happy or settled. "We've been looking for something that expressed and meshed with our thoughts and feelings – inside, you know? Success and traditional religions just don't make it. This wasn't 'home' for us," they explained. "A lot of people talk about the Path and the Way, but we haven't found anybody really doing it." When they found out we were part of a whole community of lay and left-home, *practicing* Buddhists, "I couldn't wipe the grin off my face for days, I was so happy," said Vicky.

They came out with their friends to make offerings, and joined in our Sunday afternoon Guan Yin praise-recitation and chanting the Great Compassion Mantra. Last week Cliff was driving home during a bad storm. Heavy rain and high winds were pushing his little car all over the highway. A flock of birds struggling with the storm got tossed in front of Cliff's car. "I looked out the rear-view mirror and saw a bird roll across the highway. I had hit it!" said Cliff. "I knew the bird was dying. I felt I needed to do something to help. Then for some reason, without thinking, I said 'Namo Guan Shi Yin Pu Sa' about five or six times. I remembered Guan Yin helps in times of suffering and sickness. Then something strange happened. Suddenly the skies cleared and the wind died down. It was sunny and safe all the way home," said Cliff.

"When he walked in the door he was glowing and happy," said Vicky.

"I know it had to do with reciting Guan Yin, but I don't know how or why. I've never had anything like that happen to me before. Strange, huh?" related Cliff.

They all took copies of the Great Compassion Mantra that a layperson from L.A. had donated, and they were full of questions and sincerity for the Buddhadharma. "What's the pure Dharma body?" "Where can we start to read?" "What's a Bodhisattva?" "What else can we do?" "Who is Amitabha Buddha?" and so on.

The last two peregrine falcons in the country are carefully protected on the landmark of Morro Bay – a high rock island that rises up out of the middle of the Bay. The city itself is a bird refuge and people are very aware they live on the edge of the edge of the continent. There's no more room to expand or to run over the next hill for greener grass. As a country, this is where it is at: we have run out of room to run outside. The "great evasion" as one historian called our running away from ourselves, is coming to a natural limit and we are spiritually a thousand miles off the mark.

But Americans are optimists and resilient. They don't despair. Practical and self-reliant, they pick up again and try to avoid the same mistakes. This is repentance and reform. People we meet are not ashamed or afraid to admit they got on the wrong track and want to start again on the right foot. Open and energetic, a lot of folks are ready to leave the "brave new world" for the Flower Store World. They are ready to "return the light and illumine within." But where to begin?

> "…where was there ever a man of wisdom who got to see and hear the Buddha without cultivating pure vows and walking the same path the Buddha walked?"
>
> Avatamsaka Sutra
> Tushita Heaven Chapter

The Master has stressed, "Make Buddhism your personal responsibility." This is what really counts: each person "trying his best" to put down the false and find the true. What moves and inspires people is practice – pure vows and walking the road. Talk is cheap. There are a lot of people like Heng Sure and myself who realize we have not really done our own work, that we have been on the bandwagon and have been taking a free ride. We have nearly exhausted our blessings by just enjoying them. Like the son of the wealthy man, we have run out of conditions to climb on and have to start from scratch.

The City of Ten Thousand Buddhas is so important. It is a pure place where we can cleanse our hearts and souls of defilement and ground our lives in morality and virtue. The City of Ten Thousand Buddhas represents hope for countless living beings to end suffering and find true freedom. It is becoming a symbol, like the Statue of Liberty, of opportunity and refuge: a chance to finish the Real Revolution for Independence by liberating the mind-ground.

Many people we have met share this conviction and are very excited about the orthodox Dharma and the City of Ten Thousand Buddhas. In a very real way, the American Revolution for independence was never completed. Americans feel this sense of "unfinished business" in their hearts and minds. Our history and behavior continues to be a restless search for our natural roots and ultimate liberation. Who would have guessed the "pearl" was sewn right in our very own clothing?

What is the "pearl"? Is it our affluence and prosperity? No. The pearl is the bright substance of our everlasting pure nature, our true unchanging mind. We have been saying that Buddhism is new in America, but this is not really accurate. Like the pearl, Buddhism has always been here. We just didn't know where to look. So now the Monk in the Grave has come to America and reminded us all about the pearl sewn in our clothing – the pearl that grants all wishes, "Your very body is the enlightenment-ground, and your mind is the Pure Land," said the Sixth Patriarch.

Stan, a native of Boise, Idaho, is in his late 70's and lives in retirement now with his wife in Morro Bay. He still wears logging shirts and comes on strong, straight, and honest, "We read about you in the paper and about what you're doing up north in Ukiah…"

"The City of Ten Thousand Buddhas?"

"Yes, that's it. Well, all I got to say is the country needs more people like you." Stan made an offering and invited us to stay at their home while we were in the area. I explained our vows wouldn't allow that, but it was a kind offer. "Well, it's been an honor knowing you. My wife and I are very interested in what you folks are doing. This is what will make the country strong. Good luck and thank you."

The Monk in the Grave did not come here in vain. Virginia McKenzie wanted to thank someone. We said that the best thanks was practice, and we told her of the words over the exit door of Gold Mountain Monastery: "Try your best."

"Boy, that's it, isn't it?" she exclaimed. "And if you make a mistake, try your best to try better!"

Much peace in the Dharma,
Disciple Guo Ting (Heng Chau)
bows in respect

Heng Sure
It uses words but soon leaves words behind

> "He does not seek what living beings can speak of. These are all conditioned, false, empty affairs. Although he does not rely on the path of the words and languages, at the same time he is not attached to not speaking."
>
> Avatamsaka Sutra
> Ten Transferences Chapter

Buddhadharma exists for living beings who want to find the Holy in every moment. It uses words but soon leaves words behind.

Buddhist Sutras point the way to the Holy. They are a piece of the magic itself. The Avatamsaka Sutra is guiding Heng Chau and me out of the darkness. It is our trail out of the woods. It is our road back home.

We treat the Sutra as a magic map. We bow to it, praise and worship it, make gifts to it, read, write, and study it. It responds. Like magic. It is the oldest wisdom on the planet.

How long has the Avatamsaka Sutra existed? How long has its wisdom led beings to realize "mystic, sweet communion" with their own Buddha-nature? When a Buddha appears in the world, like our Buddha Shakyamuni, he always speaks the Avatamsaka Sutra first, after his enlightenment. How many Buddhas have there been? Infinite numbers of them. In how many worlds? Countless, mind-boggling numbers of worlds. Time and space collapse. "The path of words and language is cut off and the place of the mind's working is extinguished."

The Avatamsaka Sutra is old. Its Dharma is magic. It guides us to the Holy in everything. The Bodhisattva says:

> I do not dwell in mundane dharmas.
> My joy is in leaving the world...
> I dwell in the limits of reality without any labels...

> Avatamsaka Sutra
> Ten Transferences Chapter

Heng Chau • February 24, 1978
That's how we get psyched-up!

In the early morning fog we filled the water jugs from a hose outside the Post Office in the little hamlet of Harmony, population 18. Everyone was still asleep.

Deputy Sheriff Ray Connelly stopped this A.M. "Will you drop us a line when you get to the City of 10,000 Buddhas and let us know everything's okay?" he asked. He answered a call on his radio and then said,

"I'm very humbled by what you are doing. It must take a lot of endurance and determination. I don't think I could ever do it."

Monk: "Sure you could. Anybody could."

Sheriff: "Gotta really get psyched-up for it, huh?"

Monk: "Well, we think about doing it for all living beings. It's easy that way. That's how we get psyched-up! If you set your mind to it, you can do anything."

> The Bodhisattva has this thought: "I vow that these good roots will be of benefit to all living beings and will purify them so that ultimately they will forever leave suffering and affliction…"
>
> Avatamsaka Sutra
> Ten Transferences Chapter

Sheriff: "I'm a firm believer in that. Well needless to say you have my total support and a lot of other folks' too. They all want to know if everything's okay."

Monk: "Everything's okay."

Sheriff: "Well, I'll see you later, and keep in touch."

Heng Chau • February 25, 1978
The man on the street corner in Russia

Don and Gail Depue and their little girl, Tracy, stopped with an offering and to wish us a good journey. "Now there's some peaceful men," said Mrs. Depue to her daughter.

The Depues are from Cambria, a small town north of us. They are straight-living and honest people who embody a traditional morality and values which seem to be declining rapidly in the modern world.

"By the way things are going in the world, we certainly need as much effort in the direction you are going as we can get," stated Don.

We were cleaning up from lunch. Don talked as I washed dishes on the tailgate. Gail and Tracy sat in some wild flowers by a fenced field and quietly watched as Heng Sure began bowing.

"I don't think there's a person, I don't care where they are in the world – the man on the street corner in Russia – who doesn't want peace and happiness in his life. But I don't know how they let the leaders of their country pull some of the stuff they do if those people really didn't want it," said Don.

"Well, the American people didn't want Watergate, but they got it anyway," I said. "That's true," said Don.

"It has to begin with the small in each of us first, and then in our family and city and country before there will be lasting peace."

Don looked at his wife and child playing in the grass and laughing. "That's our small beginning toward world peace."

"Good roots, good fruit."

"You know, that's really how it has to go if it's going to happen, isn't it?" said Don. "It begins right inside."

They eradicate all poisons from the mind.
In their thoughts they cultivate the highest wisdom.
Not for themselves do they seek peace and happiness,
Their only wish is that living beings
    get to leave suffering.

Avatamsaka Sutra
Ten Transferences Chapter

"It's fun too. We're having a great time trying to get rid of our bad of habits and purify our hearts," I said.

"I know!" exclaimed Don with a big grin. "I wish we could start all over again."

"You can anytime."

Gail and Tracy walked over.

"Tracy wants to stay. This is really comfortable here," said Gail.

"I know," answers Don. "It's great!"

"Do you find that a lot of people want to be around you just because it's so peaceful?" asked Mrs. Depue.

"It's not us, it's what the bowing stands for that people want to be around. The bowing seems to remind people of something they have in their own hearts."

> In all worlds in the ten directions
> They perfect the cultivation of pure practices.
> In this way the merit and virtue is all transferred,
> Because they wish to bring
>   peace and happiness to all sentient beings.
>
> Avatamsaka Sutra
Ten Transferences Chapter

Heng Sure
You're on the path, Don

"According with still tranquility and the indestructible Dharma nature, I will cause all beings to obtain eternal peace, security and happiness."

Avatamsaka Sutra
Ten Practices Chapter

Don and Gail and their young daughter stop outside Cayucos with an offering to wish us luck. Don is an insurance man from Cambria. He wears western ranch clothes and a butch haircut. Gail's appearance and manners are straight out of America's heartland. They are down-home good folks, honest, and open.

"If you are able, while in the mundane world, to leave behind all your attachments and be happy with an unobstructed mind, then you can get enlightened to the Dharma."

Avatamsaka Sutra – Verses in Praise in
the Tushita Heaven Palace Chapter

A week later Don visited again. The talk was light-hearted at first, but soon it came clear that Don had something on his mind.

Heng Chau: "What do you do, Don?"

Don: "I've done different things. At the moment I am between jobs. I taught high school for years because I wanted to be of service to the world. What a letdown. Nothing could be further from the truth than what goes on in public school today. I was not 'doing good' there. I joined my father in selling realty, then moved on to insurance. Ultimately I want a world that doesn't need insurance, but I believe in the product I sell. My attitude is that I sell it as if to my own family."

Heng Chau: "That's a rare outlook in the business world."

Don: "You can say that again. That's my problem. I am not cut out to be a salesman. I won't do anything with my life if I have to compromise honesty and integrity. Businesses just don't want my kind. I really envy you two. How you have put it all down to follow your own inner voice."

Heng Chau: "So you quit your job?"

Don: "You guessed it. I had to leave. I said to the gang, 'Well friends, that's it. I can't be a part of this anymore.' I finally realized that if what you do doesn't come from your real nature, then every move you make is another mistake."

Heng Chau: "Wow. Are you ever lucky to have that understanding! Most people never know why they go on being unhappy. They never look for the path with heart. We were that way – just moving from one thing to the next, always looking for a way to get to the important parts of life. That's why we left home. We came to Buddhism because a monastery is not a place to withdraw from the world. It's a place to get on the right track."

Don: "For all these years I did everything I could to avoid looking at what's not there in my life. Something is missing. The young marrieds I sell insurance to…? Everyone I know has the same doubts, the same malaise. They know that this isn't it, but they don't have any way to tune in to that inner voice. That's what made up my mind to quit, hearing that voice, but still, I don't really know how.

I've made the big step but I need a way to keep it alive while the dust settles. Sometimes I'm afraid I can't get free enough to listen."

Heng Chau: "You're on the path, Don. Now you've got to work hard and be patient."

Don: "But how do you draw the line between responsibility and attachments? My family depends on me. These are not small decisions. They affect lots of people."

Heng Chau: "You bet they do. You've got to move one step at a time. You can't rip anything."

Don: "That's for sure. I've got to work my problems through or face them again later. If I run out I'd just have to pay for the same mistakes later on. If I don't take my responsibilities now, I'll only complicate things and get in deeper."

Heng Chau: "Don, you've got a Buddhist outlook on life. You're describing the process of cause and effect."

Don: "On one hand, I've got to be true to what is real in me, but I've got my family to care for..." "How do I know if I'm really hearing my true voice?"

Heng Chau: "It's right there, loud and clear, but we choose not to listen because we're too attached."

Don: "At the bottom of it I want peace and happiness for everyone, not just for myself. I really want to do what's right. Right now I could sure use a method to tune in to my true self and find that right path."

Heng Chau wrote the name of Guan Shi Yin Bodhisattva on a card and handed it to Don. He explained the method of reciting the name and told Don about the vows and compassion of Guan Shi Yin.

Don was enthusiastic and felt an immediate affinity with the Bodhisattva. He was reciting the name as he drove away. We met Don again several weeks later. He made an offering and advised us about road conditions ahead. He looked happy and on top of life.

Don: "Well, I've got a new job as a teacher – and everything seems to be working out for the best. You know, a funny thing happened the other night as I was meditating. I saw a face very clearly before me, of a kind old man with white hair and a beard. Kind of an unusual state."

Heng Chau: "Really happy to hear things are looking up, Don. There are lots of states in meditation. Don't worry about it."

Heng Chau and I both were glad to have met Don and his family. We are lucky to have met the Buddhadharma in our lives, and sharing our joy with others is true happiness.

It is not easy to face the crises in life.

Don had the courage to come out on the highway and talk openly about his difficult time. As Heng Chau said to them, something about the work that Buddhists do reminds people of the best parts within themselves. Don was already on the path back to happiness but sometimes it helps to see others walk it. It helps us remember and return.

Heng Chau • February 26, 1978
Until it's coming out of my ears

"The Difficulty with Intelligence."

A young student of comparative religions at a well-known university approached us as we bowed in open country.

"I know I've got to really go and do it! I've read and studied until it's coming out of my ears, but I don't really know anything, you know? I mean, it's all a head trip. I started experimenting with 'mind expanding drugs,' and I realized that all my book learning was a sham. There's a path to ultimate wisdom and enlightenment inside and no book can give it to me. Drugs can't either. So I've started to meditate and, well, I felt I wanted to stop and say I understand a little bit what you're doing and I know it's the right way. I'm just beginning. I'd like to find a teacher," he said. "I heard you Buddhists have a university in Ukiah that puts the books and real spiritual practice together. That's the way it's gotta be. Just studying about the path with heart is a dead end, I've found. I have to really do the work and not just rap about it."

> It is not through mere scholarship
> that one can enter the Tathagata's Dharma.
> As a deaf musician playing his tunes
> pleases others but cannot hear himself,
> When one does not cultivate the Dharma,
> mere study is just like this.
>
> Avatamsaka Sutra
> Bodhisattvas Ask For Clarification Chapter

There are eight circumstances in which it is difficult to meet up with the Dharma or cultivate it, even if you want to. The seventh of these eight difficulties is that of having worldly knowledge and argumentative intelligence. This is the "smarts" so esteemed in college, and the key to a successful career after. It's the ability to argue and make a clever case, to discriminate and debate. This kind of worldly wisdom however, is not wisdom that transcends the world, and so no matter how intelligent you are, without genuine cultivation, there is no actual liberation.

The way of a left-home person is to travel light: unattached and homeless, like deer and the wind in space.

> "He vows that all beings forever leave behind the dharmas of the home life, and with few desires they know sufficiency and stash or hoard nothing."
>
> Avatamsaka Sutra
> Ten Transferences Chapter

Heng Sure
What a Bodhimanda!

> In all counties in all directions,
> He is totally unattached,
> He relies on nothing.
> He sccks not even life itself,
> Nor does he falsely raise any distinctions.
>
> Avatamsaka Sutra
> Ten Transferences Chapter

How is this place any different from Huntington Drive in L.A., or Harbor Boulevard in Oxnard or anywhere else? All bows are one bow. Concentration makes the environment unimportant. If you don't seek, what is there to worry over?

With this contemplation in mind, I took a second look at the mountains and ocean landscape before us. "Hey! What a beautiful place to cultivate! What a Bodhimanda!" My heart seemed to take wings and soar out above the water, sailing into the clean air above the mud of my old afflictions. The pilgrimage has turned yin fear into solid faith in cultivation. This is the way to end my own suffering and help others. It's beginning to sink in that those who walk the Dharma road are on the path that all Buddhas have walked before. It's the same road that all Buddhas of the future are walking right now. It takes time. From first bringing forth the resolve for enlightenment until final realization of the Tenth Ground, a Bodhisattva cultivates for aeons beyond reckoning. These big rocks before me will fall to dust and rise again countless times before I realize Nirvana Without Remainder. I believe we all get there right on time.

> "Of all dharmas you see in the world, the mind is the only host. Following what you understand, you seek their marks. This is upside-down and not the real thing."
>
> Avatamsaka Sutra
> The Bodhisattvas Ask for Clarification Chapter

Heng Chau • February 27, 1978
Highway 1 is out of the question

Cambria, California – a small seaside community of about 2,000 people. Rain clears by 8:00 a.m. Tourist traffic and narrow wet roads, so we keep bowing in the yellow rubber rain slicks for safety. Marked change in terrain to rolling hills of conifers and ferns. Low cloud cover and thick fog. It feels like Southern California abruptly stopped and Northern California began. Suddenly we're in tall pines, fog-wet mornings, moss in hanging strands, and deep greens. Behind are dry heat, yellow parched grass, treeless fields and straight roads.

Charlotte Beal from the local newspaper, The Cambrian, asked us during a roadside interview.

"Do you ever have any problems? I mean do some people give you a hard time… like throw things or shout insults?"

At that very moment a car sped by and let fly a volley of rotten oranges. The journalist was standing with her back to the highway. The oranges zipped by the back of her head, missing by inches. She never knew.

"Well, we try not to notice and just treat it like a 'no affair.' If you don't pay any attention, then it's just like nothing happened." I answered.

"Oh, that's interesting!" she said, "I'll have to try that."

Route Change.

"Be careful. If one of you got run over it would ruin the whole purpose of the pilgrimage, wouldn't it?" said a man yesterday.

When we told a reporter our intention to stay on Highway I North of here he exclaimed,

"You mean you're *staying* on Highway I past San Simeon!?" as if such a plan was sheer madness.

Last night we parked in an isolated spot next to a small inlet by the County Park. After meditating I went outside. Out of the thick fog a man walking his dog approached.

"Oh, I've been looking for you," he said. "The name's Fillipini, Alvin Fillipini."

Fillipini got right to the point.

"I'm the superintendent at the nearby State Correctional Facility, the minimal security center. My men and I are concerned for your safety North of the Hearst Castle. We know this road. We work on it with crews everyday. It's a bad one, especially if you're going to try and bow it."

Fillipini leaned over our map in the hood of the car and switched on his flashlight. The alternatives: 1) go back 3 miles and pick up Highway 46 which crosses over the Coast Range and Santa Lucia Mountains to Highway 101. Bow the frontage roads of 101 until we hook up with a county road that goes to Carmel. A big detour around the entire Big Sur Ventana Wilderness area, 2) take the Nacimiento-Ferguson Road through Hunter-Liggett Military Reservation, 3) stay on Highway 1 and hope for the best.

The Highway 46 route is round about. Adds about 100 miles to the trip, and involves the 101 Freeway. The second alternative is a partially paved, graded dirt road through uninhabited National Forest Wilderness. It would take 3 months to bow it, bypassing Big Sur and ending up in Carmel. Gas and water are non-existent. We would have to mount big red gas cans on the car and take our chances with finding water in streams. The third alternative gave our local supporters worry wrinkles and raised eyebrows. Not much of a selection.

Fillipini said he would send one of his foremen to scout it out with us. But it was clear he was telling us as gently as possible, "Highway 1 is out of the question. It's miles of narrow switchbacks and curves not wide enough for 2 cars to pass side by side. It's treacherous in a car – on foot, on your knees, it's impossible," said Fillipini. He was supportive and genuinely interested in our bowing.

"I'd like to get together at the end of it and talk some more," he said. "They call our place a 'rehabilitation facility;' but that's just a bunch of baloney. They're just nice kids who made a mistake and get institutionalized."

"Well, I'll be in touch. We're all real interested in what you're doing. We talk about it every day as we drive back and forth. It's got a lot of people thinking. If I can help in any way, let me know. Good night," he said and walked back into the fog with his dog.

We tentatively decide to take the Nacimiento-Ferguson route to G-16 past Tassajara and through Carmel Valley.

A barrage of oranges, apples, tangerines, rocks and eggs hit the car in the middle of the night and then all was perfectly quiet the rest of the evening.

"Highway Teaching."

The highway is like our minds and like the world: good and bad, true and false, pure and defiled are all mixed together.

> Truth and falseness interlink and mingle:
> Within the ordinary mind
>   one sees the Buddha mind.
> Specifics and principles are together cultivated:
> One relies on basic wisdom
>   to seek the Buddha's wisdom.
>
> Avatamsaka Sutra

Only a straight mind can sift true from false; only true principles can glean the good from the bad; and only pure practice can smelt basic wisdom into the Buddha's wisdom.

If we don't cultivate the Way, it all just stays a mixed-up mess. If one cultivates, then even though pure and defiled, ordinary and enlightened are still mixed together, you yourself aren't mixed up about it. All the fighting stops, and inside and out there's no obstacles, and so,

"A thousand distinctions combine without obstruction."

This is the highway teaching.

Heng Chau • February 28, 1978
They become like mice, hiding in the closet

"Hiding in the Bushes…"

Mrs. Connie McCauley walked out to offer encouragement and support.

"I had to come out and tell you our family really admires what you're doing. Just your presence has had a profound effect on us, especially on our younger son John who is 15. He is really open to the new spiritual awareness and it's had a deep and good impact on him," she said.

"We left the Catholic Church and are really into the ecumenical movement to get past all the differences. We are especially attracted to Buddhism and the Eastern tradition. Metaphysically and practically and in every way, it's very appealing. You know, there are a lot of us hiding in the bushes. When I was 15 years old I ran and hid in the security of the Church. I really admire my son."

It started raining. Mrs. McCauley headed back to their home in the hills outside of Cambria.

"We want to help. Please call if you need anything. Our son is a mechanic… a pretty good one, too. Thank you," she said waving goodbye.

Her comment, "there's a lot of us hiding in the bushes," stuck in my mind. There's a present-day trend, especially among Buddhist scholars, to discourage "belief and practice" in favor of "objectivity." As a result many students who would like to cultivate feel forced to hide their Buddhism in the closet.

This is equally true for many people who are spiritually inclined, but afraid to practice because religion isn't viewed as "scientific" or intellectually respected among some people. They become like mice, hiding in the closet. I remembered a song the Abbot wrote in English to counter this trend.

Yes, yes, yes indeed.
The ways of the wise are what we study.
Yes, yes, yes indeed.
The ways of the wise are what we study.

The ways of thieving mouse-people aren't for us.
We don't hide our Buddhism in the closet.
We want to have wisdom that's really pure.
We want to have wisdom that's really pure.
We want to have wisdom that's really, really pure.

When I grow up, I'll save all the people in the world,
So that all of us can go to enlightenment.
If that sounds like a good idea to you
Let's all get together and fulfill our vows,
And reach the highest summit now.

* * * * * * * * *
March 1978

Heng Chau • March 1, 1978
The root cause of suffering

> "They understand and know that everything in the world
> is identical in appearance with the True Suchness nature."
>
> Avatamsaka Sutra
> Ten Transferences Chapter

All living beings are part of the Avatamsaka Sutra. The Sutra is the true heart of all living beings. The entire Dharma Realm is the Great Means Expansive Buddha Flower Adornment Sutra, and originally the universe, the Sutra and each living being are one, not two or three.

The entire world is the Avatamsaka Sutra; every person a chapter, each experience a small section. The wonderful Dharma is constantly being spoken all around and through us, everywhere and simultaneously.

> Deep and wide and interfused,
> Vast and great and totally complete
> Surely this must be:
> The Great Means Expansive Buddha
>   Flower Adornment Sutra!
>
> Avatamsaka Preface
> by National Master Ch'ing Liang

On Pain.

When the suffering of cultivation gets unbearable I think: My birth caused my mother pain. Raising me took sacrifices and brought worries to my parents. My selfishness and bad habits caused my family and friends much suffering. Insincerity and using people caused others much pain of heart. My attachments, confusion, and hang-ups created disappointment and insecurity for those I was closest to. Now as a monk I break the rules, am arrogant and hard to teach, and do a mediocre job in representing the awesome and compassionate deportment of a left-home person. This brings on pain for my teacher and Dharma friends.

So the least I can do is gladly bear the little suffering that comes my way to try and make up for all the suffering I have caused the world.

"Suffering is a Feeling."

The feeling of suffering is just another feeling. All feelings are basically empty. They come and go, and when you look for them they can't be found.

> "In the Bodhisattva's practice he is greatly happy and increases his finest joyful determination. In the midst of dharmas his mind skillfully understands them all. He does not seek any suffering, however he knows the feeling of suffering has no appearance and is unproduced. All feelings mutually arise and do not stay. Therefore I should cultivate great renunciation along with all Bodhisattvas of the past, present, and future, and with deep faith, happily seek all-wisdom without retreat."
>
> Avatamsaka Sutra
> Ten Grounds – 6th Ground

All life is suffering, a vast "tree of suffering." What is the root cause of suffering? Ignorance. Ignorance is just becoming attached to a view of self. So it says:

> "Ignorance is just not understanding the primary truth."
>
> Avatamsaka Sutra
> Ten Grounds – 6th Ground

The primary truth is the truth of no self. Without a self there are no deeds done. Without deeds there is no confused karma and the retribution of heavy suffering that it creates. Without a self there are no problems, and one is free and easy, nowhere attached. Because,

"Within the primary truth nothing can be obtained."

Avatamsaka Sutra
Ten Grounds – 6th Ground

Heng Sure
No wonder you can't meditate

Howard, aged 60, a cattle rancher from San Simeon stops on a Sunday morning.

Howard: "Buddhists? I thought so. I was in Sri Lanka last year and I studied a bit of Buddhism. I think I've got too much of a Western mind because I've tried to meditate ever since but I'm afraid I'm just no good at it. Can't get anywhere with it."

Heng Chau: "Well, the best way to cut off thoughts is by looking at what you do during the day. Do you hold the five precepts?"

Howard: (Holds out his membership card in the Buddhist Mission Society. The card lists the five precepts and "Do all good. Do no evil. Purify your mind.") "Yes, I do. I've held them nearly all my life."

Heng Chau: "Oh, how's that?"

Howard: "When I was a boy, I worked in the mines. Seems like all the men I worked with had dirty minds. All their thoughts and their talk were evil and foul. I didn't want to pick up their habits so I used to memorize poetry. You know 'Omar'? I used to say that poem as I worked. I'd recite it up one way and back the other. I worked too. Controlled my thoughts."

Heng Chau: "That's wonderful. Real vigor, where it counts. What do you do now?"

Howard: "I run a cattle ranch up the road here near Hearst Castle."

Heng Chau: "Do you eat meat?"

Howard: "Well sure."

Heng Chau: "That's included in the precepts against killing. No wonder you can't meditate."

Howard: "What do you mean? No one in Sri Lanka said anything about not eating meat…"

Heng Chau: "Oh sure. Look Howard, the point of meditation is to settle down the mind and body. To clear it out and concentrate and not be hot or turbid. The point of not eating meat is first of all to be compassionate and not participate in the harm to any living thing just so you can enjoy good flavor. That's basic. Secondly, meat is hot and full of vibes of killing. It's turbid. It excites your desires instead of calming them. When you're full of meat energy it's really hard to rest, hard to settle down. It's like if you killed a man, you'd never have any peace. You'd be turning it over and over all the time in your heart, right? Eating animals is much the same."

Howard: (Struck by this example – speechless.) "Well, it would be really hard to quit… maybe I could though…"

Heng Chau: "If you meditate and want a response without holding precepts, it's like boiling sand hoping to get rice. You can boil it forever and it's still going to be sand. Meditation is in the precepts."

Howard: "What do you monks meditate on? I find that I need something to hang my mind on. I can't grasp emptiness."

Heng Chau: "One good method is recite Namo Guan Shi Yin Pu Sa. If you're sincere and constant in your practice, Guan Shi Yin Bodhisattva will help you open some doors in your life."

Howard: "Say, could you tell me what I can eat that's not meat?"

The Avatamsaka is clear about suffering, its causes and cure. In the 6th Ground, the Bodhisattva sees living beings suffering bitterly in the world, constantly undergoing birth and death on the turning wheel. He sees how all beings who are born in the world come from attachments to self. If you could leave this attachment, there would be no birth and death, and all suffering would cease. But, the Bodhisattva knows that,

> "Ordinary people lack wisdom. They are attached to self. They constantly seek its existence and non-existence. They don't look at things correctly. They give rise to false practices and walk down deviant roads."
>
> The Tree of Suffering

And from these first confused steps the Twelve Causes and Conditions are initiated that end in birth, old age, and death, and "the accumulation of a host of sufferings."

In a single day of bowing we hear the sounds of the worlds suffering at every turn. Don tells us of his friends who have been married two or three times.

"And they are still running around getting more empty and hollow every day." *Desire is suffering.*

Howard Swanson, a weather-wrinkled cowboy in his 60's tells us of his life-long search for enlightenment and an end to suffering.

"But when I meditate on the ranch, I can't quiet my mind. I eat a lot of meat. My teacher in Sri Lanka didn't tell me meat increases desire and makes your mind noisy." *Eating meat is suffering.*

Fillipini, the superintendent of a nearby prison facility says,

"All the kids here got messed up in drugs." *Intoxicants are suffering.*

In a Laundromat two men talk.

"I've got ulcers worrying about losing my investment."

"Yeah and I've got ulcers from trying not to worry about losing my investment." *Losing is suffering.*

A local teacher.

"I'm making too much money and can't afford to pay my taxes. Too much, too little, it's all a big headache." *Gain is suffering.*

So life is suffering, but isn't cultivating the Way suffering? Cultivation is also suffering. But it is suffering that ends suffering, whereas the way of the world is to add suffering to suffering, with misery increasing misery. That's the meaning of,

"To endure suffering ends suffering."

This is the heart of it: the Bodhisattva sees that,

When ignorance is the condition,
    suffering can't be stopped.
Ending the condition (ignorance),
    suffering is all over.

The "condition" is ignorance about the primary truth. So when one sees there is no self, all the sufferings are over. Empty of self is true liberation.

"He knows there is no self and no others, no lifespan and no life itself. The self-nature is empty, without a doer or a receiver. And right then he obtains the Liberation Gate of Emptiness which appears before him."

Avatamsaka Sutra
Ten Practices Chapter

With no self there's no seeking; no seeking there are no problems. Emptiness isn't being a log or a zombie, rather it's the lively and wonderful state of nothing sought for, nowhere attached, everywhere content and unobstructed. That's why it's called a Gate of Liberation.

It's like Don said, "Boy, all of these problems because of an artificial self that doesn't even exist."

Heng Sure • March 3–5, 1978
You protect my Dharma, I'll protect yours

Gold Wheel Temple.

> Living beings falsely discriminate
> "This is the Buddha, this is worldly."
> One who penetrates the nature of Dharma,
> Knows there is no Buddha and there is no Worldly.
>> Avatamsaka Sutra – Verses in Praise in
>> the Tushita Heaven Palace Chapter

Friday above Cambria. No one comes to pick us up. Big rainstorm moves in. Rock-throwing attacks at night by local young men are increasingly intense. Despite imminent rendezvous, we decide to expediently leave the bowing area for a hiding spot on a back road behind tall bushes. Hard rain continues. We sigh and abandon hopes of seeing the Master this month. We resolve to stay out and work harder. Heng Sure hears alarm bells in his head. Saturday, six a.m., familiar blue VW bus appears before our dragon. It's Hung Ju Fa Shr! How in the world? "I drove in every driveway and side road for miles! After three hours I said, 'Heck with these guys, I'm going to go meditate.' So I turned off the highway, turned right up this tiny back road and here you are."

Many sections of Highway 1 washed out, or flooded with mudslides as we travel south.

Interview with the Master Saturday evening. "Would you like to accompany me to Malaysia? You can bow just like you do when you visit this place. You protect my Dharma, I'll protect yours."

Being near the Master feels so good that you don't realize he is leading you to the edge of your capacity to cultivate and then slightly beyond. Only when he steps back do you see the new space on all sides. Test: do you scramble for safe, old ground or do you scramble to float on the new water? Another analogy: Shih Fu's Dharma talks fill us full of light and juice as they pinpoint our faults and cracks. We then scramble to hold the juice in, by patching the leaks as they appear. It's wonderful and bitter and hard and sweet all at once. It is a priceless chance to progress in cultivation. It feels like a light bulb dropped into a Japanese cut-paper lantern. The light streams out the holes. The Master holds up his mirror of perfect virtue and deportment and we identify the holes and cracks in our lanterns. We listen to the Dharma as the Master gives us glue and patching compound to make our lantern whole and complete once more. The Master called it "being able to read your own Sutra, every false thought is a chapter."

After ten visits to Gold Wheel since the trip began, I can now identify some of the repeated mistakes I repeated time and again: reading my Sutra.

Our new route over the mountains is approved. Wilderness pilgrims!

First volume of our journals published. Official verdict: "Like a piece of toast seen on top of a garbage can – something no one wants. I'm waiting for the time when you merge your experience with the principles of the Avatamsaka Sutra – that will be wonderful!"

Giant, violent thunderstorm Saturday night. D.M. Heng Ju who has sailed some heavy seas, calls it "the worst storm I've ever seen." At 1 a.m., a lightning bolt crashes down just outside our rain-swept garage. A deafening flash of thunder and light.

Driving back to San Luis, Heng Sure reciting Guan Yin's name, nods out behind the wheel. Bus lurches towards the shoulder. Sudden sharp rapping on the head wakes him just in time to swerve back on the road. Who did that? No one there.

Heng Ju and Bill Ireland tune the dragon and repair the window hinge that kept the tailgate shut since Ventura. Car runs and feels like new.

Coasting on the glow of the Master's energy. Have to work to return to our own stream. The key words: "This is your own responsibility. Bring the Dharma to the West. Work as if you were all alone!"

"I should be a path for all beings so that they can reach wisdom…"

Ten Transferences

Heng Chau • March 3, 1978
A retreat is an advance

Bowing in extremely heavy rain outside of Cambria. First a van then a big car tried to run us off the shoulder. They cross over lanes, sliding and careening on the slick roads and head straight for us. "Playing chicken" it's called. Half of the speeding car is on the road, the other half takes up the shoulder we are bowing on. There's no place to run. The road embankment drops straight down 30 or 40 feet into the sea or barbed wire cattle fences flooded under water.

Fortunately it's the end of the day and so a showdown is avoided. In the streaming rain, we transfer and pile into the Plymouth. We retreat to an abandoned side road for the night's camp. "Sometimes a retreat is an advance," the Master told us last month.

Heng Chau • March 4, 1978
That's how he found you

Rains all night. Car won't start. All our clothes are soaked and we are three miles from town.

After morning ceremony, we sit in meditation. At 6:00 a.m. a familiar looking faded blue VW bus pulls alongside. Heng Ju jumps out. He's really surprised and said, "I've been driving back and forth since 3 a.m. trying to find you two. Finally I gave up and decided to pull off onto this little dead-end road into these bushes to meditate and here you are! Amazing!"

Heng Ju came to take us along to Gold Wheel Temple in L.A. We pushed and started the Plymouth after some hot tea and ploughed through flooded roads and high winds all the way to L.A. Heng Ju, a veteran sailor, said, "This is the worst storm I've ever seen."

The Abbot was waiting for us and listened to our experience and stories.

"The Dharma protectors guided Heng Ju to you. That's how he found you," he said with a smile.

As for the rest of our states and questions, the Master simply said,

"Not seeking anything, then there are no problems. Use a single mind on one method and you're sure to have a response."

> When you are concentrated,
>   then it's magic.
> When you are scattered,
>   then there's nothing.

With hot shower, dry clothes and the rare chance to listen to the turning of the Dharma Wheel, our lives are rich.

Heng Chau • March 5–6, 1978
Growing mushrooms under the seats

Los Angeles – San Luis – Cambria.

Shih Fu asks us if we want to join him in a Dharma trip to Malaysia this summer. We agree.

We stock up on supplies from L.A. disciples and drive over the "grapevine" highway back to Cambria. Heng Ju is driving a '56 Chevy he's "fixed for sure" six times en route. Heng Sure and I trade off driving the VW bus. Many detours and delays with flooded and washed out roads. Lunch at an isolated railroad crossing on a country back road. Quiet, except for the sound of wrenches on metal as Heng Ju works on the Chevy again. "Think I've got it now."

Arrive at Ireland's in San Luis. Bill Ireland welds our broken tailgate hinge while Heng Ju tunes up the engine. Hot chocolate, welding, grease solvent, and a backyard garden of junk metal. The car was growing mushrooms under the seats from all the dampness.

Bill Ireland lifts his welding goggles to look at an image of Guan Yin Bodhisattva and picture of the Master hanging inside the car.

"You know, the Abbot looks more familiar all the time, it's the darnest thing."

Heng Sure
Returning it could ease my mind

> "The Bodhisattva cares only about solidly upholding the pure precepts."

> Avatamsaka Sutra
> Ten Practices Chapter

I found a rusty garden hoe in an empty field miles from anywhere. I thought, "Hey, Wan Fo Cheng could use that hoe." A little voice said, "Don't touch it. Leave it right here. It was not given to you. You're breaking a precept if you take it." I listened to the first voice. Why? Because I was false thinking of lunch and the laypeople who had come to visit us that morning. I gave them the hoe to take to L.A. One week later we returned to the field and there was a farmer tending a brand new orchard. Of course it was his hoe and I had stolen it. How to get it back?

It was not easy. Once the door is open, it is very hard to close. I repented but could not forget. During our next visit to L.A., I pulled the hoe out of the garage and set it in full view of the car. I certainly would not forget to take it back. I certainly did. Another month passed and every day I had thoughts of the hoe. It obstructed my concentration thoroughly. I wanted to concentrate and I couldn't because I had broken the fundamental rules, the ABC's of the Bodhisattva Path.

Again in L.A., I grabbed the hoe and packed it in the bus as soon as we arrived. I was really anxious to get rid of the thing. I had repented of the misdeed as soon as I recognized it two months ago. It was fait accompli; nothing could change the offense. Still, returning the hoe could ease my mind.

It was late at night as we approached Santa Maria. We lost the road. The bus was nearly out of gas. We had to go miles and miles out of our way to find the tiny road leading to the orchard field.

There at last, I lifted the hoe and left the bus. Walking down the muddy, steep path, the little tool weighed a ton. The path seemed endless. My feet got stuck in soft mud. The moonless night hid the road. Owls and coyotes sounded very near; I was spooked. Are the hells like this? My shoe came off, stuck deep in a gluey puddle. On and on; finally, the scene of the crime appeared. I gently planted the hoe in full view and then on impulse, I bowed to the hoe: three full kou-tou's in the mud. Surely I had learned a deep lesson from it. It had been my wise advisor.

The road back to the bus was no easier. Heng Chau met me halfway, worried that I had been gone so long. The lights of the bus looked like an oasis in the night. Don't break the precepts. Listen to the little voice. It won't steer you wrong.

This is what he thinks, "I am holding pure precepts so I must rid myself of all bondage and fetters. I must abandon all greed and seeking, all difficulties and oppression..."

Avatamsaka Sutra
Ten Practices Chapter

Heng Chau • March 7, 1978
Everything is on loan from the universe

We spend the night in the car in front of the Ireland's house, refusing an offer to stay in their mobile trailer.

Early a.m. we're back on the bowing road near Cambria. Blue skies outside, light hearts inside. The weekend with Shih Fu at Gold Wheel was a real blessing. Of all the gifts the giving of Dharma is the best.

> Good Man, of all offerings,
> the gift of Dharma is the highest.
>
> Avatamsaka Sutra
> Universal Worthy's Conduct and Vows Chapter

Road Thoughts...

Broken down highways, broken down cars, broken down bodies. Impermanence is everywhere, and by it, we are all gathered in. The cars, the roads, our bodies, are all temporarily strung and glued together of borrowed elements that never take one shape for long. Mold and mushrooms eat the car's wood paneling; rust and friction eat the metal. The highways eat the trees; the storms eat the highway, and the earth eats the people.

The elements circle and re-circle in change that is changeless. Without beginning or end we turn and return like motley pieces of metal in the junkyard, like the grains of sand on a beach. Where did each one come from? Where will one go to? The self is false and too small for the big picture. The Dharma Realm is too mysterious and wonderful for words to grasp, and within it, it is always thus.

> Going and returning with no border.
> Movement and stillness have one source.
> Embracing multitudes of wonders, more remains,

Overstepping words and thoughts by far:
This can only be the Dharma Realm!

Avatamsaka Preface

Nothing belongs to us. We have no home. Everything we have is on loan from the universe. We use what we need, no more, no less. Things come and things go and in time, so do we. When going and returning are the same, one becomes a Buddha, Thus Come One.

Many people stop to ask about the City of Ten Thousand Buddhas. "Is it open to everyone?" "Aren't Buddhists the ones who stand for world peace?" and, "Why 10,000?"

It's said,

We are all together,
The many return to the one.

The Buddha is the true and original home of all living beings. All beings have the Buddha wisdom and happiness inherent in their self-nature. "Ten thousand" is a Chinese expression for "all" or a countless number. And so the City of 10,000 Buddhas is just another way of saying the true home of all living beings. It's a place where ten thousand living beings can become ten thousand Buddhas.

At the City of Ten Thousand Buddhas
Ten thousand Buddhas are born.
In ten thousand rays of light,
Its homes are like ten thousand lamps.
Ten thousand multitudes are of a single mind.
Ten Thousand generations' work goes on.
All the ten nations acclaim
the City of Ten Thousand Buddhas.

The City is also a place to vastly benefit the world. The guiding principle of Buddhism is "no self." No me and you, all are one. The world, the countries, the family, and the individual all go bad because of selfishness. Selfishness and greedy self-seeking ruin all under heaven. And so when the individual's mind is straight and humane, sincere and selfless, then the family, country and world can come together again in peace.

Heng Sure
You guys aren't very evangelistic, are you?

I went into the Cambria Laundromat to pick up our brown basin and soap dish and encountered a big, curly-haired man in stylish overalls – drunk and unhappy with his first look at me. "You got change for a quarter?"

I gesture "no money."

He doesn't understand. "Does that mean 'no'?"

Suddenly I realized that this guy was hostile and getting hot. I could have shaken my head "no" and smiled, but I felt attached and I went on the defensive. No talking, the best I could do was pull back and give no edge. I retreated with my washbasin, feeling inadequate. My vibes were not yielding – the guy had turned me and I felt like a little kid pouting in the car. After all these months of taking insults on the road, as soon as you stop bowing you stop being compassionate, hey? Phooey. What kind of patience is this?

Went back in after evening ceremonies to help fold the laundry. Here are Heng Chau and Kuo Chou; oh, oh, there's the guy again. Kuo Chou has smelled the alcohol and has cautiously withdrawn. Heng Chau, fearless and compassionate, has met the man face to face. Heng Chau has explained that I hold a vow of silence. The guy is trying to get a rise out of Heng Chau.

Man: "Yeah? What for?"

Heng Chau: "For concentration."

Man: "That's no big deal. He gets twice as tired using all that sign language."

Heng Chau: "No, he's just being quiet."

Man: "What kind of monks are you?"

Heng Chau: "Buddhists."

Man: "What's the Buddha? Who's the Buddha? He your big God?"

Heng Chau: "No, the Buddha is the best part of you inside. The part that is kind, the part that figures stuff out."

Man: "Always doing good, that kind of stuff?"

Heng Chau: "Yeah, something like that."

Man: "Figures what out?"

Heng Chau: "Where you came from. Where you're going. Who you were before you were born."

Man: (Silence)

Man: "You guys aren't very evangelistic, are you?"

Heng Chau: "No. Everyone's got the same questions. They'll want answers sooner or later. There's no use pushing – like fruit on a tree, when it's ripe it will fall. Everyone will find the answers sooner or later."

Man: "What are you doing it for?" (Considerably more quiet and mellow.)

Heng Chau: "To calm things down. To cool things off. To end fighting."

Man: "For yourselves?"

Heng Chau: "We start there but we're doing it for everybody. There are too many bad vibes floating around."

Man: (Half-heartedly) "Well, you ought to try Jesus…"

Subdued, he stared at us through the window as we drove away.

Here is the magic of Buddhism as it changes us all, as it opens the hearts of Americans. In five minutes of straight talk, Heng Chau used the Buddhadharma to turn this dark and sullen man back into a living being. He was full of fear and vulnerable. The Dharma transformed a potential fight into a learning experience for each one of us.

Heng Chau's comments: "I saw a lonely man doing his washing late at night in a vacation town where it's tough to be alone. He was pretty sad. He'd been down to the local tavern, so you know he was scared inside. I felt for the guy. His big, tough-guy approach was an act to cover his fear. People approach us on the defensive. It's not easy to ask questions of bald, robe-wearing strangers. There's this mystique, especially with your silence. People are afraid we'll blow them down, that they won't be able to stand up to us, so they come on either tough and hard or totally passive and yin."

It's like the truth we discovered on Labor Day about the men who hazed us. They were uptight about their big decisions and changes coming up with the end of the summer. It's the ones who are closest to their own pain who yell the loudest. These are people who are ready and looking for the Buddhadharma.

I explained how I had tuned the man out in the Laundromat. I had withdrawn and retreated before his hostile vibes.

Heng Chau replied, "That won't do it. Here's what I learned from working in the psyche-wards in the hospitals in Wisconsin.

"1) Get right in there and deal with the person where he's at. Don't be afraid to get in close. When people see that you're not afraid of them, they feel secure and they relax. If people feel judged or slighted, like you're standing back, you've lost them right there.

"2) Totally ignore pain. They tune in to the healthy part, the yang energy. Quickly zero in on something positive about the person, 'Look what's healthy here.' Talk to that.

"3) Here's the best part. The Buddhadharma is elastic. Everyone is inside of it. No one can hear the Buddhadharma and not feel it in their hearts. It's so true and so right. Talk the Dharma. Answer straight. It works every time. Find the healthy part in people and talk to where it's coming from. Is it pink or blue or green? Use pink or blue or green Dharma. Intellectual? Happy? Subdued? Talk that kind of Dharma. It's magic. For example 'Compassion. Don't get angry. Patience. Kindness. Giving. Happiness. Concentration. Peace. Don't be selfish.' People hear these words deep inside. These are the words to put out fires and really bring more peace into being.

"I've seen it work many times now on the Pilgrimage. Peace-making at the grassroots level."

The Venerable Abbot Speaks: "You two may not get angry no matter what. Don't fight, inside or outside. This will be very important for Buddhism in America. Buddhists will be known as the ones who don't ever get angry. Practice the perfection of patience everywhere. All the time."

Heng Chau • March 8, 1978
We've been looking for you all weekend

North of Cambria, California

Camped in a cow pasture overlooking the ocean last night. Quiet.

We bowed across San Simeon Creek this a.m. The road North is still closed due to winter storm. A man in a van stopped.

"You boys are really gonna' get wet today, yes sir. She's gonna' rain big today, yes sir, hee hee hee," he laughs, "Gonna rain *real* big they say, hee hee hee."

We both look out to sea at the huge black puffs of thunderclouds gathering in the West.

"Well I just thought I'd stop and tell you. You gonna' get rained on. Yes sir, hee hee hee."

The rain is like karma, impartial. If we have it coming to us, it will find us. If we don't have it coming to us, then even in the midst of a storm we'll be safe. If one can straighten out the mind and its deeds then eventually what comes back will be straight too. This is a basic Buddhist principle: everything that happens to you comes from what you do. It's all made from the mind.

> "Resulting retributions come from the karma you create."

> Avatamsaka Sutra

"Sangha" is a Sanskrit word meaning "harmoniously united assembly." It is the community of Buddhist monks and nuns who live together without fighting or dissension. The Sangha is a pure field of blessings for gods and humans because of its members' vast vows and impeccable precepts. They shine like the bright, full moon in an Autumn's sky. The Sangha specializes in taking a loss: they give away their blessings to those with few of their own, they take on suffering to reduce suffering all around. They eat one meal a day to feed the hungry. They wear tattered, plain cotton clothes to clothe those who are short. By not holding personal wealth they give to the poor, and without money their thoughts stay pure.

Treating all beings levelly and equally, the monks and nuns travel lightly through the world, unattached and homeless, free and light at heart. Seeking nothing, creating no problems, always patient, knowing true peace. Content with what comes they are naturally happy and their minds not clogged with longing and worries.

> No karma and no affliction,
> Without possessions and without a home,
> They neither illumine nor practice anything.
> In level equality they travel through the world.
>
> Avatamsaka Sutra

A car full of young men sucking on beers skids its tires to a stop inches from my head as I bow.

"Hey, where *were* you guys? We've been looking for you all weekend," says one with a mischievous grin. A round of smothered giggles and laughs rings out in the car.

These are the young men who have been throwing rocks and fruit at our car at night and "playing chicken" with us during the rainstorm. They looked so afraid behind their beer bottles and young faces I couldn't find it in myself to get angry or uptight. I wanted to say, "What are you so afraid of?"

Heng Sure and I have felt that our fiercest enemies on the road actually are those closest to us. Those who try to force the biggest gulf between themselves and us by put-down, anger, ridicule and threats actually feel a common bond. It is just because they feel so close that they need to make such a show of distancing. Why? Left-home people stand for the emptiness of self and the emptiness of dharmas. They embody the principles that worldly happiness is suffering, and true freedom is non-attachment and seeing through the play we call life.

Their fear is in sensing the truth of no self, but not being able to face it squarely. And so everything gets a little "off," and a nervous kind of energy breathes down their necks. They become stiff and critical, always testing for weak spots, rebels without a cause. They feel like,

"I'm a stranger and afraid in a world I never made."

If you can turn this energy and pressure around and illumine within, it's the fuel for enlightenment. If you can't, this fire spills out into fighting the world, fighting yourself and fighting your own nature until you burn out.

> The Bodhisattva further reflects, "All beings distinguish self and others and mutually harm each other. Fighting, conflict, anger and hatred blaze on without cease. I should cause them all to dwell in unsurpassed great kindness."
>
> Avatamsaka Sutra
> Ten Grounds Chapter Second Ground

We knew where these men were at, and I think they knew where we were, too. They sat in their car watching us bow, beers clutched in hands. There was no traffic, just a light breeze off the ocean blowing through the quiet emptiness. Face to face, no once could get angry or throw rocks, and seeing their thinly covered pain and security we couldn't feel afraid or rejecting of them.

Finally the leader broke the silence,

"Well, we're going to get stoned out of our minds and watch you for the next forty miles. Toot-a-loo." And off they drove.

Dark rain clouds all around, but a patch of blue sky above keeps us dry. A Cambria resident stopped to say,

"I admire your perseverance and I finally got a chance to stop and wish you luck."

Heng Chau • March 9, 1978
The entire world seems identical

> "The ways of the Thus Come Ones, great immortals are subtle, wonderful and hard to comprehend. Not thought, they are apart from every thought. Those seeking them in seeing can't obtain them."
>
> Avatamsaka Sutra
> Ten Grounds Chapter

After a while bowing turns the world into a monotonous blah. Everything looks one color, sounds one sound, smells one scent, tastes one flavor. Gravel, sand, grass, cement, hot and cold, rain or sunny, all blend together and feel the same. One becomes keenly aware of another reality, the world of the mind and all its subtle, wonderful states. When the world of the senses goes flat and flavorless, the world past seeing opens up. It's a world of direct experience "not thought, apart from every thought."

Today the entire world seems identical with the Sutra. Wherever we go we are never outside the Avatamsaka, the Dharma Realm, our own mind. These three are the same. Everything and everyone is a chapter, a page of this great teaching.

These states come and go: they come after long, hard concentrated bowing; they go with false-thinking and emotion. A quiet day. Steady bowing, just the wind and ocean roar. Suddenly everywhere feels like anywhere, anywhere feels like everywhere. Time stops, no inside, no outside – the earth beneath your feet feels as close as the depths of outer space above, like one substance unbounded, neither big nor small, without a beginning or end. A wordless kind of experience.

> Their nature is basically empty and it's still.
> Non-dual it is; but it is also unending...
> They are not beginning, nor middle or end;
> They are not expressive in words;
> They transcend the three times;
> Their characteristics are like empty space.
>
> Avatamsaka Sutra
> Ten Grounds Chapter

Questions of survival and supplies, who you were in the past or might be in the future, all fade away into empty space like the faint cries of sea gulls muted by the absorbing vastness of the sea.

Then you realize that all the things you take for real and important and run after every day are just dreams, a child's fragile sand castle that won't outlast the next big wave.

The words of the Sutra, ancient and changeless wisdom, incomprehensible to mind and thought, these speak right to your heart. One world stops, but another opens that is far more true and real. And there's no way to express any of it. One just bows in gratitude and reverence for having met up with this "friend" who knows your sound.

> Such states as these are difficult to perceive.
> They can be known but not expressed;
> Through the Buddha's power they are proclaimed.
> You should receive them with all reverence.
>
> Avatamsaka Sutra
> Ten Grounds Chapter

Erik, a State Park Ranger, offered some kerosene and a lantern.

"Where are you from? Whom are you associated with?" he asked.

Then without waiting for an answer, he smiled and answered his own questions,

"Oh, it doesn't really matter, we are all the same."

"The Bodhisattva clearly understands that living beings are just a single dharma. They do not have two natures."

Avatamsaka Sutra

Heng Sure
Mountain goblins and the water sprites

"If you want to see the Buddhas in every direction, if you want to give away an inexhaustible treasury of merit and virtue, if you want to eradicate all the bitter hassles that living beings have, you ought to quickly resolve to get enlightened."

Avatamsaka Sutra – The Merit and Virtue
of First Bringing Forth the Mind Chapter

Again and again I return to the basic truth: what counts is heart. If you really want to get enlightened, then nothing will hold you back.

In American talk we say, "Where there's a will, there's a way." The Venerable Abbot's eulogy to Dharma Master Hsuan Chuang has these lines:

"One hundred blows could not disturb his vajra will. Ten thousand demons could not reverse his Bodhi mind..."

The Master instructed us to stand firm when demonic obstacles arise, to continue our work and ignore them. A genuine resolve for Bodhi will cut through any obstacle.

Last Sunday at the Southern end of the Big Sur Coast, we were met by eight highly unusual people just at sunset. Heng Chau said,

"They look like they saw us at the last minute and didn't have time to get their people-costumes on straight." Strangely shaped, moving slowly, they tried to break our practices, to move our minds. We followed instructions and kept on bowing. Later we were advised, "It was the mountain goblins and the water sprites come to play, come to test you out. But they didn't get in."

Heng Chau • March 10, 1978
Big, black and white

A row of motels and a gas station with "sundries" for sale, strung together with pink neon flashing "Vacancy," "Bar and Grill," and "Souvenirs" signs. It's the last town for miles south of Los Padres National Forest. We still need gas tanks and topographical maps for the backcountry. Route uncertain. When in doubt, bow, don't think.

Big storm predicted never hit yesterday. It rained all night, though, from the time we stopped bowing until 6:30 A.M.

Last night we camped in a large field away from the main road. It was dark and overcast. No houses or traffic, so quiet one could hear the fog.

About 1:00 A.M., I snapped awake to the sound of slow, heavy steps in the mud outside. First there was just one, but then more came from other directions. The steps stopped right next to the car. Then came deep, slow breathing. We were surrounded. I could hear it on all sides. I tensed and didn't dare move. They were groaning deeply and grunting as they moved in. Suddenly the car began to shake violently. No group of people could move the car like this. Panic and fear hit. Heng Sure was jolted out of sleep by the car bouncing and shaking. The matches were wet so we couldn't light the lamp. I reached for the flashlight but the batteries were dead.

Finally we got the flashlight working. I timidly shined it out the window as a huge face pressed against the glass inches from my head. What was it? A big black and white dairy cow.

A herd of cows had come to check us out and were using the 1950'ish space ship fins and fenders of the Plymouth to rub against and scratch themselves. The cows were as surprised to see us as we were to see them. They turned and stampeded back into the night.

Emotion is deadly. In the Flower Adornment Sutra Prologue it says,

"When emotion is produced, wisdom is cut off."

As soon as the seven emotions of joy, anger, sadness, fear, love, hate, or desire arise, they cut off wisdom. Our original bright wisdom seems to be lost, but it has only been forgotten, covered over by the darkness of emotion. Wisdom turns into false thinking. Fear turned harmless cows into monstrous goblins in our minds. Our emotions are so heavy they press our wisdom into the ground like the weighty cows pressing their hoofs into the mud.

Later the Master responded to this incident, laughing, and saying,

"If you understood true principle then there's nothing at all to be afraid of. It's all made from the mind. Because you didn't have matches for light, people feared the cows. Once you had matches, the cows feared the people. Basically there's nothing at all in the world; people make all their own troubles. Do you believe me? So it's said, 'If you view what is strange as not strange, then strangeness naturally explains itself.'"

That's just how it was, all made from the mind. Fear eclipsed wisdom. We followed our dark understanding and got turned by appearances making everything come out upside down.

"Of all the dharmas you see in the world, the mind is the only host; Following what you understand you grasp at appearances. This is upside down and not the real thing."

Avatamsaka Sutra

Heng Sure
Let's bring Papa Joe home

Sherry and Kenton Hyatt drove out from Cambria to bring the monks some hot food. With them in their orange VW bus was "half of Cambria" said Kenton. In all there were seven: Abraham and Rosebud, aged 2 and 2 months respectively, Sherry's father Papa Joe Miller, aged 86, and Lynne Borges and her baby daughter, Elizabeth.

"I was so happy to read that Buddhists don't cut their ties with family," said Sherry.

The meal was set out on a cliff above the Pacific but a rain squall moved us back into the bus. Papa Joe who is ailing with the problems of old age, is "not able to walk well on some days." He was originally going to stay in the car and miss the picnic; when the rain came we gathered the party around him.

"You bow in this weather, don't you?" asked Sherry. "Rain or shine," said Heng Chau.

Sherry: "That's the other thing about you that impressed me right away. You're not out for the easy path, I believe."

Heng Chau: "You're the first person to say that right out. People say to us 'Take it easy!' and I answer, 'No, we take it hard.' You realize Heng Sure is not being impolite. He's made a vow of silence."

Sherry: (Laughter) "Yes we know. I can really see the advantages of silence. All the trouble you save. I talk all the time without thinking, so I stick my foot in my mouth – left and right."

Kenton: "Can you tell me briefly what Buddhism is all about in your view?"

Heng Chau: "The Buddhadharma is a method to break your false thoughts and your attachments, so that you can respond to the world as it is right now. I came to it because it gets right to the heart of what's important in life. Buddhism is about ending birth and death and helping other people."

Kenton: "How do you do that?"

Heng Chau: "Right now we're doing it in just one of the many ways possible. We're bowing so as to end disasters and calamities; to turn back the suffering and bad vibes that fill the world. Buddhism holds that all suffering comes from the presence of the Self. We're not bowing *to* anything in particular. But we are trying to bow away our egos."

Sherry: "That's what people see in your work."

Heng Chau: "I think so. People aren't really interested in two individuals – it's what we represent. Are you working for others? That's what counts."

Kenton: "How come Buddhists are identified with seclusion?"

Heng Chau: "Basically monks and nuns are mendicants – wanderers. Temples and monasteries are like base camps to mountain climbers. We leave our homes and the whole universe becomes a home."

Sherry: "So you don't have to go to a temple to be a practicing Buddhist?"

Heng Chau: "If you really practice, then the whole world is a temple. Buddhadharma transcends all boundaries. It doesn't get stuck in any distinctions. That's what we like about it. It's really democratic."

Kenton: "Hmm. Buddhism might be the first true working man's religion. I'm a tour guide at Hearst Castle. Can I be a Buddhist and a tour guide too?"

Heng Chau: "Look at it this way, Kenton. All the tour guides at Hearst Castle are Buddhists. Only some don't recognize it yet. Start with that principle. It's only a matter of time." (Laughter)

Kenton: "How did you two find your way to Buddhism?"

Heng Chau: "Like everyone else, we looked hard for something that had heart, something that lasted. As I said, I wanted to do what was important. To me that meant repaying the kindness of my parents and doing good for others. I couldn't bear the thought of my life just going down the tube."

Kenton: "Well sure, that's everyone's dream. No one plans for this life to be a waste, but somehow it happens to a lot of people."

Heng Chau: "We had to put down a lot to find the Dharma. We took a lot of false roads along the way. We have to come a long way to find out that you had what you wanted all along."

Kenton: "Do you take days off from the bowing?"

Heng Chau: "Our rest is in our work and our work is restful. We like what we do so we do it all the time."

Kenton: "Very few people in the world can say that."

Heng Chau: "It is said that we are 'born drunk and die in a dream.'"

Sherry: (Laughter) "Wow! I like that. Ain't it the truth?"

Heng Chau: "We have a dream of success or fame or all pleasures of desires satisfied and then when we get what we desired, it turns out to be more suffering. If you want a lot of money, you have to hire people to guard it from thieves. If you eat a lot, you get overweight. If you buy a lot of clothes, you can't wear them all — what a lot of hassle."

Sherry: "This comes from false thoughts and attachments in your view, right?"

Heng Chau: "Precisely."

Sherry: "Well, you two have so little. Seems like it would be hard not to always think about getting more."

Heng Chau: "We've learned that what we need, we get if we are sincere. What we don't need, we don't get."

Sherry: "For instance, if you take this wilderness route you're talking about, you'll need a jeep, won't you?"

Heng Chau: "See, there's a false thought. If we need a jeep, by the time we reach the turn-off point, a jeep will appear."

Sherry: "Oh, so that 'what-if' questions are false thoughts."

Heng Chau: "Right. The point in cultivation is to be *here and now*. When you're worried about a jeep in the future, you're no longer *here and now*, and you're *then* already."

Sherry: (Laughter) "I get it."

Heng Chau: "So, when *then* comes you've already been there. Then when the jeep doesn't show up, you get all afflicted and suffering begins. The best way to be is like little Abraham here. Tomorrow's his second birthday, right?"

"Right."

"Well, you know he doesn't spend two seconds today thinking about his party. But then when it comes, he's right there totally into it, same as he is right now."

Sherry: "Children are really pure. When you shave your heads that way, it makes you look like a kid again in a certain way."

Heng Chau: "Exactly. It's another way to return to your original face. (Laughter.) The point is not to decorate the body or cover it with vanity and phoniness."

Kenton: "How do you begin being a Buddhist?"

Heng Chau: "You could say we're all Buddhists to begin with, but we wandered away from our original home. We all begin cultivating by holding the five precepts – the rules of living. No killing, stealing, sexual misconduct, lying, or intoxicants."

Sherry: "Boy, that really says it, doesn't it?"

Heng Chau: "When you hold the precepts then the whole world is a pure place, a temple. You can hold them everywhere. The point of precepts is right here, to stay pure to open the road to concentration and wisdom."

Sherry: "Sounds right on."

Heng Chau: "Abraham isn't clouded over by sex and confusion. He doesn't tell lies. But we've all learned those habits, we've all gotten covered over."

All: "Amen."

Heng Chau: "Precepts give you the purity back. They allow you to drop the covers. When you hold precepts, pretty soon you can say 'see what I had before I got dirty?'"

"The Bodhisattva does not seek nobility... he does not seek riches or benefit... he only cares about upholding pure precepts."

Avatamsaka Sutra
Ten Practices Chapter

"To be human you must first of all be aware that your father's and mother's kindness towards you is higher than heaven and deeper than the ocean. If you don't consider repaying it, you should be truly and greatly ashamed. Such a one is unfit to be called a person."

Master Hua

Kenton: "We had the chance to invite Papa Joe to live with us and look after him. We just didn't believe that a rest home was necessary. After the decision was made, sure enough, we found room. A big house in Cambria came our way and I found a good job in this area that we like, and jobs are incredibly tight around here..."

Sherry: "Things are really going well since we got all our family back together again."

Sherry: "I can't tell you how many blessings have come to us because of taking care of my father."

Kenton: "We were down and out in Santa Ana, California. I had just come out of college. I had all my plans made and was looking ahead. I was going to be a teacher just when the job market didn't want any teachers. It was a hard lesson."

Sherry: "Then my father's health got bad and we didn't believe in rest homes. We thought, what's the most natural, most simple way to put all the pieces of our lives together? We decided to start by giving my father the treatment he deserves. Let's bring Papa Joe home where he belongs. And this is the neat alternative to rest homes. We thought, 'We can do it, so we just do it.'"

Heng Chau: "Boy, that's great. The path to Sagehood starts right here with filial piety. Wonderful. You know why Abraham respects you and is such a happy child? Because he sees how you treat Papa Joe. If you respect your parents you will win your children's respect."

After lunch was over and the Hyatts had returned home, we were still glowing with the good vibes of the visit. Look at what a good time that family has wherever they go because they didn't forsake their elders. On the highway this Sunday, look at all the middle-aged couples passing in their cars and motor homes with vacant, searching looks on their faces while their parents are off in some rest home bored literally to death. I worked in the geriatric ward in a sate hospital in Wisconsin and I'll never forget the miserably lonely old people, no spark left in their lives, passing day after day, sitting in chairs with their heads hanging. So sad. Boy, when I was a kid, just like the Hyatts we would wrap our grandparents up in blanket and drive out to the lakes on Sundays for a picnic. To see that people still do it really fills my heart up. The Buddhadharma is what we need. Kenton said he saw a *chance* to take care of his father-in-law. An opportunity. That's the right attitude. A chance to cultivate filiality. Right on! Bring the old folks back home!

Heng Chau • March 11, 1978
Filiality is basic to being a person

"No Way."

Rain, cold, heavy winds, and biting fog. Scattered thoughts, can't concentrate. Sleep urge hits, the desire to curl up and hibernate when faced with difficulty. Sleep is one of the five basic desires. I can see why. When our egos are most threatened, in times of stress and uprooting, we dive for sleep. "Highway closed and dangerous for travelers ahead," says the CHP.

Sometimes inside and outside gets so thick and heavy with obstacles you feel there's no way through the mire. But if you can hold on and take one more step past the point at which you felt you couldn't go another step, suddenly a clearing opens and a road appears. I really like this quote from Ch'an Master Hua. It has kept us going when we felt there was "no way" at all.

"When you die and have been cremated to ashes, where have you gone? To find the 'you' of your true nature which does not die is the spiritual exercise of Ch'an. When your meditation reaches the point that the mountains are leveled, the seas disappear, and you doubt that there's a way at all, then suddenly, there beyond the dark willow and the bright flower is another village. Although you felt there was no way, there is yet another world, another realm – the realm of light peace. Those who can bring their meditation to the ultimate point can experience freedom, independence, and the bliss of both body and mind – a bliss which is incomparable."

A Reminder to Myself: "Be Just Like the Earth."

> Listen well, O Buddha Son,
> For now I'll tell the truth.
> Whether one gains a speedy release,
> Or has trouble getting free.
> If one seeks to eliminate
> One's measureless evil deeds
> Within the Buddhadharma one must
> Be constantly vigorous, a courageous hero.
>
> Avatamsaka Sutra

There are no gifts or cheating in cultivating the Way. Skill and accomplishment cannot be given or stolen. If it were that easy, we would all be Buddhas by now. It is all up to you to get rid of your own "measureless evil deeds." There are no short cuts. Whether one's release is speedy or unbearably slow and difficult has nothing to do with anyone else at all.

Suffering and bliss begin in the same place: a single thought of the present mind. Pure thoughts bring blessings; defiled thoughts bring suffering. This is the immutable law of karma: "as one thinks so one receives in return."

Be compassionate. Tragedy and happiness, blessings and misfortune, belong to all of us, because all of us belong to one. Others' unhappiness and suffering is just my own. My good fortune and blessings are for everyone. My hang-ups and faults are my own. Others' good luck makes me happy. Share blessings; swallow sufferings. Cleaning up your mind invisibly benefits everyone.

> He eradicates all poisons from the mind.
> In his thoughts he cultivates the highest wisdom.
> Not for himself does he seek peace and happiness.
> His only wish is that living beings get to leave sufferings.
>
> Avatamsaka Sutra

The "mind's poisons" are greed, anger, and stupidity. Don't lay your jealousy and arrogance on others. Don't drag living beings into your garbage heap. Give. Give whatever makes beings happy. Give strength, your possessions, laughter, courage – give by taking a loss. The highest gift is the giving of Dharma. The giving of Dharma is just being a real person: pure, peaceful, and happy and without the slightest bit of self. Manifest a body to speak the Dharma – a body of kindness, compassion, joy and giving in every thought, word and deed. Gather in the entire universe, and in great peace and happiness contain all things. Just like the earth.

> His mind is skillful, he dwells in peace without compare.
> His intentions are constantly pure, he is greatly happy.
> In this way for others he vigorously cultivates.
> Just like the earth which can universally accept all things.
>
> Avatamsaka Sutra

"Papa Joe."

> "What is mindfulness of parents' kindness? Alas! My parents. They bore me with hard labor, ten months in the womb, three years at the breast, drying my bottom, changing my diapers, swallowing bitterness and feeding me sweetness. Only then was I able to become a person..."
>
> Exhortation to Resolve Upon Bodhi
> by Great Master Hsing An (d. 1735 A.D.)

The Hyatts, a young family from Cambria, drove out on a blustery day to share a meal offering. There was Ken and Sherry, their two small kids, Abe and Rose, still in diapers. And all bundled up in blankets, warm and dry, sitting in the back seat, was their aging father, Papa Joe.

Papa Joe could no longer walk. He showed signs of senility and required a lot of care and patience. But the Hyatts didn't seem to be put out or burdened. Ken carried Papa Joe out to the picnic spot and when a rainstorm came up, he quickly wrapped him in a blanket and carried him to the car.

We all squeezed together in their V.W. bus along with a friend of theirs and her infant, making nine in all. They listened with bowed heads as Heng Sure and I chanted the meal offering and rang the hand bell. Over hot vegetable soup and homemade bread, the Hyatts told their story.

"Papa Joe was ready for the nursing home, but we didn't feel right about it, so we asked him to please come and live with us. We felt he'd be doing us a favor. We were so happy when he agreed."

"At the time," said Ken, "we had no house, no money and I couldn't find work. But you know right after our decision to ask Papa Joe to come live with us, things opened up. A big old house came our way and I got a fine job offering in *this* area even, where jobs are almost non-existent."

Papa Joe sits quietly, smiling now and again, as the kids crawl around his legs chasing a ball. He's so obviously happy and at peace.

"We feel all our blessings came from doing right by Papa Joe," said Mrs. Hyatt. "We just did what came naturally."

A cold rain blows against the windows. The Hyatts say they came out because they felt somehow Buddhism stood for filiality and just doing the right and natural things in life. Lynn, their friend, picks up that we don't talk much and says,

"I talk too much. My tongue is like a snake." Everyone laughs. The Hyatts are drawn to the moral precepts of Buddhism and the spiritual goal to "go back to the root, return to the source." It's as if the principles of Buddhism are already deeply rooted in their minds, in a timeless, natural understanding.

They identify with the Buddhadharma as much or even more so than with their home state, Ohio. (Someone mentions the monks are from the Midwest, and Heng Sure from Ohio. Papa Joe perks up and grins, reaching out to shake hands. "Ohio!? That's where I'm from." Papa Joe has been listening to every word about Buddhism nodding where he agrees. When he hears "Ohio" something connects and suddenly Buddhism is very close to home, like it was as American as corn and apple pie.)

"But what really excited us was when we heard that filiality is a fundamental teaching in Buddhism. We just had to come out," says Mrs. Hyatt.

The ultimate expression of filiality is cultivating the Way. To repay the kindness of parents is a primary motivating factor in spiritual history. It is a belief shared by the ancients and enlightened teachers of all countries over the centuries. The Buddha, Shakyamuni, spoke the Earth Store Sutra to rescue his mother, and also set forth the Bodhisattva precepts (pratimoksha in the Brahma Net Sutra) to repay his parents.

"At that time, when Shakyamuni Buddha first sat beneath the Bodhi tree, after realizing the supreme enlightenment, he set forth the Bodhisattva pratimoksha out of filial compliance towards his parents, his masters among the Sangha, and the Triple Jewel. Filial compliance is a dharma of the Ultimate Way. Filiality is called precepts, also called restraint and stopping."

Brahma Net Sutra

Why the precepts? Because precepts are the only way one can end the suffering of birth and death and leave the turning wheel of the six paths. Filiality is an ultimate teaching moreover, because one who is enlightened sees all living beings as his own parents. Therefore, he restrains himself to act with utmost kindness and compassion and filial regard toward all that lives.

"All male beings have been a father to me in former lives and all females have been my mother. There is not a single being who has not given birth to me during my previous lives, hence all beings of the six destinies are my parents."

Bodhisattva Precepts

It is from this understanding of the oneness of all beings and inter-relatedness of all things that Buddhism takes its roots. They Hyatts recognized it immediately. Filiality is basic to being a person and to accomplishing ultimate wisdom.

"If you want to be a person, the very first thing you should know is that compared to the sea, your parents' kindness is deeper; compared to the sky, your parents' kindness is higher... If you plan to repay them, you must first learn to have virtue and to teach living beings to cultivate the Way. It is said, 'If one child obtains the Way, nine generations will leap over birth and death.'"

From Record of Water and Mirror Reflections
By Ven. Master Hua

More advice against continuing on Highway 1. Local people volunteer gas and water, and check out alternate routes.

"Papa Joe" was our Dharma lecture for the day. We learn from everyone.

Heng Sure • March 12, 1978
Nature's first law

Old Age: A Blessing, Not a Crime.

> "There are four rules inseparable in obtaining happiness and prosperity in your next life. The first of these is to be dutiful to parents."
>
> The Sutra of Cause and Effect

The Buddha teaches filiality as Nature's First Law. The Buddha speaks truth, with principles older than time itself. Old age is a natural badge of honor. But in the younger generation, being old is often viewed as a crime.

> Can you imagine us years from today,
> Sharing our park bench quietly?
> How terribly strange to be seventy.
>
> Simon and Garfunkel

Until this century, old people lived among their kin. Big families held together. Youth honored, and respected the wisdom and experience of elders. Divorces were few, runaway children were fewer, suicides and alcoholism rare. The family absorbed the stress and confusion of life. People lucky enough to have their seniors alive enjoyed happiness, blessings and a sense of belonging sadly lacking in the contemporary, alienated world.

But all creatures fear death and prefer the dream of immortality. Science and materialism give people new solutions to the riddle of impermanence for the first time in history. "No deposit, no return;"

throw away the old; hide grandparents in the senior's home. We replace anything that wears out, including old people. We toss out jobs, mates, hearts, and kidneys as easily as changing T.V. channels.

Filiality is forgotten in a graceless scramble for eternal youth. Growing old in the twentieth century is an unpardonable sin. "Everyone for himself," has become a universal disease. We preserve the Ego and repair its failing, leaking, boy-shell. We ignore the signs everywhere shouting: "Wake up! A tree that cuts it roots cannot stand long."

Buddhists face aging and death with an even mind. Nature's cycles revolve in perfect harmony. Who would feel complete in a year without winter?

> "To everything turn, turn, turn; there is a season, turn, turn, turn, and a time to every purpose under Heaven. A time to be born, a time to die…"
>
> Ecclesiastes

It's time we restored the dignity of old age, time to rescue our elders from solitary confinement at the senior's home. Filiality is Nature's First Law.

Heng Sure
The supreme medical student

Meat and Disasters.

> "When one merely studies but does not cultivate the Dharma, it is like concocting an efficacious medicine without curing one's own sickness."
>
> Avatamsaka Sutra
> Bodhisattvas Ask for Clarification Chapter

One of the best analogies for the Buddhadharma is medicine and health. Here are a few of the ways to explore the comparison:

– The Buddha is the healthiest being alive. When you get enlightened to the Buddha's wisdom, you take on the Buddha's healthy body, the indestructible body of Dharma.

– The Avatamsaka Sutra describes a state of ultimate health. Most of us are sick but don't realize it. Once we get sick of being sick and begin to cultivate, the Dharma medicine brings us back to health. Then we can see how sick we were.

To illustrate, I spent the first three months on the pilgrimage purging my body of foul garbage. It ran out of all my holes almost beyond my control. I felt sicker than before I began to cultivate. But I recognized it as a healing process. What was flowing out of me were the poisons accumulated over years of bad habits. Determination to fulfill my karma in the Way carried me through this dark time. The coarser sickness has now been purged. I'm fighting the subtler effects of the illness of selfish greed, hatred and stupidity every day now.

– Don't tolerate being sick. It is not the natural state. The Dharma is the road to recovery. You have to walk it yourself. You have to heal yourself. The walking is the healing.

– The Bodhisattva is the supreme medical student studying and applying the cures for the ultimate health of all beings. He has passed his boards and is doing a prolonged internship throughout the Dharma realm, before receiving his degree of annutarasamyaksambodhi.

– The first year of the pilgrimage feels like pre-med studies. Learning the fundamentals, cleaning up the tool kit, studying the diseases first-hand, curing ourselves. Purging the yin, building the yang, preparing to focus on health.

Heng Chau • March 12, 1978
The antithesis of the castle

> "Disciples of the Buddha, what is the Bodhisattva Maha-sattva's practice of benefiting? ...The Bodhisattva does not seek awesome power, he doesn't seek high class (nobility), he does not seek riches or benefits, he does not seek a handsome appearance or a King's throne. He is attached to none of these. He only cares about solidly upholding pure precepts."
>
> Avatamsaka Sutra
> Ten Practices Chapter

We are camped below the historic Hearst Castle which is poised in the state on the ridge high above us overlooking the sea. It is a monument to mammon and the multi-millionaire W.R. Hearst who built it. Hearst is dead. The castle remains as a tourist attraction operated by the State.

A tour guide from the castle stopped to offer encouragement. As we talked on the highway he looked up at the white-faced mansion and then back down to our dusty old Plymouth and the bowing.

"He spent more money on himself than any person in the history of this country. This is the monument he built to himself. It cost millions of dollars. He entertained nobility, movie stars, and presidents. But he was very unhappy," said the guide.

"His life and family was a mess and full of tragedy. You know, you monks are the antithesis of the castle and the mind that made it. You try to make your 'self' invisible. You leave worldly attachments and live in voluntary bitterness. Instead of building up personal fortunes, you make giving to others your life's work," he observed. "Really interesting, I mean, seeing both of you together here – the monks bowing and the castle. Kind of a mind stopper, you know?"

It's a violation of precepts to hold gold, silver, or valuable objects. Why? It's selfish. These things increase greed and can undo one's karma in the Way. When the Buddha was in the world, the Sangha begged for food and didn't cook for themselves. Clothing and shelter were provided from external conditions. Consequently gold and silver were useless. Because they did not touch money, their purity was obvious and inspiring.

In the Vinaya it says that perhaps handling "gold and silver" (money) is unavoidable in the present day.

> "But one should know that this is contrary to the Buddha's instructions and be greatly ashamed. Be mindful of the poverty of others, and always practice giving. Do not run a business, do not amass wealth, and do not trade. Do not adorn your clothing and possessions with the seven jewels.

> "Only if you act like this can you handle valuables without committing a serious offense. To hoard money and save wealth is wrong. Benefiting others simply means don't plot and scheme for your own benefit. Never forget there are many people suffering in bitter poverty."

> Shramanera Vinaya

Cold, windy and clear. Quiet nights except for the soft sounds of surf and a few night birds. A couple of fishing boats bob at anchor in the small harbor below. There's not much traffic north of Hearst Castle. This is kind of the end of the road for Southern California. Wilshire Boulevard and traffic-choked Los Angeles Freeway system have tapered off and whittled down to the stillness of tall pines and a narrow coast road. We are almost ½ way to the City of 10,000 Buddhas.

How is the bowing? It is difficult and wonderful, bitter and magical. "Keep to the natural. Cultivate the basics and be simple" advised the Master on his last visit. These few words hit a deep spot in us. Everything we need we already have inside. True peace is to be content with what you have.

> Don't greed afar and forsake what is near.
> Don't seek anything and there are no problems.

Heng Sure
They don't make them like they used to

"Namo Da Fang Gwang Fwo Hwa Yen Jing" (Namo Great Means Expansive Buddha Flower Adornment Sutra)

Hearing the name of the Avatamsaka Sutra is most rare. Opening its covers is rarer still. Hearing its principles is one chance in billions of kalpas. Bowing to it, praising it, making offerings to it is a chance you might hope for and never get. Studying the text, memorizing its principles, propagating its doctrines surpasses words and fortune.

"Hwa Yen Hai Hwei Fwo Pu Sa" (Flower Adornment Sea-Like Assembly of Buddhas and Bodhisattvas)

> "I should perfect all of the Buddha's Dharmas, dwell in the supreme place of level impartiality and with an even mind, contemplate all beings."
>
> Avatamsaka Sutra
> Ten Practices Chapter

Don't force it. Don't try so hard. Just use your mind and *practice*. Contemplate. Cultivate. Concentrate.

"With one heart bowing to the City of 10,000 Buddhas." I contemplate it as "With *all* my heart, bowing to the City of 10,000 Buddhas." That's what we're working at, to give this City to the Dharma Realm.

The pilgrimage is a precious opportunity to use medicine to cure my illness of greed, hatred, and stupidity. The medicine is Dharma, personally prescribed by the King of Physicians to heal my sickness and return me naturally, slowly, through my own best efforts to total and perfect health.

The biggest change since the first bow? Beside Hearst Castle, as we passed the last little town I realized, "Hey, I don't *want* any false thoughts in my head. They just mess me up. Hey! I don't *want* to seek and climb anymore. Seeking creates a seeker, a self, and here the pain begins. I don't want to do that anymore."

In *tai ji quan* use your mind to keep your energy low. In cultivation, use your method to still false thoughts. In sitting Ch'an, use whatever it takes to sit still! Don't wiggle!

Sitting Ch'an puts me closer to my own life. Sitting still, I penetrate my own barriers. All I do is sit still and use the method. The mind settles and purifies itself. Like magic. When I can't bear to sit any longer, I use the principles of the Sutra text and I can bear it longer.

And all actions of the day are just the same! Can't bow another bow? Think of Ch'an sitting. Bow. Can't keep silent? Think of patient bowing. Silence! Can't hold your vows? Think of Sutras. Keep your vows! "The Way and the response intertwine, hard to conceive of."

The words of the Avatamsaka Sutra are magical. They carry a special charge of light and energy. They hold limitless meanings. The meanings string together my mind's random ideas like an index to a good book. Memorizing the Ten Practices Chapter of the Sutra is the best project I've begun since I've left home!

Ch'an sitting is endless yielding. Letting go. How does virtuous practice aid Ch'an meditation? One with virtue is at ease and natural in every situation. When sitting Ch'an, as states arise, it is easy to stiffen the body and attach the mind to this or that thought and leave the Middle Way. When virtue is practiced one can easily recognize unnatural states and return to the simple, the Middle.

Take care not to seek outside!
Guard the Middle Way.

The Heart Sutra, Verses by Master Hua

The section of Highway 1 below Salmon Creek winds like an eel. It cuts back to deep gorges and silver waterfalls, then return to the seaside. Vertical cliffs plummet hundreds of feet below. No room to stop cars for photos, and bowing the curves is tricky. We travel where few walk; at our inchworm pace we get a rare view of the landscape. The road hangs in empty space, a thin thread halfway between heaven and the sea. Who built it? The WPA? They were superb stonemasons. The snaking switchbacks are held in place by magnificent escarpments of mortar and stone. Huge slabs, perfect joints, keep the roadway in place against some of the world's meanest storms. We travel on the sweat of our elders. We eat the fruit of land they cleared. The old-timers who built the buttresses had skill and courage. I doubt the workmanship could be duplicated any longer. No one takes the time or care today that went into making this isolated highway on the edge of America. I admire the wisdom and experience of age and I recall a story told by a Chinese professor at Berkeley.

"Where I grew up in China," he said, "I walked to town over an old bridge near my home. An emperor committed suicide, jumped from the bridge into the river, eight centuries ago; the bridge was captured and lost during six dynasty changes and civil wars. It has witnessed famines, countless spring floods, and autumn harvests; a poet in the Ming Dynasty used those smooth stones as background for some of his famous stanzas. That's history."

"No one recalls exactly how long the family has lived in the same spot," he continued. "My grandfather guessed well over five centuries, maybe longer. Our family was solid, just like that old bridge."

Heng Chau • March 13, 1978
I was afraid I missed you

"Happiness."

> Moreover, when one meets a sagely ruler,
> Obtaining it (Avatamsaka Sutra) on magic mountain,
> Exhaustively reflecting on its esoteric doctrine,
> How can one but jump for joy?
>
> Avatamsaka Preface

> "The whole world is a Sutra. Roll it up, secretly hide it away; let it go, it fills the universe."
>
> Master Hua
L.A. Instruction, 1978

> "I give rise to happiness because I draw near the grounds of wisdom... I give rise to happiness because I draw near to all Buddhas."
>
> Avatamsaka Sutra
Ten Grounds Chapter
Ground of Happiness

Happy. Happy beyond words. Why? Because I feel I am coming "back home" to my true home, the Avatamsaka. It's alive inside each of us, and vibrating all around and through everything and everyone. Everything I've been searching for is contained within the wonder of this "esoteric doctrine," and none of it is outside my own heart. All that happens speaks the Sura; the Sutra pulses in all that happens.

> It may truly be called
> Wonderful speech of constant duration.
> Vast model of universal scope.
> Ultimate expression congruent with the nature...
>
> Avatamsaka Preface

All I ever did, thought, felt or wished for appears and comes together in the simple act of bowing to this Sutra. I have no way to explain it. Magical, yet real. I feel relaxed and at ease. A serenity and certainty has set in – not from having everything figured out or down pat, but rather from knowing nothing for sure, having nothing fixed.

Everything feels big and connected, simple and mysterious. Like a child with boundless energy, I feel I could go on forever from wonder to wonder without tiring or getting "homesick" in the vast, boundless universe of the mind. I want to share this happiness with all beings.

Ride the Dharma-Wind.

True son of the Buddha, Vajra Solid Bodhisattva breaks the shell, melts the ice with the virtuous power of the four unlimited hearts.

> Seeking nothing, nowhere to attain,
>   then all obstructions ended.
> Free n' easy, truly letting go
>   he rides the Dharma wind, and
> With the Flower Garland fragrance,
>   purifies the world.

Heng Chau

Note to a Selfish Cultivator (Myself):

"Stop seeking, just concentrate, with one heart and bow. Work hard and be patient. Be without goals or purpose; have no expectations. No self, no others, no living beings, no lifespan. No yesterday, tomorrow, or today.

"Give. Just give and transfer constantly to every living being. Don't seek enlightenment, peace or Dharma-bliss. Selfishness ruins the world, only giving can save it."

"Disciples of the Buddha, when the Bodhisattva, Mahasattva gives in this way he has no thoughts of being false, no thoughts of hope or of reputation, no thoughts of regret or anxiety... Until all kalpas of the future come to an end I will always practice giving, and I will dwell in the mind's wisdom of all-wisdom."

Avatamsaka Sutra

Stan, the old retired man from Morro Bay, drove out with some supplies. He said goodbye back near Morro Bay as he was too old to drive any further. Yet he came all this way to help us along and offer encouragement because he was worried about the storms and road ahead.

"I was afraid I missed you," he said. That was his only concern. We were deeply touched.

Maybe it's coincidence but Stan shows up each time our heart opens to the Avatamsaka. He comes after an understanding about oneness of all beings and a resolve to end suffering and bring happiness to the world. Stan was the man from Idaho who said, "This is what will make the country strong. America needs more of if. It helps everyone along."

Flip-Flop as fast as turning over the hand. The mind can turn from true to false, from pure to defiled.

As soon as I began to false think, a speeding car tried to run us off the road. Then a pick-up truck full of shouting men tossed a home-made "pestle" of empty carbine gun shells held together with electrical tape. The car missed by inches, so did the missile and so did my mind. One cannot leave proper mindfulness, not even for an instant. We get back exactly what we put out, sometimes immediately.

Heng Sure • March 14, 1978
I will be good to all the world's children

The loneliness we feel in our lives has its roots in selfishness. We feel empty and spiritually poor because we forgot to be filial.

Ask yourself, "Why are my children unfilial? Is it not because I myself was unfilial to my own parents? How shameful! Whether or not they are good to me, I will be good to my children, and to all the world's children. I shall respect all elders as my elders, and treat all children as my children. In this way the world will quickly become peaceful."

Essay by Master Hua
"What Great Joy", Vajra Bodhi Sea #15

Heng Chau • March 14, 1978
True giving is without a mark

"According With All Beings."

"If a Bodhisattva accords with all beings, then he accords with and make offerings to all Buddhas. If he can honor and serve living beings, then he honors and serves the Thus Come Ones. If he makes living beings happy, he is making all the Thus Come Ones happy."

Avatamsaka Sutra
Chapter 40

What does it mean to "accord?" It means to get along and harmonize with, not to oppress and obstruct. According should be very natural, like falling rain or fruit dropping when ripe. When something comes up, one responds; when it's gone, one is quiet.

Too often I seek after things and try to rush my way through the world. This isn't according, and what doesn't accord soon perishes.

There is a time to give and a time to be still; a time to let go and fill the universe, and a time to roll it up and secretly hide away.

Seeking to give is still greed and often conceals a desire to be spotlighted and acclaimed. True giving is without thought or a mark. It is so natural and appropriate that the giver seems as if empty and the gift passes unnoticed.

We are learning to gather in our energy and to accord with conditions; to honor and serve when it's ripe, to be quiet when it's not. Making living beings happy happens by itself when one is just being oneself, spontaneously unattached and peaceful. Peacefulness comes from knowing sufficiency and not seeking self-benefit.

Heng Sure • March 15, 1978
Extremely lucky to have good parents

Be Filial: Leave Home.

The Hyatt family brought Heng Chau and me a fresh appreciation of the value of leaving the home life. Papa Joe Hyatt, ailing and infirm, was a happy man. His son, daughter-in-law, and their two children shared a special joy in life. And we in turn, rejoice in their upholding the dharma of filiality. Filiality is a natural blessing. Respect for elders is right in the heart.

If so, why have we chosen to cultivate the Way instead of staying at home and honoring our parents? Because ancient wisdom teaches: "When a child obtains the Tao, nine generations of ancestors are reborn in the heavens."

Our families gave us solid ground for growing up into world citizens. We feel extremely lucky to have good parents. Only because of their deep kindness were we able to step up to the challenge of life as Buddhist disciples. Cultivators of the Way forsake personal security and transfer their filial duties to a bigger responsibility: they devote their lives not to maintaining one family line but to preserving the supreme path to liberation for all beings.

Heng Chau • March 15, 1978
Give me the mountains any day

A tour guide from the Hearst Castle stopped to wish us luck.

"I work there," he said, pointing up at the castle.

"Hearst Castle?"

"Yes. But we call it Cursed Hassle. Because even though it is the finest of palaces, it brought nothing but a curse and hassles to the man who built it. Outside rich, inside poverty stricken... Do you want a tour?" he asked.

"No thanks, we don't sightsee," I answered.

Why no sightseeing? Because of all the "sights" we see in the world "the mind alone is the host," says the Avatamsaka. Originally we were whole and complete. Any looking outside is like adding water to an already full cup – it spills over. The smallest amount of sightseeing is adding a head on top of a head. Seeking anything is climbing on conditions and arises from greed and ignorance. No joke. We have paid dearly each time we chased outside, even a "small peek's" worth. It is like tying an anchor around your neck and jumping into a sea of suffering. The more you look, the more you lose. You go out in high spirits to "take in the sights," but it's *you* who gets "taken in," and you return dead-tired and drained. Why? Because your natural wisdom-light and energy flow out to sights, sounds, smells, tastes, tangibles and dharmas. These are the "six places." So the Bodhisattva stays at home, seeking nothing, always cool and happy. No "cursed hassles," content with his original share.

> He is happy, blissful,
>   apart from all worry and vexation.
> His heart and will are soft and flexible.
> All his organs are clean and cool.
>
> Avatamsaka Sutra

Why? Because he knows everything is made from the mind alone, and all the "sights" we see appear according to our thoughts. Outside of this there's nothing at all. We are simply looking into a mirror that steals our image. The Bodhisattva therefore says,

> I do not rely on form.
> I am not attached to feelings.
> I am not turned upside-down by thoughts.
> I do not do actions.
> I do not seek consciousness.
> I forsake the six places.
>
> I do not dwell in worldly dharmas.
> My joy is in leaving the world;
> I know all dharmas are like empty space,
> They come from nowhere.
>
> Avatamsaka Sutra

While traveling with the Abbot in an historic city full of tourist spots, our host asked, "Would the Venerable Abbot like to go sightseeing?"

"Why sightsee?" replied the Abbot. "I've seen it all already."

Today is the celebration of Shakyamuni Buddha's leaving the home-life. Heng Ju and Kuo Kwei (Nicholson) drove us to San Luis Obispo to arrange passports for Asia. We picked and boiled up some fresh roadside "weeds" and ate on car bumpers in a dirt pull-off by the ocean.

Eric, the Park Ranger, pulls up, "Ah, real Dharma Bums, at last!" he says. "Be prepared for a long rugged camp out if you go through the mountains. *Nothing* up there. Stock up on everything, especially gas, food, and water," he advises.

"Creeks?" I ask.

"About one every ten miles. I'd drink out of them, but not out of the lake." he replied.

"Gas?" I ask.

"Nothing."

"Vegetation?"

"Uncertain. Big forest fire up there. It could very well be completely burned out." he said. "I'll see what I can find out. It's really beautiful, but rough wilderness."

"And this road?" I ask.

"Narrow. One-foot-wide loose shoulder at best. You'd spend all your time watching out for traffic, but it's more convenient then the mountain route."

Convenience has never been a consideration, but survival has. We worry more for other people's safety than our own. We are not equipped for wilderness travel. Our car is a low-to-the-ground "deluxe" station wagon designed for shopping trips in suburbia and commuter freeways, not for back-country trail blazing. But we were told not to get run over or bow where traffic and road conditions are too dangerous. A dilemma.

Eric is scanning the countryside and raises his chest as he takes in a deep breath.

"Boy, I feed off this land! After living in Beverly Hills... Well, you just can't find this there," he says. "Give me the mountains and green rolling hills any day."

I used to feel just like Eric: the mountains and deep forests soothed and cleaned the mind; the cities drained the spirit and created all our hassles. Now I'm not so sure. There were moments bowing through Beverly Hills, even during rush hour smog, that I've never felt more peaceful and happy. And there have been times while bowing through breathtaking coastal scenery, renowned for its beauty and stillness, that I've never been more uptight and miserable. Everything is created from the mind alone, even if we don't recognize our own creations. In the Avatamsaka it says the mind is just like an artist that can paint the entire world. There is nothing it does not create. And yet,

Just as the master painter
Cannot know his own mind,
Still his paintings come from the mind;
The nature of all dharmas is like this.

Avatamsaka Sutra

It is all in how you look at it. However you see it, that's how it is. A peaceful mind finds peace anywhere; a troubled mind feels trouble everywhere.

The poet John Milton put it this way,

The mind is its own place, and in itself,
Can make a hell of heaven, and a heaven of hell.

From "Paradise Lost"

The McKenzies brought out gas and water and maps.

"John works for the Forest Service. We'll plan out a route and have the problem solved by next week," said Mrs. McKenzie.

A trip to Asia, the wilderness route, a dangerous road closed off ahead, gas and water supplies in doubt. Who knows what will come of it all? We live one day at a time, but living one bow at a time would be even better. With no past, no present, no future, what is there to worry about? We worry for ourselves, but the self does not exist. The circumstances of living on the highway pressure us into waking up from our dreams. Basically there is nothing to hold on to and nowhere to dwell.

"If one contemplates it thus, then one will have no desires with regard to the body, no attachments to what is cultivated and will not dwell in any dharma.

"The past is over, the future has not come, and the present is empty and still."

Avatamsaka Sutra
Brahma Conduct Chapter

Anything goes. If we let go and release our hold, it is wonderful. It's in hanging on that we suffer.

A young woman in colorful clothes bedecked with fresh flowers quietly offers a handful of bright flowers for the car altar and a smile.

An elderly man in a jeep stops to encourage us and says, "Bless you, brother."

We are at the edge of Big Sur. Marked change in topography and vibes.

Heng Sure • March 16, 1978

"Because he valued the Dharma, he did not cherish his body or life, how much the less did he crave a king's throne, cities, towns, palaces, gardens, groves, or any material thing at all."

Avatamsaka Sutra
Chapter 40

Hearst Castle sits on the cliffs above. W.R. Hearst collected dharmas; he brought the entire world in bits and pieces to Southern California: Italian frescoes, African giraffes, British courtyards, Chinese porcelains, Persian rugs. He scattered an emperor's wealth to the winds, building a monument to emptiness. His tragic effort at immortality is one of human kind's most adorned follies

We prize our shelf of Sutras in the old Plymouth. They contain a treasury of wisdom. Sometimes we open the car door and the Sutras seem to glow. Cultivate the Sutras' Dharma as the Buddha spoke it and one opens the door to peace and joy, worth more than any throne, palace, city, or garden on earth.

Heng Sure • March 16, 1978
Feeling the Master's presence

Dear Shr Fu,

Spring came all of a sudden today and we took off layers of clothes for the first time since November, it seems. Hot sun and visits by swarms of insects.

It's so clear that everything is made from the mind alone. Last month I dug through my clothes bag looking for a pair of warm socks. The light, hot-weather socks would not do. Too cold. Today I sorted through again. The heavy wool socks looked like pure misery on such a hot day. They were no longer attractive. At the bottom of the bag were the light socks. Ah! Perfect. Had the socks transformed in four months. Not a bit. It was all my mind's doing, making big discriminations, and seeking comfort for the skin-bag. Being a living being can sure be complicated and troublesome.

Heng Chau and I have had a big realization over the past few months that the Venerable Abbot is here among us. We reached this awareness after experiencing Shr Fu's instructions coming true in our hearts time after time. Such clarity and precise timing! Wherever we wander on our initial attempts to walk the Middle Way, whatever state arises in our meditation, we find the Master has foreseen our direction. Then either he points to an open door and/or by using some effortless expedient means he delivers with a message or a gatha to steer us away from a certain path, or to another straighter, higher road. This is hard to communicate in words, but we both feel the Master's presence as we work. It's tangible, reliable, and constant, as long as we use effort. The power and the wisdom of a Good and Wise Advisor is inconceivable.

Many cultivators throughout history have worked really hard, but fell into attachments to form or to emptiness and stopped their progress simply because they had no such teacher to guide them. Heng Chau and I bow to our teacher each day on the highway, morning, noon and night with ever-deepening respect for him and with a profound sense of wonder at our incredible good luck to have met a Good Knowing Advisor in this life.

Disciple Guo Chen (Heng Sure)
bows in respect

Heng Chau • March 16, 1978
Cabrillo Highway

"Dharma Bums' Dilemma."

We bowed past San Simeon. The road abruptly shrinks and twists. The road signs say,

"Road Narrows"

"Highway 1 – Cabrillo Highway"

"Gorda – 26; Montery – 94; San Francisco – 212"

"Road closed 41 miles North of this point."

Heng Chau • March 16, 1978
There is no fixed way to get to the City

Dear Shr Fu,

It's spring. Suddenly there are warm winds and soft sounds. The bitter and cold winter storms are gone, leaving behind flowered green meadows and easy, flowing creeks. The birds are looking for mates and building nests. It's that time and the earth's "natural" energy all moves in this direction: make your mark in the world, nesting (the home) and being creative.

And us? We are also returning to the natural – the original natural, the unconditioned self-nature. Life after life we yielded to spring's desires and pleasures. Life after life we went "with the flow" and returned to the nest. But the nest (home) became a cage and soon the ultimate questions arose: "Is this it? Is this all there is? Mating and dying, dying and mating? Birth, dwelling, decay, emptiness all in the blink of an eye? Is there no more than eating, sleeping and wearing clothes? How and where do you look?"

> If there are those
>   who don't know how to get out,
> Who do not seek liberation
>   but only cry and are dazed,
> The Bodhisattva manifests for them
>   the giving up of his country and wealth,
> And constantly happy, he leaves the home-life
>   and his mind is tranquil and still.
>
> Avatamsaka Sutra

Yesterday, Heng Ju and Kuo Kuei Nicholson stopped by and Kuo Kuei commented, "Tomorrow is a special day."

"Oh?" I said.

"Yeah, it's the day Shakyamuni Buddha shaved his head and rode off on a white horse – his left-home day." What a powerful image of purity and freedom: the Buddha shaving his head and riding off on a white horse to cultivate! Shakyamuni Buddha had one of the finest nests. So why leave it?

> The home is a place of greed and love,
>   bondage and fetters.
> He wants all living beings
>   to be able to leave it behind.
> Therefore, he manifests leaving home
>   and gaining liberation,
> And amid all desires and pleasures
>   he accepts none of them.
>
> Avatamsaka Sutra

This morning while bowing along the deserted, quiet road, I realized it has been almost a year since I left home and I'm happier every day. There is another natural urging that wells up inside of living beings. It is the urge for enlightenment and ultimate freedom. It is stronger and more basic than mating and nesting (needing a partner) and in time we all follow it. In time, we all realize it. "All have the Buddha-nature, all will become Buddhas." Some of us will mate this spring, some of us will cultivate. And that will make all of the difference. But, originally there is no difference, and sooner or later we all are "able to leave it all behind" and ride off on a white horse. So, "everything is okay," as the Master often says.

Everybody should be free and happy this spring and every day go toward the good. Lighten the heart and purify the mind and find ways to benefit others. In a year of bowing, Heng Sure and I are discovering that cultivation is right here in these simple basics. Getting rid of greed, anger, and stupidity is what matters and causes others to be happy and free. May we all go to perfect enlightenment together real soon. I hope so. Much peace in the Dharma.

P.S.: The local Dharma Protectors have strongly urged us to leave Highway 1 and find an alternate route. The road apparently becomes very winding, narrow, and heavily trafficked. Our friends in the Forest Service are mapping out a new route for us through Ventana Wilderness and Los Padres National Forest. It will by-pass the treacherous section of Highway 1 up to Carmel. We should have it figured out whenever it's figured out. We have learned to not force or get attached to even the smallest things. Whatever happens will be as it should be and in accord with conditions, not our false thoughts. We will be on Highway 1 for another 4-5 weeks as best we can tell and will let you know as soon as we have a new route to the City of Ten Thousand Buddhas. There is no fixed way to get to the City of Ten Thousand Buddhas! All roads to it eventually return.

Disciple Guo Ting (Heng Chau)
bows in respect

Heng Sure • March 17, 1978
As you grow older, grow stronger

"Recycle the Mind."

"People age, but youth and age are basically identical. In both youth and age you are still the same person. Having been in the world for a time, you feel old, but your mind is always young. So don't retire and say, 'I'm old;' say instead, 'I am young!' If your heart is young, age cannot affect you, and will run away. Buddhism teaches that 'everything is made from the mind alone.'"

Master Hua
Vajra Bodhi Sea #15 June 1971

Old people are a natural resource. Ecology-minded citizens can recycle a priceless treasure of talent, energy, and wisdom if we heed the Master's advice. The secret to reclaiming an ocean of vital energy overlooked and wasted at present: cultivate the mind; diligently cultivate precepts, concentration and wisdom. Wipe away greed, anger, and stupidity!

The Avatamsaka discriminates youth and age only by praising respect towards one's elders. In Buddhism, human lifespan is a view of the impermanent physical body. The mind creates all the different bodies. Following our karma we turn and flow in an endless cycle of birth, old age, sickness and death.

"Living beings' bodies are all different. They come from adherence to the distinctions in thoughts. So too are the many kinds of Buddhalands; none do not come from karma."

Avatamsaka Sutra
Flower Store World Chapter

To retire mature, experienced minds at age 65 is a great waste. To abandon one's elders and grandparents as their bodies decay is bad karma. The mind endures, returns, and does not forget.

> "People of long life are the world's most honorable citizens. That is not to say that they honor themselves, but that they receive the respect of others... Don't be satisfied with growing old; as you grow older, grow stronger, so that the older you grow, the stronger you become. How does one grow stronger? By benefiting the world. Do whatever work you can for the common good of all people."
>
> Master Hua
> Vajra Bodhi Sea #15

Heng Chau • March 17, 1978
An elegant woman out of nowhere

Coincidence? We have entered new territory and geography: rolling foothills that rise abruptly into the famous, rugged Big Sur coastline. Suddenly unusual people appear. This has been the case throughout the trip whenever we set foot into a new area.

Last night was the "flowered lady." Today a woman riding a bicycle and wearing a long flowing dress pedaled up, as if on a Sunday ride through the park at the turn of the century. Everything about her was from another time, long ago.

"You're from Gold Mountain?" she asked.

"Yes," I answered.

"Ah, such discipline. It's quite something to see. It makes a strong impression. I'd like to make an offering," she says handing us some fresh fruit from a small wicker basket.

Then she rode away. This is remote country – not towns or houses – and yet here was this elegant woman in ankle-length gown gliding through on a bike. How did she know of Gold Mountain?

"Take Heed."

Every mistake is a big lesson, and thinking I've learned something is a big mistake. As the Master put it,

> "As soon as you think you've got something, you're ripe for a fall."

The spring mountains are pure and clean because they endured the bitter winter. The mind of a cultivator is cool and clear because he endured bitter practice.

I find myself returning to the Heart of Prajna Paramita Sutra and the gatha commentary by Master Hua to guide my cultivation. The Heart Sutra is among the shortest of Sutras (it can be recited entirely in one minute), yet is an inexhaustible well of right-on instruction on how to walk the Path. Small though it is, it fills one up every time. It is a jewel among jewels.

> "All Buddhas of the three periods of time attain annutarasamyaksambodhi[1] through reliance on Prajna Paramita."
>
> Lines from the "Heart Sutra"

In the Standless Gatha, the Master writes that by cultivating this wisdom one becomes,

> "Capable of the wonderful truth, you personally enjoy its use. Those who know easily enlighten to the dark and difficult path. Virtue nowhere not complete, all impediments perish."

I find myself turning to it where the road gets "dark and difficult." It has a way of melting all obstacles, inside and out.

---

[1] "annutarasamyaksambodhi" is Sanskrit for the highest state of enlightenment.

"Sticking to It."

The Hyatts brought out maps, water, food, and detailed information on the roads ahead.

"We like to see things through to completion," they said.

"So do we," I answered.

> "The Bodhisattva Mahasattva is not startled or alarmed. He does not retreat and he is unafraid. He has no fatigue. And why?..."

Why? What keeps a Bodhisattva eternally high and bright, totally unafraid? Why does he never roll over and belly-up in the face of obstacles and incredible odds?

> "...Because, as he has vowed, he really wants to do it; to take responsibility for all living beings and cause them to be liberated."

Avatamsaka Sutra
Ten Transferences Chapter

Heng Sure • March 18, 1978
You may not fight with anyone

"Softness Overcomes Hardness."

Ever since Cayucos, a gang of young men have made it their job to haze us as we bow. They play, "chicken," running their cars onto the road shoulder to buzz our prostrate bodies; they throw missiles – rifle cartridges bundled to baseball size with plastic tape; they strafe the Plymouth with high speed attacks, shattering beer bottles on the bumpers and tailgate.

Our response:

"You may not fight with anyone for any reason. Use kindness and compassion to subdue all demons. Bodhisattvas are good to people no matter how they are treated."

Heng Chau • March 18, 1978
I'll demonstrate my independence over birth and death

"The Bodhisattva does not seek suffering, however, he understands that the feeling of suffering has no appearance and is not produced. All feelings mutually arise and do not stay."

Avatamsaka Sutra

"Is sitting in full lotus painful?" asks a fireman. "I mean, I've tried it, and sometimes it's a breeze, no pain at all. And then other times I'm shooting with pain by just crossing up one leg."

Pain is made from a scattered mind; no pain comes from a single mind. We bow through sharp gravel and broken glass, through deep dripping wet grass and prickly thistles with bugs crawling all over us. When our minds are concentrated we hardly notice, but when our minds move, every inch is a hassle. Feelings come and go according to our thoughts. When the mad mind stops and one is naturally content, there is no pain or pleasure. Everything just is. This is what the Sutras say.

"I heard that sitting in full lotus is the way to end birth and death," says the fireman. "Is that true?"

When all the energy is gathered back and quietly focused, not running off in the ten directions, this is dhyana concentration or Ch'an. It is producing the mind that is nowhere attached. When attachments are put to rest and false thinking cut off, the matter of birth and death then resolves itself.

So it's said,

"Birth and death from thoughts are made. When thoughts stop, birth and death are ended."

Avatamsaka Sutra
6th Ground, Manifestation

Sitting in full lotus makes it easier to enter samadhi, but it is with the "unattached, unbound liberated mind" that one ends birth and death, not from just sitting cross-legged.

The famous Third Chinese Patriarch Seng Ts'an invited a thousand Bhikshus to a vegetarian feast. After eating, the Great Master said, "You think that to sit in full lotus is the best way to die. Watch! I'll demonstrate my independence over birth and death."

They all followed the Patriarch outside. He halted under the trunk of a tree, and after pausing for a moment, he leapt up and grabbed a big branch. Then while swinging playfully from the tree by one hand, he entered Nirvana.

The bowing is just learning how to concentrate under all conditions, to develop a steady mind that isn't confused by the temporary and conditioned things of this world. All the disasters and sufferings we undergo come from our false thinking. Scattered minds create chaotic karma. Cause and effect are impartial and unconfused. We do evil deeds and suffer bitter retribution. Evil arises from ignorance, and when ignorance is ended all the suffering stops.

> "When ignorance is the condition, suffering can't be stopped. By ending the condition (ignorance) suffering is all over."
>
> Avatamsaka Sutra
> 6th Ground

"Who Will?"

Immediately after bowing we sit in meditation or the accumulated energy scatters. The sit at day's end is more important than eating. Often a wave of "fire" hits us like the backwash of a motorboat that suddenly cuts its engines. The "fire" is experienced as irritation and discomfort, a nervous "antsy" feeling often accompanied with pain and heat.

Today a fire-wave hit. I held firm and let it burn itself out. It uncovered past bad karma I had created and buried in secret long ago. As I repented of these offenses I felt compassion and kindness for all the people still entangled and unhappy, doing the very same stupid things I did. My thought was to end all my greed, hatred, and ignorance, all my self-seeking, and transfer to all living beings. I wanted to help them out of the sea of suffering we ourselves enter. We can't bear to see the suffering and hurting. If we don't try to end it, who will?

> "They never retreat from this resolve to transform living beings. Their hearts of kindness and compassion increase and grow. They are a place of reliance for all living beings…"
>
> Avatamsaka Sutra

Just as the Bodhisattva is about to attain the highest state of liberation, Annutarasamyaksambodhi, he stops and asks himself these questions,

> "If I don't bring living beings to ripeness, who will? If I don't subdue and tame living beings, who will? If I don't teach and transform living beings, who will? If I don't enlighten living beings, who will? If I don't purify living beings, who will? This is what I ought to do. This is my work."
>
> Avatamsaka Sutra

The Bodhisattva figures it this way: If I alone get free, all the living beings around me will go on as if blind. They will enter dangerous paths and get all afflicted. Unable to end their suffering they will be like someone with a terminal illness, everyday more pained and closer to darkness. They won't be able to get off the turning wheel of birth and death, and will constantly fall into the realms of the hells, ghosts and animals. How can I possibly enjoy my own liberation in the midst of such suffering? No way.

"As the Bodhisattva contemplates living beings in this way he thinks: If these beings have not yet come to ripeness, not yet been subdued, to forsake them and seek the realization of annutarasamyaksambodhi (for myself) would not be right."

Avatamsaka Sutra

And so the Bodhisattva puts off his own attainment of Buddhahood for the sake of others. He delays entering the ultimate state. Instead, for inexpressible, ineffable numbers of kalpas, he keeps returning to help all living beings end suffering and attain liberation. Only after everyone else is safely across does he himself cross. The Bodhisattva goes last.

As I write this and reflect on how the Bodhisattva ideal draws so many people to Buddhism, two men about our age pull up in a camper van.

At first they joke around and slightly mock us, but then one says seriously,

"I've been on the road searching for one and a half years. Didn't find it, ya' know? Monday I go back to work. I just came out this weekend to give it one more look, and here you are!"

He watched us bow for awhile and then said, "Why?"

"We are trying to get rid of the bad vibes in the world by being better people."

"What's in it for you?" he asks.

"We are not doing it for ourselves. We are doing it to turn back disasters and suffering in the world."

"Wow! Two years!" he exclaims, "What will you do when you get there, to that Ten Thousand Buddhas place?"

"Well, there's a university, hospital, translation institute, fields to work, a monastery, elementary and high school…"

"Really!? Hey, where is this place?" he asked excitedly. "I was in a monastery for 8 months once and it wasn't anything like this. I mean there's real perseverance here. It must be nice to be so content."

"It's a good life. Anyone can live it."

"You got an address?" he asked.

The mockery is gone now, just smiles and handshakes as we stand on the highway shoulder looking at a map.

"Good luck," they shout.

"Gook luck to you too," I answer. They grin and wave good-bye.

We are camped on grassy cliffs overlooking the ocean near Piedras Blancas Point and lighthouse. Heavy weekend traffic included motorcycle clubs and mammoth, two-story house on wheels called R.V.'s. Too fat for this skinny coast road. They often extend into the shoulder. We bow facing on-coming traffic so we can spot them and step aside in time to avoid being run over.

The Master instructed us at the start of our journey. It's hard to be patient under insult, but we have learned a deep respect for the power of softness. Practicing non-contention saves our lives.

For all the years of training I've had in martial arts, karate, shao lin and *tai ji*, I've never felt safer, more ultimately at peace than with five limbs to the ground, bowing to the Buddha.

Softness is why the Great Vehicle Buddhadharma endures forever.

> "In Buddhism, there are no enemies. Buddhists never take revenge on anyone. This is Buddhism's most superior aspect. We don't harm even demons. We still want to gather them in. Buddhists never give rise to a feeling of opposition. We are kind and compassionate to all beings and never harm them."
>
> Master Hua

This attitude can disarm the nastiest baddies and blunt the ugliest threats. The method is patience and simply not moving. It really works, both outside the mind and inside.

World-transcending wisdom arises from ultimate softness, from the hart of "same-substance Great Compassion" with all beings. Fighting with anyone is fighting with oneself. Contention and anger makes waves in the mind and wars in the world. Stilling the mind brings peace.

Heng Sure • March 19, 1978
Because we remember

Big Job.

> "You are beginning in the smallest of places to do the greatest of work."
>
> Master Hua to Bowing Monks

We often hear from the windows of passing car, "Get a job!"

Praying for peace is a job, an important work, little understood in the speedy, greedy, modern age. Heart Castle crowns the cliffs above us, the flat, blue Pacific winks and glistens to our left. Between these two extremes of ultimate, greedy existence, and ultimate, impersonal emptiness, what in the world really matters?

> "Do no evil. Offer up all good conduct. Purify your mind. This is what all Buddhas teach."
>
> Dharmapada

Cultivators work at stilling their minds, reducing greed and anger. They contemplate according to the proper views of ancient wisdom. It's a full-time job. We cultivate because people should cultivate. It's our basic share, our responsibility. We dwell in the world for only a few decades of productive years. It's a chance to create merit and benefit others or make offenses and increase suffering.

When the bowing gets dreary, we remember the atomic-bomber patrols thundering into the sky every morning from Pt. Mugu airbase. We remember the shadowy fleets of missile-subs that trace the coast by night and day. We remember the millions of men in uniforms reluctantly trained to kill, to destroy peace and make widows and orphans. We remember the cruelty of modern weapons technology, making smart-bombs and death-rays, and because we remember, we return to the bowing with renewed vigor.

Heng Chau • March 19, 1978
Not ordinary people

"After All, What is Life For?"

> "The Bodhisattva further reflects: All beings are confined in the prison of the world. They endure all kinds of bitter suffering."
>
> Avatamsaka Sutra
> 2nd Ground

It is as if we are in a prison – confined within our own minds by thoughts of insatiable greed. Greed for food and fame, for wealth and sex, and for sleep. We are shackled by our material possessions, our jobs, our reputation, the clock, and the gnawing feeling that our lives are passing in vain. We dream of some day putting it all down to find our true self, but...

We see each other through the bars, each of us in a cage and not knowing how to get out. Country to country, rich and poor nations, all classes, all races, throughout all time "all living beings are confined in the prison of the world."

Our bodies come and go like the seasons' falling leaves, but our souls revolve without end on the turning wheel of birth and death. Birth, old age, sickness, and death spin like a broken record. Life after life, over and over, and amid it all there's nothing but suffering. There's the outright suffering of poverty. There's the suffering of decay where one's blessings and honor go bad and decline. There's the suffering of process: from childhood, middle age, old age, to death – so fast the years flow by and can't be stopped. White hair, wrinkles, and failing health appear as if overnight. No one escapes; none are immune.

Before opening the Sutra every night we recite a verse:

> The unsurpassed, profound, subtle
>   and wonderful Dharma
> Is difficult to encounter
>   in hundreds of millions of kalpas.
> I now see and hear it,
>   receive and maintain it.
> And vow to understand
>   the Thus Come One's true and actual meaning.

Why is the Dharma unsurpassed? What is so unique and special about Sutras? Because everything in the world – wealth, name and fame, our family, friends, security, and success – it's all impermanent. Everything is overshadowed and rendered meaningless by the "one great matter." What is the "one great matter?" Birth and death. The Dharma is invaluable and unsurpassed in all the world because it is the key to unlocking the riddle of the "one great matter." Without the Dharma, there's no way to escape from the prison of the world. Without the Dharma, there's no way to get off the wheel of birth and death.

A young couple asks on the highway, "Two years you've been doing this!? Two years out of your lives. Isn't that a waste!?"

No. The waste of one's life is in the blind and commonplace living of it. We were meant for great things and noble understandings. We were meant to do heroic and beneficial deeds. We were meant to plumb the depths of our souls. But each passing day of just going along with the crowd leaves our lofty dreams lying empty and forgotten like seashells bleached and broken on the beach. We live it up, but down we slide, and when fear of death comes we sprint as if running over burning coals. Isn't this a waste?

There's a saying in Buddhism,

> Don't wait until you're thirsty to dig your well.
> Don't wait until old age to cultivate.

The billboard ads on the side of the road say:

> "Indulge. Enjoy yourself. After all, what is life for?"

and

> "You only go around once in life, so grab all the gusto you can get!"

The Sutras say *because* we try and grab all the gusto we can get we go around without cease life after life. We resolve endlessly on the turning wheel of rebirth for one reason: desire. Desire is just grabbing all the gusto you can get. And when we get it, are we happy? No. No matter how much gusto we grab, it's never enough. The more we grab the more we suffer. So it's said,

> Of all the happiness in the world,
>   there is none that is not suffering.
>
> Avatamsaka Sutra

Then what is life for after all? Life is a chance to end suffering if you cultivate. If you don't cultivate, life is only suffering. The ancients held that the unexamined life is not worth living. To live one's life without cultivating the Way was to be "born drunk and die in a dream."

"Weird Visitors."

We bowed into an abrupt change in terrain. Suddenly the road twisted into hairpin curves along a sheer cliff that dropped straight into the sea. On the other side there are rolling foothills ascending into the beginning of the rugged and famous Big Sur Wilderness. Traffic slowed to 10 and 15 m.p.h. The sea and the land interlaced, and every curve was like entering another world. The vibrations changed as sharply as the highway. One could feel a tension, and "up in the air" unpredictability, a sense of stepping onto another planet where the familiar cues and rules no longer fit. Everything seemed to be dancing and tingling, stirred up and jumbled around. It was as if we entered a mirage or twilight zone. In the next five hours and ½ miles of road, we met up with some of the strangest "people" we had ever seen.

> "You should know that the demons are coming to test you, to see if you're sincere... No matter what situation you encounter, use real wisdom and real samadhi power to subdue it. Don't move your minds."
>
> Ven. Abbot, instructions on the
> 1st day of pilgrimage, May 7, 1977

1:00 P.M.: A convertible sports car swerves into the pull-off we are bowing on. Two people get out. The man is bare-chested and oddly shaped. He looks out of proportion and off center, as if he were a collage of borrowed body parts from a dozen different people. Just to glance at him made me nervous. I averted my eyes instinctively. The woman was even stranger looking. She was as thin and shapeless as an upright No. 2 pencil, wrapped up in a skin-tight cloth with a turban headpiece bringing her head to a sharp point. They walked straight for us. The way they moved their heads, arms and legs, their gait and mannerisms were chaotic and irregular, unsettling and hypnotic. He moved slowly in undulating waves, his fleshly belly rising and falling like a water balloon. She walked rigid and jagged, shooting quick, darting glances, step-stabbing each foot sharply in front of the other.

"Jesus Christ, what are they!? Huh? What have we got here Shelly?" he says taking a swig off a quart beer bottle and blocking our way.

They dance around and pepper us with questions. Heng Sure isn't talking, of course, and I'm learning it's not necessary or beneficial to talk with everyone. I am only now coming to truly appreciate these instructions I got almost a year ago:

> "Have one person answer all the questions. Kuo T'ing, you're the Dharma-protector, you answer. Don't rattle on and 'write essays.' If a person understands, you need not say much. If he doesn't understand, more talk will just confuse him."
>
> Ven. Abbot – early instructions May 1977

"We thought you were tripped out on acid, but now we see you again and you're for real," says the man.

"You really think it's worthwhile? I mean, wow, over 2 whole years out of your life."

"We feel it's 2 years *into* our lives" I answer.

"You know, I've never seen anything like this. I mean, out here in the middle of nowhere. Totally isolated. You're just out here on your own, aren't you?" he asks scanning around for others, or perhaps a monastery in the hills.

I nod assent. He seems halfway honest.

"You get some kind of reward when you get there? Do they teach you judo and stuff?" he asks sarcastically.

"They teach us how to quiet our bodies and minds and help others."

They give Heng Sure a hard time. The man keeps shoving a camera in Heng Sure's face saying, "C'mon whadya say, huh? Smile. Give me something good to shoot. You forget how to smile? Want a drink of beer?" The woman mocks and lets go with a string of defiled remarks and suggestions too filthy to repeat.

As it turns out, their camera had no film in it, but they harassed Heng Sure for over ½ hour trying to get him to pose and respond.

Soon it became clear they were not at all what they seemed, not ordinary people. We both stopped looking at them and just bowed as if we were there alone.

Finally Shelly said, "They oughta lock em up. Hey, there's a cave entrance over there in those rocks. Let's go check it out. Maybe there's something in there." They left.

"Mushroom People."

2:30 P.M.: An old, beat up camper pick-up stops down the road. Two people get out and walk toward us. Same vibrations and weird body energy as the previous couple. The man is bulbous and blimpy and moves like a slow motion movie. He's wearing bib overalls, a loud Hawaiian floral print shirt and an oversized straw hat. The woman is dark and gives the feeling of heavy density. She moves like molasses rolling downhill. Her face seems hidden away and I get a strong intuitive message not to look directly into her eyes. She is literally absorbing.

The conversation is scattered and disconnected. Their words and body movements are slowed and dreamy, almost half as fast as ours. It's as if they're in a different medium, like under water or suspended at '0' gravity.

"My father does *tai ji*," says the woman out of the clear blue. "He has a guru and is greatly enlightened now." A long silence follows.

They disappear into a field across the road and return with a bag of fresh-picked, large mushroom.

"They're okay. Not poisonous. We eat them all the time" says the man reassuringly. The man says he's a marine biologist and they live off the sea mostly – "even have a garden down there" he says pointing out to the ocean.

3:30 P.M.: A station wagon pulls up behind us. Four "people" (clearly they are not people, at least not like any people we had ever seen) approach. They are like zombies or bodies risen from the grave. Their skin color is pale chalk white all over and the texture looks like soft clay – as if touching it would leave an indent, a permanent print. There's no blood color at all, even in their lips or fingernails. They are bleached and lifeless, without any spark. They speak in a slow, dragging monotone – not the slightest inflexion or fluctuation, just one tone, like a 33-1/3 LP played at 1-7/8.

"We have come to save. You are on the wrong path. You must listen to us," they drone.

There are two men and two women. They work in teams, going back and forth, preaching and pleading with us. Neither of us says a word.

"You claim to be peaceful and seeking truth but you won't even talk with us. How can you just shut us out? You must listen and change to our way. It is the only true way," they incant.

None of them shows any emotion or change in facial expression. They don't blink their eyelids, but just fix-stare as if looking through us with plastic faces and half-closed eyes. Are they in a trance or possessed?

They keep pressing up as close as they can without actually making contact. A few times they reach out their arms to touch our faces or grab our arms, but suddenly stop and withdraw as if meeting a barrier of resistance.

"You're selfish. Not talking is selfish. You must talk to us." Their voices and presence leave an eerie, sepulchral feeling in the air. After about 45 minutes of heavy soft-sell, they give up. Then, as if someone gave a cue or blew a whistle, they straighten up and turn in perfect unison and dream-walk back to the car, arms hanging straight down at their sides, head welded, unmoving, looking straight ahead.

5:00 P.M.: As we bow near sunset along a wind blown, rocky shoreline near a lonely point, a pickup truck stops. A tall man steps up.

"My name's Preacher," he shouts through the wind.

Preacher is about 6'10", dark and wild looking. Long hair and a full beard twist and curl every which way. His face is raw, angular, with deeply set features. His manner is aggressive and unpredictable, yet not unfriendly or violent, just rough and powerful. A solid, silver medallion, a forbidding steer's skull, with long, pointed horns, hangs from his neck on a rawhide thong. He grabs my meditation beads from around my neck.

"Sandalwood beads," he says sniffing them. "Far out!"

Backing up and running all over the road and rocks, he snaps pictures like someone playing a hot pinball machine. "Snap, snap, click, click, whrr."

"Yes sir. In these days of mechanization and mass conformity, I believe everything should get equal coverage," he roars with gusto. "Click, click," goes the camera.

Preacher is a self-styled bohemian "minister" of an unspecified church.

"I live out over there" he says pointing towards the windswept bouldered point where breaking waves slam and spray. "If you get near, stop in," he laughs.

Preacher is a personification of the rocky shoreline and pounding breakers. I don't know where he lives because the area he pointed towards has no houses or any signs of people. There is just the wild sea and the rocks.

Throughout, Heng Sure and I felt protected and watched over. We didn't feel fear or anger, just a naïve sense of wonder at the strange things that can happen in this world. When things started feeling off-center or too close for comfort, I would close my eyes and visualize my teacher or an image of the Buddha as if in front of me. It seemed to neutralize any danger or fears.

> "He vows to always have proper mindfulness of all Buddhas of the Three Periods of Time, and reverently think of the Tathagatha as always appearing before him.
>
> "He vows to dwell in the perfection of ever-increasing will and bliss and to separate himself widely from the animosity and anger of all demons."
>
> Avatamsaka Sutra

The key is to not give rise to any "demons of anger and animosity" in our own minds. If in our own thoughts and feelings towards others there's no fear or hatred, no bad vibes (*ch'i*), then nothing can disturb us, and no one will harm us.

Later at Gold Wheel, the Master asked,

Master: "Did you get to the mountains yet?"

Monks: "Yes."

Master: "And then strange people came, right?"

Monks: "Yes, that very day." (We then related the above events to the Abbot).

Master: "The strange people who suddenly came up were mountain weirdoes and water goblins who came to play with you, to check you over. They wanted to find an entrance, but since you didn't talk they had no way to get in."

Heng Sure • March 20, 1978
The axis of cultivation

"Moreover, Good Man, as for following all Buddhas in study…"

[The sutra quotes in my journal for the next two weeks all come from vow #8 in Avatamsaka Sutra Chapter 40.]

There are ten rules for Buddhahood found in Chapter 40 of the Avatamsaka, known as Universal Worthy's Practices and Vows. These Kings of Vows are like a blueprint for enlightenment. National Master Ch'ing Liang, the 4th Patriarch of the Avatamsaka School, called Chapter 40, "the pivot point of the Avatamsaka, the axis of cultivation."

I contemplate the text of the vows as I bow and meditate throughout the day. By praising the Buddha, making offerings, repenting of karmic faults, and transferring merit, cultivators naturally bring to life the teachings of Universal Worthy's practices. We feel the Sutra acting as a roadmap, guiding our steps along an ancient, high road.

Heng Chau • March 20, 1978
Don't seek anything

"People of the world, at their tasks, constantly spoil things when within an ace of completing them."

Lao Tzu

"Inches."

Bowing on highway shoulders as narrow as our own shoulders. Ice plant ledges on cliffs that drop straight into the sea. Weekends bring fast and frantic traffic racing by inches from our ears. Inches, everything begins small, in inches and first steps. There's an ancient saying,

The journey of a thousand leagues
began with what was under the feet.

The first step reflects the first thought. It is so important to start out with a straight-forward mind and pure intent. Because, if one is

Off an inch at the beginning,
off a thousand miles in the end.

If there's as little as an inch's worth of selfishness or crooked motive, the effort won't succeed. Why? Because the virtue within one's heart is insufficient to carry it through to completion. The one inch of thought off at the beginning is the "thief among the virtuous" and robs the accomplishment. Without virtue nothing survives.

What steals and depletes one's virtue? Seeking and the mind of greed. On our last trip to Gold Wheel Temple in L.A. the Abbot said, "At the place of seeking nothing, there are no worries. That is, in cultivation you should not seek to become a Buddha, or a Bodhisattva, or to certify to the 4th fruit of Arhatship, or to have great wisdom, or to get enlightened. Don't seek anything. In the very act of seeking, you are adding a head on top of a head; you are riding a donkey looking for a donkey. In cultivation seeking nothing, just cultivate. It's just like eating, sleeping, and wearing clothes. It's a necessity, that's all," said the Master.

Someone wonders, "Well if you don't seek for enlightenment or Buddhahood, you'll never get it, right?"

The Abbot: "Cultivate every day, day and night the same... Work in this way and when you have reached the extreme point, without seeking enlightenment, you will be enlightened. Without seeking to become a Buddha, you will become a Buddha. Without seeking to become a Bodhisattva, you will certify to the Tenth Ground. So, when the effort arrives, one's success is naturally attained. You don't need to seek. Seeking is just greed, just false thinking."

Contemplating the Sea.

> Going and returning with no border
> Movement and stillness have one source.
>
> Avatamsaka Preface

Reflection I:

The sea moves in waves, in tides, to clouds, then rain, to the earth then to rivers and back into itself. Constantly moving, it is always still; always still yet constantly moving.

In meditation, although the body and mind are still, there is warmth and increased circulation. The body is still outside but inside it is very much alive. Inside the mind is fixed yet its state expands in vast measure. Although the body moves through the world, the mind is still. It is not confused by states and remains Thus, Thus unmoving "in the face of the ten thousand affairs."

Seeking stillness is to be like a corpse or log of wood. Trying to be moving continually is frenetic. Simply do not attach to movement or stillness. This is to be in harmony with the natural. Movement and stillness do not fight and oppose each other. The sea is like this.

"Going and returning without border" is the natural enduring circle of change. The entire universe is in a continual state of flux, yet it neither increases nor decreases. The sea speaks this Dharma and tells us how to regain our true selves: Let go, release your hold; "produce the mind that is nowhere attached."

> It is like the water in the ocean
> Which has a unified nature,
> And waves by the millions, each one different,
> Yet the water itself has no such difference;
> And all Buddhadharmas are the same.

All living beings in the world are like the "waves by the millions, each one different." Yet the nature of living beings has no difference. Like the water in the sea, all beings are one substance; their Dharma body is the same.

> The Dharma nature pervades all places,
> All living beings and all countries.
> It exists throughout all times without remainders,
> Yet it has no shape or appearance which can be be got at.
>
> Avatamsaka Sutra

"The Little Men."

Erik, the park ranger from Hearst Castle, stopped by today, advising against the overland route.

"It's just too dangerous. The roads are primitive, hard for jeeps, even." he said.

"At first everyone warned us to not take Highway 1. Now everyone is telling us to take it. We are learning we can't get attached, got to let things happen naturally, on their own," I said.

"Boy I know that feeling," Erik nodded in agreement. He sat and watched the bowing and then came to say good-bye. "The Castle is garbage workmanship, really. Good for vampire movies. I work nights and meditate in the boss's office. It's as good as any place I guess... Living in the country is nice, but you pay through the nose. It's a small town, but it has a huge, thick grapevine. There's been quite a response to you monks," he said.

"Oh?"

"Yeah. Everybody knows where you are each day and what you do. In fact, you got a nickname, did you know?"

"No."

"Yeah. You're called 'The Little Men'" smiled Erik.

"Little Men?" I asked.

"Yup. I don't know where it started, maybe the waitresses. People say: 'I saw them! I saw the little men bowing outside my door this morning!' It's in all the papers and gossip corners." Erik noted. He went to his truck and brought back a lantern and some kerosene as an offering. "The response has been real positive. A few yoga people are appalled, a few Baptists are turned on, and a few are worried about the cowboys getting you. But I don't think you'll have any problems with anyone." he said.

"In a way we *are* the cowboys, the waitresses, the fishermen, and tour guides. Buddhists don't see themselves as separate or different from others. We are everybody; everybody is us. There are no problems except the ones we make for ourselves." I said.

"Disciples of the Buddha, the Bodhisattva, Mahasattva protects and transfers to those who are not his family and friends equally as he does to his family and friends without distinction. Why? Because the Bodhisattva has entered into the level and equal nature of all dharmas. He has no thoughts of any living being not being family or friends."

Avatamsaka Sutra

"That's really how it is, isn't it? I like that. It rings true," said the ranger. He folded his hands and half bowed. "Take care. I won't be seeing you again probably. Good luck."

Big rainstorm all night clears in time for A.M. bowing.

Heng Sure • March 21, 1978
At peace, at home

"Following all Buddhas in study," begins with filial respect to parents.

There were several senior citizens' homes in my neighborhood. What somber, unhappy places they were. Sometimes we'd chase a football onto their lawn; we'd see a pale, gray-haired head peek at us from behind a Venetian blind. Otherwise, the homes were as still as tombs.

Few of my friends had grandparents at home, yet visits with the old folks on Christmas and Thanksgiving always gave delight.

This evening at sunset I scrambled down a long and steep gravel ramp to do standing meditation on the beach. Our Plymouth sat high on the cliff above. Facing West I saw a towering statue; a statue; a stone figure at tide's edge. It looked like a bearded old fisherman leaning back in a rocking chair, smoking a pipe. The slanting sun gave him an uncanny reality. He looked at peace, at home – a silent, venerable Elder. How incomplete our lives would be without old people.

"Be respectful. Cultivate the Way with diligence – this is filiality. If you don't cultivate, you have no way to repay your parents. Don't do evil and don't have false thoughts. In this way you are being a good child and your parents invisibly receive a response with the Way. In general, faithful believers in the Buddhadharma must be filial. Being filial to one's parents is being filial towards the Buddha."

Master Hua

Heng Chau • March 21, 1978
A place to transcend the world

"Contemplating the Sea."

Reflection II: I never went slow enough to experience the ocean's tides.

Twice daily the high and low tide cycle repeats itself. Yet within this set rhythm there is continual change. No two tides are exactly the same. They change a little every day, as does the constantly eroding and shifting shore they wash against. We live in a mystery. We can feel it, but never fathom it. Everything is like this – planets, galaxies, our lives. We only see the small and close at hand, an eye-blink glimpse of the boundless wonders within the Dharma Realm.

We are like children trying to hold the sea in a Dixie cup. Beyond our limited senses and small minds are worlds of mysteries and unimaginable universes. We lose sight of them, but we never forget. Some part in each of us is drawn to the sea and stars. We gaze at them in a silent, wordless recognition of yet another world beyond and another realm within. We all contemplate the sea. The sea is just our minds.

> Deeply enter the Sutra store
> And have wisdom like the sea.

The Avatamsaka Sutra is the record of all this, the measureless worlds within worlds that are beyond our ordinary senses, but always in the haunt of our souls. The Sutra is our autobiography, family album, and cosmic history book all rolled into one. It includes all time, all space, all dimensions. It is,

> Deep and wide and interfused,
> Vast and great and totally complete.

Avatamsaka Sutra, Preface

Last night I had to stop reading the Avatamsaka. I couldn't physically and mentally absorb it all. It was simply too rich and profound.

In the Sutra, the Pure Youth Sudhana (Good Wealth Bodhisattva) journeys to the South in his search for spiritual advisors. He comes to a country called Gate of the Sea and meets the Bhikshu named Sea Cloud. Good Wealth bows to him and circumambulates respectfully. Then with folded hands he sincerely requests instruction.

The Bhikshu consents and says, "Good Man, I have dwelt in this country called Gate of the Sea for twelve years. I have always regarded the sea as my state. That is,

> I contemplate how the sea is vast,
>> great and measureless.
> I contemplate how the ocean is extremely deep
>> and hard to fathom.
> I contemplate how the sea
>> grows progressively more vast and deep.
> I contemplate how the ocean is uniquely
>> and wonderfully adorned with limitless treasures.
> I contemplate how the sea
>> collects the measureless rivers.
> I contemplate how the colors of the ocean's water
>> are different and inconceivable.
> I contemplate how the sea is the home
>> of measureless living beings.
> I contemplate how the ocean can accept and hold
>> all kinds of big-bodied creatures.
> I contemplate how the ocean can hold all the water
>> that rains from the great clouds.
> I contemplate how the sea
>> neither increases nor diminishes."

Avatamsaka Sutra
"Entering the Dharma Realm" Chapter 39

The Avatamsaka and our minds are basically the same. The Sutra reflects and reveals the sea of wisdom within our minds the way a light shining on a crystal jewel reveals its deep brilliance and dazzling facets. The "sea" in the Sutra is the self-nature, the awakened mind. It is our original home and natural state. When we contemplate the sea we are, in a place past words and thought, contemplating the source of our own minds: the Buddha's wisdom.

"In Name Only."

Bowing gradually opens and reveals the natural, Middle Way. Study and practice mutually respond. It's a whole different world bowing through it at less than one mile per day. Or is it us whom the bowing changes and not the world at all?

The Avatamsaka says the nature of all is basically still and empty. In the Verses of Praise in the Suyama (Heaven) Palace Chapter, Forest of Strength Bodhisattva receives the Buddha's awesome power and contemplates everywhere. He sees that all living beings, the five skandhas, and all karma "has the mind (thoughts) as its basis." Yet, the things of the mind are just like illusions, the world around us is the same. So he says,

> "What then is the world? What is not the world? World and non-world are merely different names. The dharmas of the three periods of time and the five skandhas, when named, bring the world into being. When they are extinguished the world is gone. In this way they are just false names."
>
> Avatamsaka Sutra
> Chapter 20

On this trip we have learned that the "world" is made from our minds. Within seconds it can totally change according to how we change. Everything we see is a projection, a filtered selection of our thoughts and feelings. A bicyclist rolls to a stop and says,

"I envy you. You get to see and enter worlds most of us never knew existed. What a great way to see the world!"

What would we see if the mad chattering, busy mind stopped and entered perfect stillness? No more filter, no more projection, no inside or outside, no boundaries at all? When all the false names are extinguished and the world is gone, what is that experience? The Sutras say just that is enlightenment.

"When the mad mind stops, the very stopping is Bodhi."
Shurangama Sutra

"Which World?"

"Yes, but why do you leave the world? I mean, you leave home and just withdraw totally from the world, right?" asks someone.

Wrong. A monastery is not a place to withdraw from the world. The monastery is a place to transcend the world. It's a place to deeply enter your true nature and put down the false.

Besides, which *world* do we leave? There are millions of countless numbers of worlds. The Avatamsaka says there are,

"Lands in variety beyond thought, worlds without limit."

Each person's world is different according to his thoughts and karma. In thought after thought, life after life we are constantly leaving and entering worlds. Birth, old age, sickness and death are worlds. The ten realms from hells, animals, and ghosts up to the heavens, Bodhisattvas and Buddhas, are all distinct and different worlds. There is the Triple World of desire, form and formlessness. The past, present and future are worlds. Some people live in the past; others in the future. There is an Indian Tribe which has no past or future tense in their language. They only live in the present.

All worlds are made from the mind. Within a single thought one world is created and another left behind. For example, crying, we fall into a dark room (world); laughing, we enter a young world. The world isn't fixed. There isn't just one world.

We eat, sleep and wear clothes, so we are in this "world." This world is very dangerous and sticky. It's hard to leave even when you want to. Who of us is truly free to come and go at ease through the world? When we die which world will we be reborn in? Who of us can say?

When monks and nuns arise in the morning they silently recite this verse as they leave their room,

> "As I leave my room I vow that all living beings will deeply enter the Buddha's Wisdom and eternally transcend the Triple World."
>
> Vinaya for Daily Use

We don't wish to leave the world and get away from people. We wish that all living beings forever transcend the world of suffering and together enter the real world.

Heng Sure • March 22, 1978
Worshipping the rocks

"What do you do when the road is too narrow? Do you fudge a little on the vow?" Some people watch us carefully, count our every step and bow, noting logistical details as we progress.

"Do you cheat and cut steps or bows when there's no shoulder or the traffic gets too heavy?" they ask.

No. With safety in mind for the motorists and monks, we devised an expedient called "bowing in place." The road past San Simeon is too narrow to bow safely. I counted one bow for every third step as I walked the road. Keeping the total on my recitation beads, dodging the fat recreation vehicles that squeezed by on the highway, I pulled my precept sash free from a spider-webbed manzanita, adorned with twinkling dewdrops. I added ten percent to account for the bowing-in-place expedient and then set to work bowing. We take turns counting bows with a makeshift abacus of stones and bottle caps lined up on the ground. Superstitious people think we are worshipping the rocks or doing divination.

Overheard while we bowed in place yesterday:

"What are they doing, Harry?"

"Oh, they're kissing the ground and praying to some little stones, Ruth."

"Oh, how nice. Bless their souls."

Heng Chau • March 22, 1978
Monks have gotten by for centuries

Take car into San Simeon for "pit stop." Gas, oil, water, air in tires, steering and brake fluid and battery fill up.

Lunch: fruit, cracker, hot porridge, and peanut butter.

Heavy rainstorm all night. Again clears 20 minutes before we start bowing. Blue doughnut appears in clouds overhead.

Strange couple returns. Dave, Cortina, their daughter Tiffany, and mutt dog. They want to make an offering, so they show us how to select and gather wild, edible mushroom.

"There are two kinds of mushroom gatherers: old ones and bold ones. But there aren't any old, bold ones," says Dave leaning over to slice a big white mushroom.

"Conversation with a Highway Dharma Protector."

The McKenzies from Morro Bay drive out with fuel, fresh water, food, maps, and lots of encouragement. John, the Forest Service Ranger, has checked out routes.

"Stay on Highway 1," they say. "You can't even take a 4-wheel drive back there. The road is closed in parts and the bridge is out. You'd have to bow through a live rifle range, too. It would be 'three crawls and one bow' and you'd never get back up."

As they prepare to leave Mrs. McKenzie says,

McKenzie: "I've had the impulse to come out and bow with you in the fresh air and all. I need to get away from my family and job and take a quiet look at things."

Monk: "You could bow at home."

McKenzie: "I tried it and fell asleep. Two jobs have got me really running. I can't talk to most people about this but I feel you understand." (i.e. about bowing to benefit world and returning one's own light.)

Monk: "That's why we left home."

McKenzie: "Yes, and your teacher looks deep and wise, very wise. You need a good helmsman. It's also good that you don't go inside people's homes. That way you spend less time talking and staying up late at night and then it will rain less on you when you bow during the day. Right?"

Monk: "Right."

McKenzie: "Have you got the laundromat situation under control? I didn't see a laundry in San Simeon."

Monk: "We are okay."

McKenzie: "How? Are there laundromats in the woods around here?"

Monk: "We make do."

McKenzie: "No, you know, do you need to wash your clothes. We've got a machine, you don't."

Monk: "Monks have gotten by for centuries without laundromats."

McKenzie: "You'll end bowing where?"

Monk: "The City of Ten Thousand Buddhas."

McKenzie: "Oh boy, home! When do you think you'll arrive?"

Monk: "Don't know."

McKenzie: "That's good. Don't let the schedule get in the way of what you are doing. It's important for everyone. I like people, but I have to get with the birds and trees and get together with myself every now and then. I often think of the City of Ten Thousand Buddhas and remember all those pictures and I can almost see myself finding a quiet place there."

The kids finish pouring gas into the tank. This is their last trip out.

"I'm sure our paths will cross again," says Mrs. McKenzie. "There's a little verse I want to give you. You may think it's kind of silly, but it's helped me through many a difficult time. It goes,

> Fear knocked on the door.
> Faith answered: 'There was no one there.'

"We will do whatever we can to make your bowing easier. That's the most important," they said.

Heng Sure • March 23, 1978
Teach me, huh? **C'mon**, do it again

Violent Airs.

I climbed down to the salt-water to practice Shao Lin temple boxing.

Heng Chau had warned me not to do Shao Lin in public. Originally a monastic discipline to invigorate meditators, Shao Lin was later isolated into a martial art. The meditative aspect got left behind. When people see the flying fists and feet, it brings up the fighting spirit.

I didn't heed the warning, and the beach was too bumpy. Returning to the level road, I swung into the opening line. Sixty seconds later, the headlights of a passing car swung around and pinned me to the sand bluff in a brilliant spotlight. A drunken, burly man with long hair and bulging biceps ran up, his eyes aflame.

"Say, what do you call that? Teach me, huh? C'mon, do it again."

> He whose braveness lies in daring, slays.
> He whose braveness lies in not daring, gives life.
> For it is the Way of Heaven not to strive,
>   but nonetheless to conquer.
> Not to speak, but nonetheless to get an answer.

Tao Te Ching

Tough situation. Couldn't ignore him; couldn't talk to explain. I recited the Great Compassion Mantra, smiled, shook my head and stood very still.

"No joke man, that's good stuff, I want to learn," he insisted, standing so close I smelled his beery breath.

On inspiration, I gestured to him to follow. Heng Chau sat in Ch'an meditation in the Plymouth. I pointed to him sitting peacefully and nodded, "Okay." I mocked the Shao Lin fighting stance and shook my head, "no good." I put on my precept sash and imitated the sitting posture, gesturing, "#1." It worked, or maybe it was the mantra's power that cooled us both down and carried the message home, without words.

"Oh, so you guys are monks, huh? And you don't teach kung fu? Too bad, that's hot stuff!" he said as he left.

"It is best to leave the fish down in his pool. Best to leave the state's sharpest weapons where none can see them."

Tao Te Ching 36

Whew! No more Shao Lin in public. Violent airs breed violence. Peaceful practices promote peace.

Heng Chau • March 23, 1978
No, it's my karma

Sheriff Officer Connelly stopped to see if we were okay and to wish us a good day. "Be careful. This is Easter weekend and the worst section of the road is ahead," he advised us.

Two young men out driving the scenic coast in a convertible sports car. They were packed up and setting out, "to find something that college doesn't have." Miles and Steve, in their early 20's, stopped to make an offering of fresh fruit and bread. They asked some questions.

"We heard that this is how you get your food," said Steve. I nod.

"They get *everything* like this!" said Miles.

"Wow! That's incredible," answers Steve. "I know a lot of people must ask this, but I really want to know: Why? Why are you doing this?"

"Well, if you can find what was behind your impulse to stop and make an offering then you'll know why. The reason we became monks and are out here bowing basically is the same reason you had the thought to stop and ask why," I said.

"Hmm," said Steve.

"What do you bow for?" wondered Miles.

"To try to turn back disasters and suffering in the world. We transfer the bowing to help cool off the overheating world a little."

"That's far out! I mean you give it away, you're not doing it for yourselves?" said Miles.

"Yeah," cut in Steve, "That makes it *real*, ya know?" He continued, "One of my favorite quotes goes something like,

> A bell's not a bell unless you ring it.
> A song's not a song unless you sing it.
> Love's not love until you give it away.
> It's not real love if you try to keep it.

I really like that. It doesn't mean romantic love, I mean, I think it means just being good and decent to everyone, not being selfish and uptight," he said.

Full moon today and celebration of Shakyamuni Buddha's nirvana.

Two men came up as we ate lunch in a sandy pull-off next to an ocean inlet. With folded hands they did a half-bow, then offered food, flowers, and incense. They were really happy and full of light. They placed the food respectfully on our mat and offered incense and flowers at the small alter in the car. Not a word was spoken. It wasn't necessary. They bowed and left.

John (Kuo Jan) Scroggs and his brother Tom stopped en route to their parents' home in Carmel. They offered some fresh orange juice and words of encouragement.

"Road looks pretty clean up to this point. You must be working hard. Everybody at the City of 10,000 Buddhas has you two somewhere in the back of their heads, bowing all the time," said Kuo Jan.

Kuo Jan is single-handedly running the sewage plant at the City.

"It's not a fixed dharma," he joked.

"It's what he deserves," retorted his brother Tom.

"No, it's my karma," corrected John.

A party of Tibetan Buddhists in a couple of cars stopped. Purple robes, and smiles. One, in a white shirt with yellow top and ponytail, seemed to be their spokesman. They knew we were from Gold Mountain and doing prostrations.

"All the way," one kept saying.

Heng Sure • March 24, 1978
Ugly, slow moving bugs

I hopped into the car to meditate before lunch. Look out! Too late! My Ch'an seat had visitors. A cloud of cow-pie bugs from the seaside pasture had paid a call. Ugly, slow moving insects covered the cushion, the curtains, the crackers, and the cups. Unaware I had crushed a few forlorn little bugs in my haste to sit.

We work to protect life, to decrease suffering, and to benefit all living things. Not killing, not harming, cherishing life, are sources of great happiness. Refraining from killing makes good karma. We try our best to watch out for the beings whose karma brings them insect and animal bodies.

But sometimes you simply sigh and endure life as it comes. When it comes as death you offer up a prayer for the transforming soul and vow to cultivate pure causes in the future.

I very slowly eased out of the Plymouth, left it to the squatters, and meditated on the tailgate.

> "Moreover there are animals, in odious and repugnant shapes, which all come from their bad karma, and they suffer an eternity of affliction."
>
> Avatamsaka Sutra – Flower Store World

Heng Chau • March 24, 1978
Not knowing what he could do until he tried

Near Arroyo Del Oso, somewhere between the Piedros Blancos Pt. Coast Guard Lighthouse, and Pt. Sierra Nevada. Sunny, blue skies, clear wind. Very quiet and alone.

Bowing reflections off a full moon…

I. The only way I ever got anything genuine and worthwhile was by following the rules and hard work. The teachings of the Buddha and the traditional values of American culture meet and merge, like distant cousins or forks of the same river. Ralph Waldo Emerson wrote,

> "There comes a time in every man's education when he arrives at the conviction that envy is ignorance, imitation is suicide, and that he must take himself for better or worse. For although the vast universe is full of great good, no kernel of that nourishing corn can come to him except through cultivating the ground given to him to till. The power that resides in him is new in nature, and none but he knows what he can do until he has tried."
>
> From "Self-Reliance"

In Buddhism, Emerson's principles are applied to cultivating the mind ground. The harvest matches the tilling just as the Way and the response intertwine. The fruit of enlightenment ripens and falls naturally through diligent cultivation of morality, concentration and wisdom. You grow your own Bodhi-tree; it can't be begged or borrowed. The Buddha was a man who cultivated the "ground given to him to till" throughout measureless aeons, in life after life, until he perfected all merit and virtue and opened the wisdom of all-wisdom. No one gave him Buddhahood. He simply set out, like a pioneer, not knowing what he could do until he tried. After sitting unmoving for 49 days beneath a Bodhi-tree, he looked up and saw a star, and at that moment, attained the Way. Then he said,

> "Strange indeed. Strange indeed. Strange indeed. All beings have the Buddhanature and all can become Buddhas. It is only because of false thoughts and attachments that they do not realize the fruit."
>
> Shakyamuni Buddha

The first Sutra the Buddha spoke after his enlightenment was the Avatamsaka. In the chapter "Verses of Praise in the Tushita Heaven Palace," the Buddha expresses the same principles of self-reliance and independent hard work that Hawthorne, Emerson, Thoreau, and others were to mold into an American ethic.

> Where was there ever a man of wisdom
> Who got to see and hear the Buddha
> Without cultivation of pure vows and
> Walking the same path the Buddha walked?
>
> Avatamsaka Sutra

They called themselves "transcendentalists." Had they known about Buddhism, they would certainly have responded to those teachings.

P.S.: Our very first day of bowing L.A., the Abbot gave us some instructions that Emerson would have appreciated; "You can't be lazy. Go do it like no one ever did it before. Don't imitate anyone else. If you look at others for the way to do it, you still don't understand the true principle. Do what's never been done. Don't follow or imitate. This is America. Go and be unique." (May 1977)

Heavy holiday traffic. We are bowing through barbed wire fence pieces and on the pull-offs to avoid direct highway travel. So far, so good.

II. The faults of the world are just my own faults. If I want to improve the world, I should first improve myself. Only with a straightforward mind can I hope to straighten out the world.

The virtue and goodness in the world I owe to the good people who came before me, my parents, my teachers, and elders. I should safeguard this legacy by subduing myself and returning to principle and not getting lost in the hustle and the chase.

Heng Sure • March 25, 1978
The stinking carcass that was a tool

> "Peeling his skin for paper, splitting his bones for pens, and drawing his blood for ink, he wrote out Sutras stacked as high as Mt. Sumeru."
>
> Avatamsaka Sutra
> Chapter 40

Vairochana Buddha had a proper sense of values. The stinking carcass that we so treasure he saw as a tool, an object, a means to benefit others. He recognized the body as impermanent, going bad after very few years, turning weak and sick, returning to earth, air, fire, and water.

I practiced *tai ji* on the beach again this morning. The beach at low tide speaks the Dharma of impermanence. Rotting wood from the eroding, shoreline trees, pink-bellied shells turning to sand, a fly-covered seagull, eyeless and hideous, the bleached skeleton of a California sea otter. My own decaying flesh bag stretching, cracking, leaving tennis-shoe prints in the wet, brown beach sand. The running tide quickly erases the marks of my passing; in a few years I will be gone and forgotten, of no more consequence to the world than the gull, the otter, or the flies that pick their bones.

Yet if I can find the courage to follow Vairochana in study, to use my body to cultivate the Way according to the Eternally Dwelling, Indestructible Dharma-nature, then my few years in this body will not have been wasted.

Heng Chau • March 25, 1978
A knock on his head

Last month Heng Sure was driving a bus back to San Luis Obispo after a weekend visit to see the Master at Gold Wheel Temple in L.A. It was late and everyone was tired and sleeping in their seats. Heng Sure relates he was reciting the name of Guan Yin Bodhisattva when he fell asleep and drove the bus off the road towards the ditch. He felt a hand knock him on the head. He woke up just in time to pull the bus back on the road. It would have surely overturned. He looked around to see who had awakened him, but he was alone. Everyone was still asleep in the back of the bus.

"When people recite Guan Shi Yin Bodhisattva, know that for a space of 40 yojanas, 3,200 miles, there will be peace and no calamities."

From "Listen To Yourself", by Master Hua

David (Kuo Chou) Rounds shows up to bow for a week.

The car is so full of offerings there's barely room to sit. Too much can be as big a problem as too little. "All who get enlightened walk the Middle Way." For a cultivator, that means too much or too little, good times or bad times, friends or enemies, inside it's always the same: peaceful, clear and unmoving, even in one's dreams.

"Walking, standing, sitting, lying down, even in sleep and while dreaming, the Bodhisattva doesn't let himself be obstructed for an instant."

Avatamsaka Sutra, 7th Ground

I'm ashamed to admit how much false thinking I've done about food on this trip. And yet when I add it up, it comes to this: food has never been a problem; it's all in my mind. If I truly understood the Way, how could I allow myself to be obstructed by anything? Kuo Chou (Rounds) said it this way at lunch today,

"Every day I'm afraid I won't get enough to eat. And every day I manage to eat my fill. There's never been a day when I went hungry. And yet I go on false thinking about it. Really stupid!"

Heng Sure • March 26, 1978
Getting past the prickly spines

Cactus Practice.

Prickly pear. Across the fence in the low pasture, the first we've seen. Then another, a hundred yards on. A cactus with an unfriendly appearance but a personality like a Bodhisattva, benefiting people in a hundred ways. A drugstore in the desert. Cultivation works the same way. From the outside it looks like suffering. Those who walk the Bodhisattva Way taste its sweet rewards.

Getting past the prickly spines is the trick. Singe the fruits in the fire. The needles turn to smoke and disappear. The tough purple skin softens up and opens, revealing flavorful goodness. Indians and early pioneers ate cactus fruit raw or boiled, stewed or dried. The seeds make flour, and the juice makes a sweet syrup. Mexicans eat cactus pickles, use the fleshy cactus pads as a poultice to bind wounds and bruises, and add cactus sap to mortar and whitewash so it sticks better to adobe walls.

Bodhisattvas pass through the fires of self-discipline and lose the spines of false thoughts, bad habits, and attachments. Cultivation opens and softens stubborn minds to reveal the infinite potential for wisdom within. Enlightened beings benefit all creatures impartially, with no thoughts for fame or personal gain, just like the cactus. Bodhisattvas are like oases in the desert of birth and death, manifesting countless skillful means to end suffering and give joy.

But walking the Way looks as thorny as a prickly pear. An artful evangelist from another religion argued this morning,

"You're ruining your body. Don't your hands and knees want to quit? Why torture yourself like this? Surely your Buddha or whomever you worship doesn't want you to suffer so. You shouldn't punish yourself any longer. It's *too hard*, too much bitterness."

I remembered what an old Ch'an Master said,

"People in the world chase the objects of desire and mistake suffering for bliss. Cultivators want to endure suffering and attain genuine, lasting bliss. So they cheat themselves a bit, take a loss in the world, cultivate bitter practices, and in every thought, word, and deed, work to benefit the whole world with no thought for themselves. When you're enlightened, everything before seems just like a dream. Now we're all dreaming but don't know it."

As the persuasive missionary talked away, I looked to the cactus in the pasture and heard the monk's words. We cultivate cactus practice. Once past the spines, there's nourishment and goodness for all.

"I will follow and learn from Vairochana as he cultivated all kinds of bitter ascetic practices."

Avatamsaka Sutra, Chapter 40

Heng Chau • March 26, 1978
An oasis in the desert

Bowed over Arroya de la Cruz Creek. The next gas and water is Ragged Point, about a week away. San Francisco is 202 miles north. Narrow, dangerous road ahead. Feeling humbled and happy. Good bowing hurts a little, not so much the body as the mind. The hardest thing to face out here is the truth. "There is no me." Even when you know all your problems and suffering come from a big view of self, the fear of losing the self mounts stiff resistance.

What a strange dilemma: If there is no self, what is there to let go of? How can you lose what never existed in the first place? All dharmas are like this.

> "If the Bodhisattva is able to be untied from all dharmas, then he is also not liberated from all dharmas. Why? There is not the slightest dharma which exists... There are no dharmas which can be attached to."
>
> Avatamsaka Sutra

The sun set, we finished bowing and walked in silence down the empty road as the fog rolled in. "Where is the self I'm trying to bow away?" I asked. I had no answer and that felt honest. Honest and confused is better than being cocksure and phoney.

"How do you deal with the physical danger?" asks Kuo Chou.

"With single-minded bowing. That's all we've got. We bow a mile per day. We vowed to not fight or defend ourselves. We carry no weapons and at night camp on the side of the road completely exposed and vulnerable. We have learned our only safety and protection is holding the precepts outside, and keeping a very gentle heart inside.

> "He vows that all beings obtain a mind of proper concentration and become unable to be harmed by all sorts of conditions."
>
> Avatamsaka Sutra

We got a Coleman stove as an offering. Welcome addition. We've been cooking with a little Svea back-packing stove about the size of a high school chemistry-lab Bunsen burner. It was 50% effective. The other ½ of the time we ate cold canned food, peanut butter, and cereal.

We are learning to appreciate the conveniences and outright luxuries we took for granted all our lives – like running water, a roof to keep the rain out, a floor above the cold ground and bugs, warm clothes, healthy bodies, and a stove to cook on. We don't miss T.V., radio, newspapers, movies, coke, rush hour, a time clock, and vacation. Our work is our vacation in the true sense of the word, "to be empty."

But it takes work to truly be empty. True emptiness is non-attachment. One who is empty never gets angry or afflicted no matter what happens. He seeks nothing. Does he just withdraw then and renounce the world? No. It is just because he has put down all worldly things that he is able to greatly benefit all that lives. Non-attachment isn't nothing; it is no selfishness.

> He never discriminates among living beings,
> Nor does he false think about dharmas.
> Although he is not defiled by attachment
>   to the mundane world,
> At the same time, he does not abandon living beings.
>
> Avatamsaka Sutra

Taking no delight in worldly affairs and forgetting himself for the sake of others is a Bodhisattva's contribution to the world. He is a cool pool, an oasis in the desert, a reflection of our original face.

Did laundry at an all night laundromat in Cambria. Took turns shaving heads and bathing out of the bathroom sink. Hot water from the tap is a rare find in the highway filling-station circuit.

Heng Sure • March 27, 1978
Another kind of poverty

When I was a graduate student it made sense to race like an ant in file from Monday to Sunday, cramming every minute with words and ideas, making classes, meeting deadlines, gobbling three meals a day, keeping up with world news, scanning the theatre openings in the New York Times, jogging in the pre-dawn mist of the Berkeley hills, finishing the day with a pitcher of beer at the tavern, then falling asleep at the desk, head down in the dictionary. Nobody pointed out that this was a bitter life. With fine food, clothes, shelter, and companions, I had every sense stuffed full, every need gratified. Why was I miserably unhappy and dissatisfied? Because,

> Enduring suffering ends suffering.
> Enjoying blessings exhausts blessing.

Living an undisciplined, Bohemian life sounds like freedom, like cause for liberation of the spirit. Instead, the opposite is true. Glutting the senses inflames the mind of greed. Indulging in desires increases them.

> The five colors confuse the eye,
> The five sounds dull the ear,
> The five tastes spoil the palate.
> Excess of hunting and chasing
> Makes minds go mad.
> Products that are hard to get
> Impede their owner's movements...
>
> Tao Te Ching 12

Buddhism teaches the principles of reversal, turning back from what the mundane world enjoys and knowing contentment with our inner resources. Living the good life is knowing when to quit. Sufficiency is genuine wealth; "too much" is just another kind of poverty.

Lao Tzu said,

> "To be content with what one has is to be rich."

An old monk once told us,

> "No matter what it is, I feel I have enough of it already."

In the light of this proper view, my undisciplined life seems bitter indeed. Greed is poison, the spirit of life dies. Reducing desire and knowing contentment brings rare satisfaction, deep peace of mind.

Heng Chau • March 27, 1978
I need to get away

Morning clarity: Bowing, meditating, even dreams all say the same thing – half-way. We are half-true, half-false, half-concentrated, half-scattered, half-clean, half-defiled, half-vigorous, and half-lazy.

The work of cultivation isn't always magic states and tingling visions. The real day-to-day experience is hard work and a lot of patience. The job is small, difficult, and within. Every minute demands ultimate sincerity, concentration, and deep faith. Then by itself, when one least expects it, a little good news arrives. Whatever is supposed to happen, will. The less we interfere the easier it all flows:

"Be one of the Way with no mind."

No mind means no false-thinking. When I get praised I start having confused thoughts. "Hey, I'm pretty good," I think, and then I start to get lazy. Someone once praised us in front of the Master. The Abbot immediately responded,

"One of the worse things for a cultivator is praise. Why? They will just dry up. They won't progress any higher. Why not? Because they'll think that they are so good (really hot stuff), and so there's no room for them to grow and improve. Praise anyone and they will put on a high hat and think they're special. I'm not that way. When I teach I don't give people high hats."

If you can keep to the traditional practices and live as the ancients lived, then there is certain to be a response. All difficulties arise from breaking the rules. Obstructions appear where there is laziness or impatience. The modern way is fast, instant, and fruitless. The ways of the sages are slow, tasteless, and even bitter, but the fruit is rare and sweet. How much you get is how much you work. There's no limit to either.

Meditation.

A busy housewife said to us, "I need to make a quiet space to be alone in and just meditate, I'd guess you'd call it. I need to get away from the kids, my husband, the frantic world, and take stock of things. I like coming out here. The long drive and a chance to sit alone in the woods for a few minutes, makes me new again inside."

A school teacher commented, "I'd like to take a long walk in the mountains and never come back."

The purpose of meditation is simply to rediscover our true self.

> "People meditate in order to return to the root and go back to the source; to return to their original, inherent Buddhanature."
>
> Master Hua
> Ten Dharma Realms

Meditation is a universal human need, like eating, sleeping, and wearing clothes. We've met a lot of people who felt they share a common experience with our bowing when they backpacked, strolled by the sea, went for a walk alone in the woods, jogged, or took a bicycle ride at dawn. The methods vary, but the results are similar.

"It just clears things up somehow," is how one person described it.

As we meditate, we expand the measure of our minds. While walking in the mountains or by the ocean, the world gets larger; consequently, the self gets smaller. The smaller our view of self, the smaller our problems.

The self eventually shrivels so small that one merges with the Dharma Realm itself, where there is,

> "No big, no small, no inside, no outside."

Heng Sure • March 28, 1978
He looked up and saw a bright star

"...up to and including accomplishing Great Enlightenment beneath the Bodhi Tree."

Sheer cliffs, barbed-wire on the precipice, poison oak beneath
the scrub oak and manzanita. We retreat to the Plymouth at sunset,
meditate until Sutra study time. Through the dust-covered window I
caught "the flash of green" as the sun disc vanished below the
waves.

The Buddha meditated on a heap of straw by the riverbank; the
Bodhi tree has a fat, broad trunk and heart-shaped leaves that rattle
in the breeze. After 49 days of still contemplation, the Buddha had
overcome hallucinations, resisted temptations by demon-women,
and subdued the myriad states of mind and body. He looked up, saw
a bright star, and his mind opened to great enlightenment. He knew
everything. He would never again undergo rebirth.

Heng Chau • March 28, 1978
Little wheel spins, big wheel turns

"I'm Lost But Really Movin'."

Cars and campers roar by at incredible speeds, losing control on
curves. The frenetic pace of the world gets played out on the
highway. Twenty-four hours a day, non stop, wheels spin and squeal
and pound the asphalt outside as we people spin and pound our
minds inside.

Bowing slows us down to a natural speed. We have learned
wherever we go we are still in the same place, our mind. Fast or slow,
L.A. freeways or in pine woods, we never leave the world of our own
minds.

A station wagon bulging with suitcases and screaming kids speeds by. On the bumper sticker it says,

"I'm Lost But I'm Really Movin'"

"Boy, there's a lot more to that than there seems," says a Park Ranger who stopped to talk. "That bumper sticker says a lot. Running here and there, never finding out who you are or where you're going. We are all lost."

"All beings are on the dangerous road of birth and death... For example, it is just like a blind person who has no guide and mistakes a dead end road for a road with an exit. He enters a demonic realm where he is captured by bandits. He goes along with the demon's mind and abandons the Buddha's will. I should pull him out of this danger and difficulty and cause him to dwell in the fearless city of all-wisdom."

Avatamsaka Sutra
Ten Grounds Chapter

Bicycles, cars, motorcycles, planes, trains, and roller skates, whiz and spin us into a thousand difficult directions, but the big wheel doesn't stop. We ride our little wheels in circle on the big wheel. Like the song says,

"Little wheels spin and spin, while the Big Wheel turns around and 'round."

A bicyclist stops to offer us water from his canteen. Hot day, hits the spot. I look down and notice his wheels have stopped, a rare sight on this road. He stopped to give and ask about Buddhism. We are all trying to stop our own little wheels from driving us crazy, and get off the grinding Big Wheel. This is what the Buddha teaches to all Bodhisattvas.

Smashing completely all existence,
   the wheel of birth and death,
Turning the pure wonderful Dharma Wheel,
   unattached in all the world.
He teaches this to all Bodhisattvas!

Avatamsaka Sutra

Heng Sure • March 29, 1978
The new religion of the world

"…manifesting all types of spiritual power…"

How broad is the mind? The mind contains everything, but we forget.

We forget the first shock of new experiences. We take for granted what only yesterday was inconceivable. The towns we pass through display spiritual powers at night. Every home lights a dim gray or pastel rainbow lamp; we see the shadows through the windows as we make camp like nomads on the road outside. The entire country joins in a celebration of invisible psychic magic. A national family comes together to experience the new religion of the world called "watching T.V." Who says it's not psychic powers at work? Are the dancers and cowboys and newsmen and halfbacks inside that little box? Why do they wear white and gray faces on the old T.V.'s, and flesh-colored faces on the new sets? Where do they go when the show is over? After seeing a movie, primitive people in New Guinea ran up and looked for the actors behind the screen. Finding no people, they concluded there were magical spirits in the "little black box."

My grandparents had no television. They had no notion that such a thing could be. Now everyone accepts T.V. as a part of life. The mind adapts very quickly.

Heng Chau • March 29, 1978
Keep your room clean and orderly

Bowing in cold rain. Tall fir and pines line the steep, rocky, Big Sur slopes that plunge straight down into the sea. Quiet, gray outside, lots of time and room to explore inside.

During our recitation of Guan Yin's name yesterday, I had an experience that the asphalt, grass, trees, and stars, were our ancestors. The air, water, wind and earth were the children to come. And yet there was no today, yesterday, or tomorrow. The entire substance of the universe was one, without beginning or end, loss or addition. One boundless, ageless body where the many were the one, and the one was the many.

> Deep and wide and interfused,
> Vast and great and totally complete.
>
> Avatamsaka Preface

It rocked me for a second, maybe because I couldn't find a "me" in this picture. But something in the chanting, "Namo Guan Shi Yin Pu Sa, Namo Guan Shi Yin Pu Sa," made everything okay and turned my fear into a big smile.

"Messy Room."

Someone watching us clean up the car after lunch comments,

"It must give you a certain amount of satisfaction to have everything neat and in its place."

I remembered our first night in L.A. Heng Sure and I shared a small room in the back of the temple. The Master looked in after morning recitation to see a veritable pig sty. Our clothes, bags and belongings were scattered and draped wherever they landed as we threw them.

"Keep your room clean and orderly," said the Master. "A clean Way place can cause someone to bring forth the mind for Bodhi."

Later in the Master's room, I noticed how peaceful and clear I felt. I observed the Master had few possessions lying about. The room was orderly and simple, not cluttered. There was a sense of expansiveness and room to receive people.

Why would a teacher bother with such a seemingly trivial matter as a disciple's messy room?

> Deal with the hard while it is still easy.
> With the great while it is still small.
>
> Lao Tzu

Small habits and faults soon snowball into major character flaws. A sloppy room or appearance conceals a scattered mind. Left uncorrected while small and close at hand, this messy mind grows to become a major obstruction to one's karma in the Way. It's an outflow. One's energy dribbles away into a thousand loose ends of a disorganized life style. There's no concentration; the mind is unable to be still and quiet. To be successful in cultivating the Way requires a fine and subtle maneuvering in the realm of cause and effect. Every step must be right. Each act, word and thought, cannot be a fraction off the mark. So there's a saying in Buddhism,

> "Bodhisattvas fear causes, not results."

The result is included in the cause. The fruit is determined by the seed. Bodhisattvas know that what happens to them comes from the karma they create, so they tread with great care and do not overlook the smallest affair.

> "Everything great must be dealt with while it is still small. Therefore, the Sage never has to deal with the great; and so achieves greatness."
>
> Lao Tzu

Another lesson: I'm greedy. I always need less than I want. I always want more than I need. Too much brings regret later. Fear of too little brings worry before. Desire is a lot of suffering. The Sutra says,

"With a few desires know contentment."

Heng Sure • March 30, 1978
Trained to be skeptical scientific doubters

"...changes and transformations..."

Caterpillars turn into butterflies; tadpoles become frogs. Darwin suggested that apes evolve into men. We accept these changes without blinking. The mind contains all-knowledge. It's said Guan Shi Yin Bodhisattva manifests thirty-two different response bodies and appears before living beings to speak Dharma and teach and transform them. Who believes it?

Whom do we believe? We were trained to be skeptical scientific doubters. But science's pioneers are now discovering the universe looks very much the way ancient Sages described it in Sutras so old they cannot be dated.

I walked under the stars to stretch my legs after meditation. Looking up I saw a fiery streak of light and heard a faint whistling roar. Vandenberg Air Base had released another pebble from Dr. Strangelove's slingshot in a futile effort to conquer space.

We work so hard and run so far away from home, seeking what is originally perfect and complete within. There is more magic and unexpected wonder in an hour of meditation than in any space program. From "Star Trek" to Sputnik, from Tom Swift Jr. to NASA, the inner journey into the mind tops them all. Besides, full lotus is peaceful, rockets are not; they scream "Kill, kill!"

Heng Chau • March 30, 1978
Every inch is used

Big Sur Rain.

Rain and stiff winds continue. Big cliff ahead and a small road.

What's it like inside the car on a cold, rainy day? We wash up in a small plastic basin while kneeling and bent over in the back of the car. Hands are too stiff and cold to pump the stove. We light kerosene lamp to thaw our frigid fingers. Whoever gets circulation back first pumps the stove. Heng Sure meditates while I cook. The stove is propped up on stuffed sacks and clothes bags. We have a space about the size of a school desktop to prepare lunch, eat on, and do dishes. Rinse dishes with rainwater by setting them on the roof. A stick of incense burns on the altar in an old Planter's Peanut can. The food is balanced on the wheel wells and in our laps. Before we got a bell and hand bell from Gold Wheel, we used hubcaps and beat a kettle top with a chopstick for the meal ceremony gong.

The wet clothes get thrown in the front under the dashboard until the sun comes out again. Wet shoes are stacked against the door, standing on their toes to dry, as a puddle forms inside the car. Every inch is used. What space is left over bugs and spiders turn into winter living quarters. We brush our teeth and put on rain clothes while kneeling: often banging our heads on the roof and poking each other in the eyes or ribs.

Heng Sure goes back to bow. I drive ahead for ½ mile, sometimes further on mountain roads, before finding a pull-off. I make a thermos of hot water and wrap it in our winter coats so we'll have something hot to chase the chill after bowing, and the next A.M.

I'm surprised how well we get along, considering the cramped living conditions. We usually just shrug and laugh, which defuses any tension that gathers after a week of solid rain. Pressure builds patience, and patience is what cultivators need most.

A Bodhisattva is able to bear all manner of evil,
And in his mind he is totally level and equal to
    all beings without any agitation.
Just as the earth is able to support all things,
So he is able to purify the perfection of patience.

Avatamsaka Sutra

Heng Sure • March 31, 1978
We know so little

    "...transforming all kinds of Buddha-bodies which presided over all the assemblies."

From one photo negative we can print limitless pictures. The moon's light reflects at once on all lakes and rivers. Two mirrors facing each other reflect endlessly into infinity. Transformed bodies may be a bit like these, not so strange.

Beneath my foot is a dented aluminum soda-pop can. It is identical with millions of discarded soda-pop cans that clutter the world's highway and by-ways. Transformations surround us.

The Avatamsaka describes a level of cultivation where the body puts forth hundreds of thousands of millions of transformed bodies. And yet all of these bodies are one body.

We know so little of the inconceivable and mysterious. But the mind remembers as it learns. There is nothing new under the sun.

Heng Chau • March 31, 1978
Kuo Chou's test

Kuo Chou offered to drive us to L.A. to meet with the Master this weekend. When he first arrived he said,

"Hope it doesn't disturb your plan."

"We have no plans," we replied.

At the end of the day we were washing up.

Monk: "Wash up?"

David: "I already did but I can't get the dust out of my mind."

Monk: "Like in the Avatamsaka where it says the Buddha 'is wealthy with ten thousand virtues, and cleansed without the finest dust.'"

David: "Bowing this dirty highway is a great spiritual bath. It's wonderful!" grinning, "This is the best meditation session yet."

We never thought of the bowing as a session. Sessions have a beginning and an end. But we don't think of the bowing as beginning or ending. Bowing has become a state of mind, no longer just prostrations. Bowing is constantly practicing "being here and now" and subduing the busy mind. It is the heart that is unmarked by self or others, living beings or a lifespan. It's the mind that doesn't dwell in the past or future and takes the present as it comes, still and empty.

Bowing is not being moved by forms and sounds. Always returning the light to illumine within, bowing is just "recognizing our own faults and not discussing the faults of others." Bowing is taking kindness, compassion, joy, and giving as our function and universally transferring merit and virtue to all beings everywhere as our work. Bowing is borrowing a path to go back home.

"David's Test."

The three of us were bowing in a light drizzle on a quiet, empty road. Suddenly a Hell's Angel-looking biker roars up and parks right next to Kuo Chou's car. He's as tough and mean as any character we've seen. Full beard, black leather, tattoos, insignias, and weighing at least 250 pounds. There's a long bowie knife strapped to his side and heavy steel chain around his waist. He fixes a penetrating and tension-filled stare at Kuo Chou who is bowing a few feet in front of his big Harley. One hand resting over his elevated handlebars, the other on his knife, he silently judges.

Kuo Chou keeps bowing. It's his last day before heading back. Slowly the biker dismounts and walks over to Kuo Chou's car. He hasn't showed any emotion, just like granite. He reaches into his leather jacket and pulls out a $10 dollar bill and slams it down through the car antenna. Slowly he strolls back, mounts up, adjusts his jacket, and jump-kicks his bike with a roar. He stares at Kuo Chou to make sure they make eye contact, and then without the slightest expression, nods his head in approval and pulls out.

When you bow you get back exactly what you put out. Show kindness and kindness returns. Think peaceful and peacefulness comes back. But if your thoughts are angry and obstructive, then life on the road can become miserable and even dangerous.

"As one thinks, so one receives in return," says the Avatamsaka. And what you receive mirrors what's on your mind. The biker came to inspect David's sincerity and spirit. It was David's test. He passed.

We left the Plymouth with the McCauleys who live in a red log house in the steep, wooded hills above Cambria. Young Dan McCauley offered to repair and tune up the wagon. It needs it.

As we drove South, Kuo Chou said,

"I was bowing and I had a small eye opener. I realized, 'Hey, I don't have to have any plans either.'"

He looked happy and pounds lighter in the face.

We slept at the dead-end of a frontage road below the Gaviota Pass. Before dawn, we put a stick of incense in the ashtray and did morning chants together bundled in blankets, and then headed for Gold Wheel Temple in L.A.

* * * * * * * * *
April 1978

Heng Sure • April 1, 1978
The Buddha's Dharma-rain

"Perhaps he presided over the Way-place Assemblies of Great Bodhisattvas, or the Way-place Assemblies of the Sound-hearers and Pratyeka Buddhas. Perhaps he presided over the Way-place Assemblies of the Wheel-turning Sage-kings, and lesser kings with their retinues. Or perhaps he presided over the Way-place Assemblies of Kshatriyas, Brahmans, Elders and laypeople, up to and including the Way-place Assemblies of the Gods, dragons, the Eight-fold Spiritual Pantheon, humans, non-humans and so forth."

Just as the spring rain in a California valley moistens and brings to life all the many kinds of trees, herbs, grasses, and crops, each according to its roots, so too does the Buddha's Dharma-rain bring to maturity the many kinds of root-natures of living beings, each according to its own capacity to hear and practice.

.. We transferred the merit of our day's work at sundown and hustled back to the skinny hamlet of San Simeon: two service stations, two horse ranches, six motels. I'm filling the water jugs and watching the headlights glide by. Heng Chau fills the gas tank and washes the road dust from hands and forehead. People from all corners of the world cross paths at the gas pumps. We take a moment to rest, to refuel, to recharge batteries, and move on.

Lunch with the Venerable Ab

Wheel Monastery. April 1978.

Heng Chau • April 1–2, 1978
The biggest event in U.S. history

Gold Wheel Temple: "L.A. Tune-Up."

The Master's teaching in L.A. is informal and open-ended. We sit on the floor of his room in the morning as people come and go. The topics vary as widely as do the people who draw near – from meditation to real estate, politics to earthquakes, Buddhism to babies. Our instructions come in bits and pieces.

Master: "If the cause ground is crooked, then the result is confused. Cultivators can't have any self."

Monks: "Shih Fu, we sometimes run into some really tough people."

Master: "Don't cut off conditions with anyone. Be good to people. Use kindness, compassion, joy, and giving, even to the point of your own death. Always forgive people. Don't have hatred, jealousy, or obstruction towards others, or else when your retribution comes, it will be severe."

Many people come in relating their troubles and worries.

Master: "I don't know how to teach and transform people, so every day I'm ashamed and repentant. If I could teach, then you people would have lost your afflictions long ago."

We ask about bowing and meditation states. There's a hint of seeking responses in our eagerness. The Master steers us straight.

Master: "In cultivation, you've got to go towards the true in everything. One part true gets one part response; ten parts true get ten parts response. The response is not something you seek; it comes naturally by itself. Anything that comes from seeking isn't true."

The discussion turns to how to tell true from false.

Master: "In the world if you're true, people say you're false. If you're false, people say you're true. It's upside-down." (Laughter.)

Someone asks about investing in real estate. The Abbot cautions against over-extending oneself and then brings the topic back to cultivation.

"In everything I do, I go one firm step ahead at a time, and then I never have to retreat."

A layman relates climbing a hill once with the Abbot. The layman raced ahead and was sweating and out of breath half way up. But the Abbot arrived on top without even breathing hard.

Master: "I go slow, but long."

The topic turned to politics and corruption in government.

Master: "Without virtue, nothing survives. Without virtue, you will come to a bad end no matter how high you go."

Layman: "What's virtue?"

Master: "Being good to people. Even if you can't be good to them right on the spot, you can wait and when there's a chance later on, be of benefit to them."

Monk: "Master, I'm really a cheat."

Master: "Don't be so serious. You say it too severely. If you can be a cheat, then you're there."

Monk: "Huh?"

Master: "Everyone cheats himself in order to cultivate. In fact, we *are* Buddhas, but we don't know it, so we cheat ourselves into having to cultivate in order to realize Buddhahood."

Nun: "There's an American self-made guru who says, 'Everyone's a Buddha, so don't work so hard.'"

Master: "If you say, 'I'm a Buddha already so I don't have to cultivate,' this is *really* cheating yourself. If you say this, it shows you haven't even made it to the starting line. Do you understand?"

Nun: "Not entirely."

Master: "It's like someone who wants to be a college professor but hasn't yet entered elementary school. He's not qualified to even talk about professorship, much less pretend to be one. That's where all these self-made Buddhas are at."

Questions arise about the best method to practice.

Master: "In Buddhism, don't know too much. It's best to concentrate on one Dharma door. Children who cry should cry. Those who laugh should laugh. Concentrate on one and don't scatter. Bowers to the Buddha should bow. Mantra reciters should recite their mantras."

Monk: "Master, on one hand you say we should not be so serious and uptight, and then you also say not to be the least bit sloppy or casual. How should it be then?"

Master: "If you can handle it and be relaxed, okay. Hold on as tight as you need to hold on, to climb to the top of the pole."

We relate that we use the 42 Hands like weapons in our minds, to defend and protect ourselves in tense situations.

Master: "No. Buddhists never harm any being. You should always use them to teach and transform, to save and take across all living beings."

I had a dream on the pilgrimage that wherever the Master was, Amitabha Buddha was also there, and that was the Pure Land. When someone told us the City of Ten Thousand Buddhas has been called the Western Land of Ultimate Bliss, I lit up. Maybe it was more than a dream.

America is a land of freedom. People here want to be independent and self-reliant. They want room to realize their true self and develop their potential. Buddhism has now come to the West. This is the biggest event in U.S. history, even though it's small now. Why? Because through Buddhism, countless numbers of people will find the ultimate liberation and fulfillment they seek. You could say the *real* American Revolution began when the Dharma came to this country. For while there was a political and external independence established over two centuries ago, the internal and spiritual independence is just beginning.

Paradoxically, the very things we thought would give us freedom and meaning came to enslave us. Material abundance and affluence, the best and biggest, the newest and fastest, all tied us down and put a shadow on our spirit like the industrial smog cloud that hangs over Gary, Indiana. We found liberation wasn't outside. But before Buddhism appeared, there was no map for the journey within. The frontier is now open.

The City of Ten Thousand Buddhas is the new home of World Buddhism. Soon, the Dharma will be all but a faint shadow and relic in Asia. The signs of imminent decay were everywhere. As an older, retired man said about the City and Buddhism in America, "I'm glad to see this. This is what we need. It will make the country strong."

Not only will America be enriched, but the strength and vitality of this spiritual renaissance will spread throughout the entire world and eventually return to reawaken Asia itself. Somehow, it's appropriate and auspicious for Buddhism to make America its new home: the highest teaching of peace and freedom in the strongest country of peace and freedom; the oldest truths in the youngest land. It's a healthy balance of wisdom and youth that can only be good for the world.

Heng Sure and I are talkers, word people. Suddenly we are beginning to sound not so smart. Our speech is jerky and uncertain, no longer smooth and confident. It feels uncomfortable but real; vulnerable but trusting to the Path and a good teacher. Maybe one has to lose control to find the truth.

When the Venerable Abbot speaks Dharma, the entire room fills with light. It pours into and through everyone. So strong, pure and inexhaustible. The audience radiates and glows, burning bright and soaking up every word of Dharma.

> "The Tathagata's great wisdom light purifies the entire mundane world. Having purified the world, he then gives instruction in the Buddhadharma."
>
> Avatamsaka Sutra

After the lecture someone asks, "Can the Buddha get rid of all the afflictions in the world?"

Master: "Yes, but they would return in an instant. This world would end, another world would appear."

Why? Because everything is created from the mind alone.

The Saha world is produced from the turbid emotions and heavy karma of living beings. The Pure Land is produced from pure karma. When the mind is pure, then everywhere is the Pure Land. The Avatamsaka says,

> "All the world is a transformation which is upheld by karmic retribution. All the different bodies are illusions arising from the strength of what we do. And all living beings come from the many kinds of mixed up defilements in the mind."
>
> Ten Practices

I don't understand it completely. The understanding comes with the practice. It's not something the intellect can know. We all go away from these lectures challenged and stimulated to cultivate harder.

At the end of the day a young monk says to the Abbot,

"That's such good talk. I've never heard anything so straight and true."

Master: "The things I teach are understood by only small, stupid people. If you're a smart one, you won't get it. I myself am inarticulate and I look like a dummy, so the bright ones overlook what I teach."

Heng Sure • April 2, 1978
The world needs hundreds of cities like it

> "As he presided over assemblies such as these, his voice was full and perfect like a great clap of thunder. And he

brought all beings to maturity, according with their likes and wishes, until the time he manifested Nirvana."

There's a song that give us strength about a city devoted to renewing the world. We hum it from time to time and the sun rises.

It's Called the City of Ten Thousand Buddhas:

It's called the City of Ten Thousand Buddhas,
It's called the City of Ten Thousand Buddhas.
It started with a vow to bring enlightenment
    to every living beings.
And the Sage who brought
    the Buddha and the Dharma and the Sangha
    to America to build a new foundation.
It's called the City of Ten Thousand Buddhas.

It's called the City of Ten Thousand Buddhas.
Founded on a vision of the Proper Dharma
    flourishing again.
It's a place for cultivation, it's a place for transformation
Of the common one into a Bodhisattva.
It's called the City of Ten Thousand Buddhas.

The City's home to Guan Yin Bodhisattva,
Compassionate Enlightened One
    who contemplates the sounds of living beings.
With a thousand eyes to see them,
    and a thousand ears to hear them, and
A thousand hands to rescue them from suffering.
The City's home to Guan Yin Bodhisattva.

It's called the City of Ten Thousand Buddhas.
Instilling virtue in the children, filiality is number one.
They will vow to get enlightened
    to repay their parents' kindness.

And repay the Great Compassion of the Buddhas.
It's called the City of Ten Thousand Buddhas.

It's called the City of Ten Thousand Buddhas.
It starts with care for aging people,
    filial behavior in the home.
When the family is happy then the cities will be peaceful
    and the nations and worlds will come together.
It's starts at the City of Ten Thousand Buddhas.

It's called the City of Ten Thousand Buddhas.
Enlightened to the Buddha-nature,
    perfect and complete in everyone.
He's the Sage who vowed to save us,
    to show us the road to wisdom.
Return the light and wake up Turtle Island.
It's called the City of Ten Thousand Buddhas.

It's called the City of Ten Thousand Buddhas.
Making Buddhas, Bodhisattvas, Sages
    from the likes of you and me,
And the virtue of the Master
    carves our greed, hate, and delusion
Into precepts, to samadhi, and to wisdom.
It's called the City of Ten Thousand Buddhas.
It's called the City of Ten Thousand Buddhas.
It's called the City of Ten Thousand Buddhas.

Who owns the City of Ten Thousand Buddhas? We all do. It's built on a pure notion that doing goodness for its own sake can save the world. In this dusty world of material greed, endless wars, and moral decay, this is exactly the time a City of Ten Thousand Buddhas must appear. The world needs hundreds of cities like it. Everybody hopes for the light, wishes for a new dawn of peace and security. The promise of the City of Ten Thousand Buddhas renews the hopes of the world and fills the hearts of all beings.

Heng Sure • April 3, 1978
Universal brotherhood and beyond

> "In all these ways I will learn from the Buddha. And just
> as it is with the present World Honored One, Vairochana, so
> it is with all Thus Come One in every mote of dust in all
> Buddhalands of the ten directions and three periods of time,
> throughout the Dharma Realm and the realm of empty
> space. In thought after thought I will learn from them all."
>
> Avatamsaka Sutra
> Universal Worthy's Conduct And Vows Chapter

My home-town, Toledo, Ohio, is a medium-sized American city.
Toledo has surprising international flavor. A Polish friend told me
about East Toledo Polish schools where children need not learn
English until their teens. Their community is totally self-contained.
Toledo has the only Mohammedan mosque between New York and
the West Coast. Lebanese groceries and restaurants thrive all over
town.

Every summer migrant workers from Mexico, thousands of
Spanish-speaking Chicanos, float North, their dusty station wagons
and rattling sedans appear on the outskirts. They pick berries, beans,
grapes, and corn, then vanish one night back to Laredo or Monterey.
"We are all strangers and cousins," as Pete Seeger put it.

The Buddha sees the whole Dharma Realm at once, infinite
worlds interpenetrating, endlessly coming and going in perfect
harmony.

The Buddha expands his heart to the ultimate and even
transcends universal brotherhood. Not racists, sexists, elitists, age-
ists, or strictly humanists, the Buddha's compassion includes *all*
living beings, *all* species and realms from the hells to the heavens and
beyond.

The Dharma Realm and the realm of living beings,
Ultimately are not different.
He knows and understands absolutely everything.
This is the Tathagata's state of being.

Avatamsaka Sutra
The Bodhisattva Ask for Clarification chapter

We can all open the knowledge and vision of the Buddha. We each possess a perfect seed of Buddhahood inside. Perfect wisdom waits for us to cultivate. This is what all Buddhas teach.

Heng Chau • April 3, 1978
Trust your feelings out here, not your thinking

The L.A disciples loaded us up with supplies, food, and clothes. We bowed our respects to the Master, and set off early Monday A.M for the Big Sur.

Young Dan McCauley did a class A repair job on the Plymouth.

"He really got into it like we couldn't believe!" said his parents.

"Tricks and weird forces."

Kuo Chou and I dropped Heng Sure off at the bottom of a narrow, twisting and extremely steep grade that rises 300 – 400 feet in about ½ mile. It's the official entry into Big Sur. A sign at the bottom reads:

Dangerous Road. Next 60 miles.
Falling Rocks and Slides.
Not Maintained at Night.

We parked one car at the top under some trees for a night campsite and then drove ½ way back down to wait for Heng Sure. It was nearly dusk. We waited for over an hour and began to worry. The road drops sharply over the edge into steep gorges. If one fell or slipped, it could be fatal.

We ran up and down the road, calling "Heng Sure, Heng Sure!" but no answer. There was no place to go but forward or over the edge. The road was cut in the side of a sheer rock cliff. Since Heng Sure hadn't reached us, we assumed the worst.

Suddenly, Heng Sure appeared walking towards us from *above*!

"Strange forces at work here." he wrote in a note. "I hope they have a sense of humor."

"How did you pass us by? There's no way we could not have seen you walk by us!?" we wonder.

"You didn't see me and I didn't see you either, and we couldn't have been more than 6 feet apart at the turn off where you are parked!" he wrote. "I lost count of the bows twice. Couldn't control my mind. I'll have to do it all over tomorrow."

"What happened?" asked Kuo Chou.

"Don't know," wrote Heng Sure. "I got to the top, but you weren't there. I waited, figured something was up, and walked back down."

"And only then did you see us?" we asked.

"Strange. Not only did I not see you, but as I walked down, all the houses and spaces appeared that weren't there on the way up. It was like a totally different road. Everything topsy-turvy, and disappearing."

"I had a feeling we should be careful, but I ignored it," said Kuo Chou. "I'm learning you've got to trust your feelings out here, not your thinking."

We remembered the Master's words when we told him we had encountered strange people as we entered the mountains:

"The strange people who suddenly came up were the mountain weirdos and water goblins who came to play with you, to check you over."

There was no real harm done; kind of like pranks or playing tricks. Still, it sobered us all a little to realize the world and anyone of us could totally disappear before our very eyes, and we had no control over it, nor did we have the tools to even understand it.

* * *

Peter Schmitz (Gwo Dzai), arrived last night while we were meditating. It was quite dark. He saw cars and pulled over to ask, "Excuse me, I'm trying to find the bowing monks. Have you seen them?"

He was really surprised to discover he had driven right to us, and this was his first stop.

David (Kuo Chou) Rounds, left this morning. Peter came out to bow for a week. He said,

"They've been teasing me at the City saying I'll never last. I like to go out in the afternoon and get a piece of pie and ice cream. 'There's no pie à la mode doing three steps, one bow. You won't be able to take it.' they said."

"I've even had a dream about cutting up my hands and knees bowing," he laughed, "but I came anyhow and I'm glad I did. I feel better already just being here. It was just a test. I think."

"New Protectors."

The Babcocks, an elderly couple who live on a ranch across the road, walked over with some nuts, and honey from their hives. Their home is at the top of the first mountain which make them the southern "gate keepers" of Big Sur. They were happy and full of light. It felt like an official welcome after the steep ascent and the "strange forces" of last night.

"We'll be watching over you on your way and keeping an eye on things," they said.

Once we got to the top and made through a foggy, dark night, things changed. The Sun broke through at dawn and arched a huge rainbow from the mountain's base to the top. Then the Babcocks came out and took the edge off the harsh and forbidding landscape.

"We saw you back in San Luis and kept up with your progress until now. We saw you Friday, but then Friday night we couldn't find you. All weekend we looked for you. We were worried; you should have been down the road by then, but we couldn't find you."

I explained our trip to L.A to meet with our teacher. They were reassured. "Oh good, how nice, how wonderful." they said

The Babcock work at the Cancer Society and drive patients to and from the nearest hospital for treatments. They were excited to hear about the East-West Medical Center starting at the City of Ten Thousand Buddhas.

"Oh, I'll have to get in touch with them. That's such good news. That's what it's all about, isn't it? Just helping things get better." said Mrs. Babcock.

They had those special, clear, bright eyes we've come to call *hu fa* eyes. All our "Dharma Protectors" have them. They were full of giving, helping, and supporting energy.

"How did you ever make it up that awful stretch of mountain?" they asked.

I explained our bowing-in place technique and counting off when there's no shoulder. Big twinkle and laugh.

"Oh, we knew you had a method."

They asked about Peter. "He's new. We'll keep an eye on him too." And then looking at Heng Sure they said to me, "Be careful, and take good care of him. Bye."

Heng Sure • April 4, 1978
Like they were museum exhibits

At Ragged Point, the road slants up, the ocean falls away. The houses disappear and the atmosphere changes. We perch on a narrow turnoff. It's barely wide enough to allow opening the car door without falling three hundreds yards to the foaming surf.

Nestling below the sign announcing "Scenic Vista," I meditate between a giant boulder and the cliff edge. Kuo Dzai Schmitz has joined the bowing work; he checks the maps while Heng Chau cooks. Suddenly a mini-bus careens to a stop, tilted on the turnoff at an impossible angle, too close for comfort. All the doors open at once, and out strides a family of French tourists, movie cameras in hand and whining before they take a step. "Ou la la, e'ast mervelleux, n'est-ce pas?" says a young man. He films every inch of the coastline, leaning back and forth over the precipice in comical, Buster Keaton style. Stepping over me as if I were a rock, he never takes his eye from the viewfinder. "Magnifique!"

The others stare at Heng Chau's stove and pots like they were museum exhibits, without blinking. As if Buddhist monks picnicking and meditating on the mountainside were not surprising in the least. "Allons-y!" shouts the man, winding his camera and stepping over my crossed legs again. "Tres belle, non?" he asks no one in particular.

* * *

"In this way, the realm of empty space may end, the realm of living being may end, the karma of living beings may end, and their afflictions may end, but my vows to always study with the Buddhas is endless. It continues in thought after thought without cease. My body, mouth, and mind never weary of these deeds."

Avatamsaka Sutra
End of Vow #8, Chapter 40

Each of Universal Worthy's Ten Vows ends with a similar refrain. Four infinite dharmas to contemplate, four keys to the endless, ever-changing, Dharma-nature. These words are Proper Dharma power-tools, the Buddha's own mind-yoga, for stretching and popping the tight-fitting lid of the self from our minds.

Heng Chau • April 4, 1978
I should have calluses on my knees

Cultivating the Way requires incredible dedication and fervor. But one can easily get so self-absorbed that one forgets to laugh. A sense of humor goes a long way in this life and often is a most effective teacher.

For example, there was once a young novice who used to burn pots while cooking, and then leave them around unscrubbed. People asked her numerous times to clean up, but she paid no attention and continued leaving a messy kitchen. So all the other women cultivators got together and fasted on her behalf. They even recited the Buddha's name for her while carrying the unwashed pots, which eventually encouraged her to clean up after herself.

* * *

I talk too much (inside and out), and write too much. If I cultivate with right effort, I should wear out a pair of shoes before I empty a pen; I should have calluses on my knees and cobwebs on my tongue. So it says,

> "One obtains the Buddhadharma only by cultivating according to the teaching. It cannot be obtained by just talking about it."
>
> Avatamsaka Sutra, Ten Grounds Chapter

Heng Sure • April 5, 1978
Business done

You wait as long as you can, and a little longer. But the time comes and you've got to relieve nature. Across the flooded highway, vertical shale cliffs tower to the clouds. To the left only a shining oak sapling marks the brink of empty space before plunging straight down to the cresting seas. Where to go? Wearing rain gear, gloves, and warm clothes in layers, how does one stay dry and answer the call? How does one maintain a monk's deportment and observe decency? Motorists aren't prepared for yellow-clad figures relieving nature in public. People's sensitivities are easy to offend, even in the Big Sur boondocks. But to conduct oneself according to the Vinaya rules at all time, contemplate the Buddhas of the ten directions before your eyes, and never leave their presence. Mindful deportment will then be naturally proper, and in accord with Dharma.

A thought of the Buddha lends light to any situation. Just ahead a group of tall ferns and rhododendrons screened the road at the right angle. Gloves and buttons co-operated as I recited Amitabha's name. The rain continued to fall. Business done, I counted on up the asphalt three steps for every bow, and waited for Kuo Dzai to catch up. The rushing water washed away all traces of our passing.

> "If one contemplates it according to Brahma conduct, then one will have no desires with regard to the body, no attachment to what is cultivated, and will not dwell in any dharma."
>
> Avatamsaka Sutra
> Brahma Conduct, Chapter 16

Heng Chau • April 5, 1978
In the future, he will be able to cultivate

Steep mountain, sheer high cliffs, narrow shoulder that keeps getting more narrow. Ahead is a place called Ragged Point. Sometimes inside feels like the "ragged point." Heng Sure's silence, the quiet isolation of the land, and the unchanging repetitive bowing rhythm can do weird things to my head sometimes. An intense monotony sets in, yet each day is new ground, a place and depth we've never traveled before. Even though we are together here, we are alone. And there are no words or even thoughts that can describe these states.

After sunset and meditation, I felt overwhelmed by the emptiness of everything. From the socks I slipped on my cold feet to the ceremony we were going to do, nothing connected or felt real.

"Am I going crazy?" I wondered. Then we read the Avatamsaka and I felt better. It seemed to speak directly to the "no place" vacuum I was experiencing. It said,

> "All dharmas have no remainder. They are all entered into and yet they have no substance or nature. In this way does the one with pure eyes make transference and open up the prison of birth and death in the mundane world."

My feeling of emptiness was brought about from clinging to things (dharma) that cannot be clung to. Everything is impermanent and transitory. My plight was in not accepting things as they really are. I locked myself into a little "prison of birth and death" by trying to make dharma solid and permanent; trying to make things say, "You are real. There is you." We enter and leave this world without a trace left behind, "without remainder." All dharmas have no self. If one is looking for a self, then all one finds is emptiness. If you can be content looking for nothing, not seeking a place to rely, then right within emptiness the wonderful appears. The dreaded emptiness I felt was not true emptiness, for in true emptiness, emptiness itself is empty. I was just seeing a shadow made from a big view of self. The Sutra chased the shadow, leaving only the light. It is said,

> In one Buddhaland he relies on nothing.
> In all Buddhalands it is the same.
> Nor is he attached to conditioned dharmas;
> Because he knows that in the nature of these dharmas,
> There is no place to rely.
> Although they know all dharmas are empty and still,
> Towards emptiness itself,
> They do not have a single thought.

> Avatamsaka Sutra
> Ten Transference Chapter

Everything is without a nature, with nothing to be contemplated.

* * *

"His nature is straightforward, soft and pliant. He has no dense forest practices. He is not arrogant. He takes instruction well and gets the teacher's meaning."

Avatamsaka Sutra
Ten Grounds Chapter

The spirit of repentance and reform is so simple that often a child can express it best. Last month at Gold Wheel Temple, a young boy got up before the assembly and confessed,

"I broke rule. I ate food that my mother had intended to give to the Buddhas for a offering, and I didn't let her know. Then my upper lip broke out with a bad rash. When she asked me what I had done, I didn't tell her. When she found out, she got real mad and threw the fruit in my face!"

He was ashamed and sorry. Moreover, he had the humility and softness to openly repent. Everyone learned from this child's straightforward simplicity and candor. Later the Master said,

"So my little disciple stole the fruit and then realized he was wrong, and so there is still hope for him. It's not that important and he shouldn't feel embarrassed… Such a small child recognizing his mistakes is a good sign. In the future, he will be able to cultivate. The important thing is recognize your mistakes and then change."

In a way, this is the heart of cultivation; "to recognize your mistakes and then change." It's also the spirit of bowing journey; don't fear being wrong; only be afraid you won't recognize your wrongs. No fault is greater than concealing one's faults.

Heng Sure • April 6, 1978
The flood washes the stones away

Yellow plastic rainsuit emblazoned, "City of Los Angeles, Street Maintenance," bought cheap at overstocked wholesalers. Blue wool scullcap tugged tight around the ears. A-one and a-two and a quick hop over Heng Chau into the streaming rain, 7:30 A.M., gray skies and a world of water greet the intrepid pilgrims.

Kuo Dzai worked the Alaska pipeline; mean weather doesn't move him. Heng Chau inches the Plymouth up the 45° slope, rooster tails of rain fanning from the wheels. The road is too steep to bow; we slog ahead sliding back two steps in the muddy shoulders for every one step forward. At the first level spot I scout up six large rocks for the bowing computer. Tallied eighty bows to reach the spot. Tough condition – the flood washes the stones away while my face is earthward. Standing again, I've lost count. Rain pelts down the sleeves, soaking every layer, filling up the rubber gloves. Patience, patience. A tiny spark of anger at this point could turn the world into perdition. Cheerful endurance transform trials into the stuff of discovery. Spring rains are proving ground for true principle.

> "If my mind moves because of this bitterness, then I have not subdued myself. I have no proper concentration… How can I cause other's mind to be pure?"
>
> Avatamsaka Sutra
> Ten Practices Chapter

Heng Chau • April 6, 1978
When to talk, and when not to

It feels good not talking and harsh too. Most of my words are empty. I hide behind them. I never saw this until I stopped talking. But there is a time to talk, too. We cultivate the Middle Way which says; don't attach to what is; don't fall into what is not. Don't lean on words and language, but don't reject them either. In Buddhism, everything is useful; all things have a place and purpose. It all depends on how you use them. Mostly, we use words to prattle and rap. The words themselves aren't empty, it is the frivolous tongue that is false. A Bodhisattva can use the identical words a fool speaks and cause someone to get enlightened. So it is says,

> "He does not seek what living beings can speak of. These are all conditioned, false, empty affairs. Although he does not rely on the path of words and language, at the same time, he does not attach to not speaking."
>
> Avatamsaka Sutra
> Ten Transferences Chapter

How do I know when it's time to talk and when to shut up? I ask myself, "Who is it for? Will it benefit others or serves me?" I know immediately then whether to talk or hold my tongue.

* * *

Rain, cold, stiff winds and high cliffs. Lots of poison oak, no contacts, just stares and wonder from a few passing travellers.

During the Avatamsaka reading last night as the winds howled outside, there came a tapping hand on the window. The door opened and an arm reached in offering fresh-picked oranges wrapped in a silk scarf. Never saw who the person was.

We reached the Monterey County line. No towns, no people, nowhere to rely except in the Dharma and a single thought. Tonight we read from the "Ten Transferences,"

> The Bodhisattva concentrates his mind
> and thinks of all Buddhas
> With unsurpassed wisdom and clever expedients;
> Like the Buddhas, so is he totally without reliance.
> He vows to cultivate to accomplishment
> this merit and virtue.
>
> He concentrates his mind on saving all,
> To cause them to leave the host of evil karma.
> In this way, he benefits all that lives;
> Ever mindful, he never forsakes this thought.
>
> Ten Transferences Chapter
> Avatamsaka Sutra

Heng Sure • April 7, 1978
The endlessly grasping mind

Wind and signs:

> Leaving San Luis Obispo county.
> Monterey County Welcomes You.
> Cabrillo Highway.
> Scenic Route. (Picture of a California poppy).

A windy day. Air so brisk it stings like a slap. A winding road; 300 bows in place. Only flat spot is a promontory stuck on the cliff edge, a natural wind-tunnel. We three cling to the ground like moss on rock as the wind roars overhead. Whitecaps pitch high, crash back to a corduroy sea. I'm testing my mind. Do signs matter?

The highway engineers stuck five signs together on a single pole. Space is tight on this narrow ledge. The bowing tally-pebbles lie directly between the uprights. My feet stand in San Luis county, my head bows in Monterey. Heng Chau's precepts sash flaps against the Plymouth. Kuo Dzai, wrapped in Alaska-pipeline raingear, bow below the bumper of his red Saab.

The mind likes to draw lines, to measure and to label. We've walked the length of San Luis County in seven months. We've grown and changed in the miles between her welcoming sign and today's exit gate. We passed Vandenberg, The Mesa, Lompoc, San Luis, Cayucos-Cambria, San Simeon, and the rain-slick winter highway. Monterey ahead, home of John Steinbeck, my childhood hero. Big Sur, the unknown, empty cross, and the endlessly grasping mind, stand before us.

I try to make significance with names and lines. I seek to both exist and to know I exist. I struggle in emptiness to stand apart, to be special, to be extraordinary. Slowly I'm returning to the nameless source, the original home. People are tiny motes of dust on a dust-mote sized planet, in a galaxy lost in the infinite Dharma Realm.

I mark the passing days with city names and mileage totals, dividing time and space where no lines exist. The sutra makes clear that all dharmas naturally interpenetrate without obstruction. An Avatamsaka Patriarch explained to an Emperor of China who requested teaching about True Reality,

> "The Dharma Realm is the basic substance within the bodies and minds of all living beings. From the beginning it has been magical, lucid, expansive, penetrating; vast, great, quiescent, and still. It is the one and only True State. Devoid of any form or appearance… without boundary or limit, the ten thousand things are in its embrace. It is radiant and dazzling in the midst of the dust of form, yet its principles cannot be divided."

Flower Adornment Sutra
Entering the Dharma Realm
Chapter 39

Notions of me and mine blind me to the Patriarch's vision. Bowing in the wind helps peel away the covers and erase the selfish lines. The wind doesn't care where I came from, who I think I am, or where I'm headed. Whistling past the county signs, blowing the ocean to foam, chilling three pilgrims to the bone, the wind, like the Dharma Realm, is impartial; unbounded by false discriminations, unhindered by signs.

> It is like the unified nature of wind
> Which blows upon all things.
> Yet wind itself has only a single thought;
> And all Buddhadharma are the same.
>
> Avatamsaka Sutra – The Bodhisattvas
> Ask for Clarification chapter

Heng Chau • April 7, 1978
Where it's peaceful and calm

Attachments feel heavy like wearing wet clothes. False thoughts feel like being stuck in a cellar without a door. Clothes I don't need, books I never read, ideas that flow on and on. There are just too many things to fit into a day and still be pure, peaceful, and happy.

Too much is greed and confuses the heart. Too little is need and troubles the mind. Keep to the Middle where it's peaceful and calm. Take what comes and give when there is a chance. An empty mind is just right, sufficiency.

> "Neither greedy for the karma of giving or it's retribution, they take it as it comes and give in a level and equal manner."
>
> Avatamsaka Sutra
> Ten Transferences Chapter

* * *

Joseph, a young man in bib overalls, stopped his flat-bed truck to watch the bowing.

"Can I talk with you?" he asks, climbing down from the cab.

"We really need more of this. I've been trying to... some day maybe I'll be able to do a pilgrimage. I can assist by agreeing with you and also by giving a little money. I hope we all find the way," he says with a deep smile, and shakes hands. "Good luck."

Heng Sure • April 8, 1978
Able to contain all beings

Soda Spring Creek.

Pebbles in the bed of Soda Springs Creek: jade rock, azurite, quartz, mica, carnelian, feldspar – smooth as eggs, big as golf balls, fine as rice. Every pebble a unique event, separate, distinct. Yet below the names and colors, a single element, earth, unites them all.

People on the road bowing to the Buddha: Heng Chau, raised Catholic, son of an independent grocer from a small Wisconsin town; Kuo Dzai Schmitz, a Vietnam veteran, grew up playing in his family's fruit orchards in Oregon; Kuo Woo, who grew up in China, grandmother, daughter of a wealthy gentry family, Kuo Te, from Vietnam, refugee, Buddhist background; Kuo Chou, Harvard graduate, novelist, first generation Buddhist, New England Yankee stock. Buddhist disciples all; externally as different as hues of a rainbow. Faith in the Buddhadharma brings our lives together.

My companions are big-hearted, pure-minded believers in the ultimate perfectibility of people. Superficially we are like pebbles in Soda Springs Creek: alone, drifting aimlessly downstream to the ocean. Yet faith in practice of the truth returns us to a deep unity and harmony with all things; bowing today in this raw, windy edge of America, I appreciate Buddhism: it's big, like empty space, able to contain all beings. It's pure as creek water, washing away the pettiness of my mind, and smoothing the edges. Cultivation is simple and direct, yet within simplicity, myriad wonders unfold.

Tallying true substance with the region
    of ten thousand transformations.
Displaying virtue's marks in the doorway
    to the multiply profound,
Functions are legion and prolific,
    yet it is always such.
Wisdom everywhere examines,
    yet it is forever still.

        Flower Adornment Preface

Heng Sure • April 8, 1978
The only sensible thing to do with them

Dear Shr Fu,

Shr Fu, we won't be able to be with you on your birthday this year, but we will bow to you nine times here on the road and wish you many happy returns, with all our hearts. Here are some of the recent mind-changes on Three Steps, One Bow:

Heng Chau, Upasaka Kuo Chou Rounds, and I bowed around a steep rise and wham! there before us stood the next three weeks of our lives, etched in green stone and blue water: twenty miles of awesome rocks in the slanting, afternoon sun. The first sight of the sheer cliffs falling straight to the azure ocean took my breath away. We could see tiny flecks of sun-glare on glass: cars and campers rolling on a tiny thread of highway stuck on the mountainside, halfway between oblivion and nowhere. We were going to bow on this road? My first impulse was to follow an old habit energy and let my mind dive into a daydream, to avoid facing the reality.

But I couldn't do that. A new yang energy that's been slowly building took control and brought my heart back to focus on the work. What came to mind was this passage from the Sutra lecture the night before:

> Although he causes all existence to be purified,
> He does not make distinctions amid all that exists.
> And he is caused to be happy, with a purified mind.
> In one Buddhaland, he relies on nothing.
> In all Buddhalands it is the same.
> Nor is he attached to conditioned dharmas,
> Because he knows that in the nature of these dharmas
> There is nowhere to rely.
>
> Avatamsaka Sutra
> Ten Transferences Chapter

I applied the Sutra passage to this situation: only hours before, I had been bowing on Huntington Drive, outside Gold Wheel Temple in L.A.; where were there any dharmas to rely on there? Where was L.A. now? When I was in L.A., where were these mountains, this ocean? How was this moment any different from that moment? I couldn't find any differences! So what was there to hide from? Why take a vacation in false-thoughts? It's nothing but the sad little ego looking for a way out of the pressure of slow, steady work on the mind-ground. What would Shr Fu say? "Everything's okay. No problem. Use effort. Fear is useless."

So, I took another look at the landscape before us. "Hey! What a beautiful, pure place to cultivate in. What a fine Bodhimanda!" My heart seemed to take wings and soar out into the clear air above the mud of my afflictions. When these boulders have turned to dust, I vow to still be on the Bodhisattva path, working to end the sufferings of all living beings.

Now we're concentrating on the basics: giving, holding precepts, patience, and vigor. Along with all the Master's disciples, we are working to give the world a City of Ten Thousand Buddhas, a place where precepts will be the ground rules for being a person. As for patience, well, there's lots of chances to practice patience on this mountainside. Kuo Dzai Schmitz is sharing the work with us this week, patiently enduring some of the most contrary weather of the whole trip.

We are traveling seven miles of the most dangerous road we've faced: poison oak that grows everywhere, venomous ticks that inhabit the underbrush, sunburn, the mad Big Sur wind, freezing rain that stops as soon as we put on our slickers and boots and then starts again when we change back out of our rain gear. This trip has taught us an appreciation of the monastic environment. How fine are walls, a roof, and a clean floor! I did not make the most of my chance to cultivate in the ideal meditative space of Gold Mountain Monastery. Now that I really want to do the work, all sorts of obstructions arise: each one becomes a test of patience, resolve, and kung fu: wind, insects underfoot, cramped quarters, rain and sun in excess, traffic – all these dharmas can help cultivators forge a vajra resolve. We transfer our work and wish that the City of Ten Thousand Buddhas will come into being quickly and easily, so that whoever brings forth the heart to cultivate the Way will have a pure place to realize their wish. They won't have to endure any hassles before they sit in meditation. I'm not complaining! I have never felt happier or stronger.

These clumsy corpses we walk around in are such a drag! We waste so much time looking after our bodies. The only sensible thing to do with them is to cultivate the Way. I like the Bodhisattva in the First Practice of the "Ten Practices Chapter": he makes a vow to reincarnate into a huge, vast body so that no matter how many living beings are hungry the flesh of his body will satisfy their needs. Then the Bodhisattva contemplates all living beings of the past, the future, and the present. He contemplates the bodies they receive, their lifespans, their decay, and their extinction. The Sutra says,

> Again he thinks, "How strange living beings are! How ignorant and lacking in wisdom. Within (the cycle of) birth and death, they get countless bodies which are perilous and fragile. Without pause, these bodies hastily go bad again. Whether their bodies have already gone bad, are about to decay, or will come to ruin in the future, they are unable to use these unstable bodies to seek a solid body!

"I should thoroughly learn what all Buddhas have learned! I should realize all-wisdom and know all dharmas. For the sake of all beings I will teach them equally in the three periods of time. According to and harmonizing with still tranquility and the indestructible Dharma-nature, I will cause them to obtain peace, security, and happiness."

I memorized this passage from the Avatamsaka Sutra, and it has given me heart to keep bowing through many situations, where my skinbag and my common-person's mind feared it could not go. One immediately useful application: when the heat and pressure builds in the legs from Ch'an sitting, all I have to do is review the Sutra's wisdom and I find strength to continue to sit without wiggling or dropping my legs out of full lotus. "On the path to the worry-free liberation-city," as the Sutra calls it.

The biggest discovery of the month of March: "Where there's a will, there's a way." We are rich in methods to cultivate. What counts is resolving the heart on wanting to succeed. Then the Way opens.

Disciple Guo Chen (Heng Sure)
bows in respect

Heng Chau • April 8, 1978
This is just too fine!

"I want to come back after Alaska. It won't take me long to finish up there," said Peter (Kuo Dzai) as he got ready to leave. He bowed with us for a week, pretty much in silence. Peter has been working construction on the Alaska pipeline during the summers, and living in the monastery during the rest of the year.

I always remember Kuo Dzai sitting on the side of the road, 300 feet above the azura sea. We took a bowing break and he sat down to read the Avatamsaka Preface. He just stared off for a long time with the Preface held limply in one hand, draped over his knee, oblivious to the campers and tourists driving by. The Preface begins with,

> Going and returning with no border,
> Movement and stillness have one source;
> Embracing multitudes of wonders, more remains.
> Overstepping words and thought by far:
> This can only be the Dharma Realm!

"Boy! I tried to read it twice, but I couldn't handle it. It blew my mind!" he said

Peter, an ex-marine, Vietnam Vet, now a strict vegetarian, looked serene and mellowed in a true and solid way. The bowing and Avatamsaka can do that to you.

> Opening and disclosing the mysterious and subtle,
> Understanding and expanding the mind and its states;
> Exhausting the principle and fathoming the nature,
> Penetrating the result which includes the cause;
> Deep and wide and interfused,
> Vast and great and totally complete.
> Surely this must be:
> The Great Means Expansive
>   Buddha Flower Adornment Sutra!
>
> Avatamsaka Sutra

"This is just too fine, too much...!" said Peter shaking his head. One world stops and another opens, and then another.

* * *

"Don't play around."

The three of us bowed a long warm afternoon. Built up a big thirst and a lot of pressure. As we rounded a corner in the mountain, we heard falling water from a little glen and waterfall set back off the road. We took a break to get a drink, but I wasn't satisfied with just a thirst quencher. I got the urge to explore the hollow and took off on my own, downstream, jumping rock to rock. I broke the rules: (1) Stay close together and protect Heng Sure's vows. (2) No "Playing". At all times be single-minded. No side trips or sight-seeing.

I took another cool drink and turned to rejoin the group, but a huge, grotesque looking man was standing 20 yards above me where the stream cuts under the road. I nearly fell into the water – I was that startled. He was pale, chalky colored and shaped like a bloated pear. He kept staring through me, and slowly waving his arms up and down, back and forth and mumbling to himself.

I got by him by crawling through the tunnel under the road. When I merged on the other side, the man turned and continued to wave and sway. I began bowing and never looked back. We were told right at the outset,

> "Contemplate your own heart. If you are without the slightest trace of fear, anger, or greed, then no one will be able to touch you… simply do your own work and maintain your precepts."

What is there to be afraid of? There's nothing to be afraid of if you only do your own work and keep the rules.

Bodhisattvas don't play around. They set their minds on Bodhi and never leave their vast, great resolve.

> "The Bodhisattva sets his will on the search for Bodhi…
> He does not want any of the five desires or a king's throne.
> He wants not wealth or success, amusement or fame. He wants only to end for eternity the sufferings of living beings. His resolution is to benefit the world."

Avatamsaka Sutra
Worthy Leader Chapter

At dust we made a trip back to the waterfall to fill our water jugs. The stream water was cool and pure and good for drinking. The vibes and moving shadows in the glen were thick and dancing. We might be the only people out here, but we would be blind to say "We are all alone, there's nothing else here." The place was pulsing with activity.

Where did the strange man come from this afternoon? He had no car or bicycle, no baggage other than the shirt on his back. There are no towns or houses for miles.

Heng Sure • April 9, 1978
Gentleman, your license plate is out of date

Signs:

> Los Padres National Forest
> Department of Agriculture
> Forest Service

...announces the sign.

Narrow road, cliffs and drop-off, counting beads and bowing in place. Parked below the Los Padres sign on a ten-foot dirt shoulder. I bow beside the massive brown signposts while my partner boils macaroni on the stove on the tailgate.

We've bowed four hundred miles to reach Big Sur. Nowhere was there less occasion for a sign dividing nature into lines and boundaries. There is nothing here but rock, sky, water, and stars. Originally our minds are pure and clean, just like the Los Padres landscape, but we draw lines and make false distinctions with our thoughts and selfish desires.

"All of the troubles in the world come from attaching to a self. If you didn't have a self, if you didn't see yourself so clearly, what problems could there be?" said the Master at Gold Wheel Temple.

Not all thoughts are bad, just the selfish, exclusive thoughts: thoughts of greed, anger, stupidity, jealousy, afflictions. These are the troublemakers.

I meditated before lunch out of the wind, huddled behind the right front wheel of the Plymouth. Out of nowhere, a big yellow Cadillac shoehorned into the tiny crevasse between the park sign and the cliff-drop-off. An angry man with red hair, white shoes and a loud, shark-skin suit, stalked out and circled our car.

He didn't like our looks; he disapproved of our presence, and he was ready to fight. The quiet air was suddenly filled with hostile vibes. Something about our silence gave him pause, however. While I sat in full lotus, I peaked at him from the corner of my eyes as he started to swoop down, hawk-like, on Heng Chau. Heng Chau didn't blink, but continued to chop the celery and carrots. The man stopped in puzzlement, opened his mouth, thought better of it, jammed knotted fists into his trouser pockets, and circled the car once more. He wanted an excuse to argue, he wanted a sign of fear or anger, he wanted any edge to grab.

After reading our handout posted in the window, and after gazing at the Buddha's image next to it, he cooled visibly, but was still dissatisfied, and determined to make a scene.

"Gentleman, your license plate is out of date. Your car violates the law," he stated, with a superior air, pleased to have found some way of putting down the creeps.

"No, it doesn't. You read the wrong tag. The rear plate carries our current '78 sticker," said Heng Chau with a gentle smile.

The man's face turned as red as his hair. Clearly he felt he had set the weirdos to rights, losers weren't supposed to have the last word, but what could he say? He had simply read the wrong sign. His mouth opened and closed twice. A voice from the Cadillac called, "Tom? Let's go. What are we stopped here for? Tom?"

Dust spun from the wheels and coated the Los Padres Sign as the Cadillac regained the highway. Moments later the hand bell rang.

"Let's eat." said Heng Chau.

Levelly and impartially
    Bodhisattvas teach and transform,
Without any signs,
    without conditions or calculations,
Without any falseness,
    far apart from distinctions,
From seeking and grasping.

Avatamsaka Sutra
Ten Transferences Chapter

Heng Sure • April 10, 1978
Bowed into a Chinese landscape painting

Below Mount Mars we enter a new world. The road climbs, falls, bends and twists. Waterfalls echo in deep canyons. Dense mist melts beneath the sunlight and the air floods with mystery. Suddenly, it's as if an invisible stagehand lifts a clean blue sky.

We feel we've bowed into a Chinese landscape painting, or stepped into the wilderness retreats of nature poet Han Shan, Meng Hou-ran, and Wang Wei. Landscape tests our mindfulness and tempts our samadhi. Cultivators must not move their minds from concentration no matter their environment. Below a roaring, choking L.A. freeway overpass, or in the euphoric grandeur of the Big Sur coast, in the end there's not a single dharma that can be grasped.

They know that all worlds in every direction
Are completely created
    by being's discriminating thoughts.
With regard to thought and non-thought,
    there is nothing to be obtained:
In this way they understand thinking.

Avatamsaka Sutra
Ten Transferences Chapter

Heng Chau • April 10, 1978
Leaving your door open

"I'm just Carl."

An older man with no teeth approaches me as we bow on the side of a tall, slanting moutain near the entrance to Los Padres. He presses up close and keeps pumping my hand – way too friendly for a complete stranger happened upon in the wilderness.

"I just thought I'd stop and see what you love," he said. "I mean you must love something or else you wouldn't be here. I love everybody. And so here we all are and there's the ocean, we all know that. I'm just Carl and I don't know nothing. I don't know who I am or where I am, or what I'm doing," he paused, grinned a big toothless smile, pumped my hand some more.

"Yup, so here we all are, and there's the ocean, we all know that. And I'm just Carl, I don't know nothing." Another pause.

"Well, I just thought I'd stop. I'll be going now." He grinned, saluted goodbye, and walked off down the empty road.

> "I want to vigorously cultivate all good and universally save all... I want to forever leave all arrogance and laxness and certainly go towards the ground of All-Wisdom, and certainly never bring forth a wish to seek another path... I want to concentrate my mind to receive and uphold the Dharma taught by all Buddhas."
>
> Avatamsaka Sutra
> Ten Transferences Chapter

Where did Carl come from? I called him, you might say. How? Instead of bowing with a concentrated mind, I sat down to write out my false thoughts about a grandiose project I intended to take on after the pilgrimage. This plan was arrogant, and sitting down to pen it was laxness. I attached to my big idea which amounted to "bringing forth a wish to seek another path" than the path I was travelling right now. In cultivator's language, this is called, "leaving your door open."

[Note: "Leaving your door open" refers to the six sense faculties, also called the "door" or "gates" (eyes, ears, nose, tongue, body, and mind). "Left open" means going out the six doors seeking after the six sense objects, (sights, sounds, smells, flavors, sensations, and dharma). The sense objects are also called the "six thieves" because they rob one's wisdom treasures.

The phrase can also refer to leaving oneself unprotected and off-center by breaking precepts, getting afflicted, or by false thinking. When the door of a house is left open, anyone can walk in and do as they please. In the same way, when a cultivator leaves his door open, he is likely to get ripped off or catch a demonic obstacle. Therefore, one of the first things a Bodhisattva learns is to gather back his light and secure the doors at all times.]

I left my door open by losing mindfulness and running out after a false thought. As soon as my mind moved and my body stopped bowing, Carl walked in to wake me up. He was my teacher. He came to remind me "to receive and uphold the Dharma taught by all Buddhas." That is, to produce the mind that is nowhere attached. Past thought cannot be got at, present thought cannot be stopped, and future thought can't be obtained. There's not one thing that can be attached to.

> In one Buddhaland he relies on nothing.
> In all Buddhalands it is the same.
> Nor is he attached to conditioned dharmas
> Because he knows that in the nature of these dharmas,
>> there is nothing to rely on.
>
> Avatamsaka Sutra
> Ten Transferences Chapter

> He well protects and guards his faculties.
>
> Avatamsaka Sutra
> Ten Grounds Chapter

Heng Sure • April 11, 1978
Have his vocal cords frozen?

"Words."

> "The Bodhisattva by nature, does not speak frivolously.
> He always delights in considered speech, real talk, meaningful
> speech…"

Avatamsaka Sutra
Ten Grounds Chapter

Little dirt drives lead from the highways up sharp grades to
houses sheltered by trees and hills. Occasionally we see bare roof-
lines, chimneys, lightning rods, but we don't see television antennae.
Maybe T.V. beam don't reach the Big Sur Coast. Folks who live
without T.V. have to find other ways to occupy their eyes and ears.

Remove the buzzing electric input of T.V., and a wonderful
change happens. Words count more. Speech regains its magic.
Silence tunes the mind, the ear rest, the voices of Nature reappear
and fill the world.

A newsman asked Heng Chau, "Your partner hasn't spoken for
nearly a year. Have his vocal cords frozen? I mean, has his voice box
gone stiff?" Newsmen rely on words; he found it inconceivable that
I could survive without talking. The television-radio world spits
clouds of words into the air; words as noise, words as produce – a
bushel a minute – no value remains in meaning; words without heart.
Heng Chau and I share a surprising truth with our Big Sur neighbors.
Chuang Tzu said it well:

> "Words hold meaning. Get the meaning; you can forget
> the word. Where can I find someone who has forgotten
> words so that we might have a chat?"

I used to talk like a machine gun. Words ricocheted through my
mind non-stop. Full of cliché, jargon, junk words, and jingles learned

from T.V., my speech was trite, and light as feathers. Because we experience life through symbols of language, the way we speak creates our reality. Talk less, make words count, and the world expand in all directions, clear and vast as the Big Sur sky.

Words pass on awareness. People experience life and share their knowing through symbols charge with meaning: words. Steinbeck wrote,

> "There are simple, stately, dignified words, fresh and young words, proud and sharp words, words as dainty as little girls, and stone words needing no adjective as crutches."

The wonder of voicing knowledge: speech. Talk is rich sharing; each person's talk contains different rhythms, feelings, music, pain, colors, tones, choices, echoes of entire civilizations. Bodhisattva's eloquence includes eloquence in Dharma, in principle, in phrasing, and delight in speech; that is to say, a pure joy in handling words.

Holding my tongue has opened my ears to the magic of words.

Heng Chau • April 11, 1978
The 'Monk' from Spain

Suddenly a stiff gust of wind will sweep along the ground when we are down in a prostration. It fills our ears, nose, eyes, and mouth with cinders and grit. Thinking is the same. It's talking inside, and turns the mind into a dust storm of affliction and confusion. My words and thoughts often make no sense and give one little peace. It seems the more I use the tongue and brain, the further lost I get and the thicker blows the dust.

> "The more you think, the more you talk and the further away you go. Stop thinking, stop talking, and there's no place you won't penetrate."
>
> from "Have Faith in Your Mind"
> by Great Master Seng Ts'an

* * *

Salmon Creek, California.

"Monk."

Before noon, we bowed into the Salmon Creek canyon area. Lots of energy here — tall conifers, a deep gorge carrying a powerful, bounding stream that drops over a couple of waterfalls before emptying into the sea far below. The hills on either side are rich with plant growth, rock formations, and unusual people.

As we bowed the curve passing by the falls, a man came out from the woods with a large pack on his back.

"Howdy, my name's 'Monk.' I stopped to shoot de shit with ya," he said with a friendly face.

Monk was dressed in old U.S. Army fatigues and bedecked from head to toe with insignias, patches, and charms from every place imaginable and some unimaginable. His long hair was bound in a black silk scarf and topped with a Jack Nicklaus golf cap. High leather puttees pulled down over his boot tops. He was cross-eyed, had long, brown-stained, pointed teeth, and pointed ears. And yet he gave off clear, gentle vibes and a big-hearted feeling.

"Got the name 'Monk' in my Buddhist days back in Spain. Kind of stuck. I'm still a Buddhist, but I take a little bit of everything, if you know what I mean. I want to find out for myself," he said as he reached into his pack.

"Got some brown rice I'd like to offer. I eat dog food, if you can believe it, so I can't use it." His brown-stained teeth and a big bag of dry Purina Dog Chow sticking out of his bag, made it credible.

"The Park Ranger, Howard, wants to give you some gas," said Monk, pointing to some log-style cabins about ¼ mile down the road.

"We really dig what you're doing. In this day and age to find someone doing something so pure with no motive, well, that's really something!"

Monk swung his pack over his shoulder and said, "I read where one of you said 'Buddhism is as American as apple pie,' Boy, that was really great! It really is American, suited to us perfectly. As I say, I ain't had no formal teaching, just ripped through all the books. I can't get along with organizations," he said with a proud air of independence.

"Yeah, I saw your robes while you were bowing, and figure you were Buddhists from the Northern School. So this is your pad, huh?" he said peeking into the car.

"What a trip! What a trip! What a way to see the coast of California!" he exclaimed.

Monk turned to head up the trail to the falls and mountain.

"It's really beautiful up there. Unique. That's where I do my work. I don't know what your restrictions are, but you should go take a look. Catch 'ya later." And off he went.

We were watched from a distance as we first entered this area. Strange looking people with long beards and hair peeked out from behind large trees, bushes, and boulders. Monk broke the ice. Immediately after he left, shy and cautious people came out bearing offerings of food and fresh water for lunch.

There was Ken who said,

"We've been watching and waiting for you. It's very exciting and far-out what you're doing. Here, accept this water. It's good and healthy – has high mineral content…" as he talked others came with bread, nuts, and seeds. They all had funny, floating eyes and faces, like a colorless kaleidoscope ever-shifting, in an endless variety of patterns. Some were talking to themselves or rummaging through a big green trash-can on a pull off. One man, dressed in sweat clothes and sneakers, was squatting at the side of the road and squawking at the birds.

"Where do you live?" I asked.

"Oh, in the valley," answered Ken, pointing to the creek and falls. The "valley" was nothing but a deep gorge full of thick trees, shrubs, and poison oak, maybe 200-300 yards wide across the top. The only flat piece of ground was the highway – everything else plunged or peaked. Yet when they left, they disappeared into the "valley" and there we were alone and quiet again with only a lunch offering to show that anybody had been there minutes before.

Are they crazy people, or maybe cultivators? Who knows? In the Avatamsaka Sutra, the Good Knowing Advisors the Youth Good Wealth encounters, come from all walks of life. Some are monks and nuns, sages and worthies, yet others are laypeople, maidens, physicians, merchants, a boat captain, and even outside Way adherents. The Dharma is not fixed. It's alive, fluid, and like water, finds its way to the most unexpected places – often the lowest places that men disdain. We never know who our next teacher will be on the highway. The wonderful teaching is not attached to appearances.

About 1:30 A.M., we heard footsteps outside. We were parked on a narrow pull-off about 2 miles north of the Salmon Creek Falls. There was no moon to light the extremely winding and dangerous mountain road. With only steep cliffs and no shoulder, one missed step, and you could fall to your death. "Who could be out walking this road at night without a lantern or flashlight?" we wondered.

The steps stopped outside our car and something loudly plumped on top of the roof. Then the person walked away.

In the A.M. we found a large sack full of food, maps, matches, tea and supplies – about 40 or 50 pounds total. Pinned to the sack was this note from "Monk."

> "You passed thru the valley of Salmon Creek with, it seems, great haste. Tis rather understandable; this valley has an energy that can melt metal.
>
> "This child felt your Way and 'quiet time' does not need a fool's babble – so here is some beans for your prayer bowls and tea to wash it down. It is extra and hurts not my path in sharing.

"May the Gods smile on your venture and the heart of
the magic you are making.

"May the Buddha be in each and every thing you view.

"With Lessons. With light. With Love."

Monk

"P.S.: The Ranger Howard Berry is throwing in all kinds of
things in our little package of care. We like your trip! It makes
us feel good to watch somebody do something nice. Selflessness is what will save us all. He is a good man. There are
people still thus."

We felt an affinity with Monk. He was a friend and a teacher. He
walked 3 miles on a dark, foggy night to bring us supplies and lift our
spirits. Monk and the Ranger Howard put themselves out for the
sake of others and you could feel their good energy and light long
after passing through Salmon Creek. It stayed in the heart. They
made people happy, and making people happy is the same as making
Buddhas happy.

"All these many kinds of living beings I will accord with
and take care of, providing all manner of service and
offerings. I will treat them with the same respect I show my
own parents, teacher, elders, Arhats, and even the Thus
Come Ones. I serve them all equally without difference –
why? If a Bodhisattva accords with living beings, then he
accords with and makes offerings to all Buddhas. If he can
honor and serve living beings, then he honors and serves the
Thus Come Ones. If he makes living beings happy, he is
making all the Thus Come Ones happy."

Avatamsaka Sutra
Chapter 40

Heng Sure • April 12, 1978
A quality of virtue that set him apart

Before the start of the trip, Heng Chau and I shared stories of our upbringing, and the steps that carried us into the Dharma. His education is parochial schools impressed me most deeply.

He learned more than ABC's and the three R's. School include weekend retreats where classmates gathered in bathrobes and slippers to burn night oil and discuss what being a real person meant. Education in Heng Chau's school encouraged morality, the values of the heart, spiritually, and inner exploration. His school challenged children to open their minds and try their best to meet the world with integrity. This education often turned out well-rounded people who could measure up and grow into good citizens with solid values, the magic of faith, and analytical, probing minds.

In my neighborhood, one family sent Tom and Steve, their two sons, to St. Francis DeSales, Toledo's outstanding parochial school. Tom was a special person. Although outwardly just a regular guy, he had a quality of virtue that set him apart. He was a straight arrow, trustworthy, sincere and a clean person. And his mind was alert, keen, awake. Tom did everything wholeheartedly, with vigor and an effortless, unaffected style that shed a certain light. I knew Tom through Student Council work. He was school President and an All-City athlete. He went on to the U.S. Naval Academy after graduation. Then I lost touch with him. Even we kids noticed. We never discussed it, but everyone quietly respected this family and felt the world a better place for their presence.

Our school at the City of Ten Thousand Buddhas, encourage children to benefit the world in the same tradition as Heng Chau and Tom's education. We still have much of our education to complete, but after hearing Heng Chau talk of his experiences, remembering Tom's light and energy, lights a lamp in my heart: Buddhist education will turn the world around!

Heng Chau • April 12, 1978
The most dangerous thing I've had to face

This country is right out of a Chinese landscape painting: winding streams amid soaring foggy mountains, and twisted, gnarled trees; wandering monks with walking sticks on narrow foot paths. Solitude, no obstacle, truly heading home.

The most dangerous thing I've had to face on this trip are my bad habits. Nothing outside is worse than my own arrogance; nothing more perilous than my own greed, anger, and stupidity. Bowing is a small step toward cleaning up the world inside and gently reuniting with the world outside – not the dusty world, but the "always so" eternally dwelling, pure world that is said to perfectly blend and intermingle with the dusty world. When the mind is pure it can be seen as a lotus flower resting in a sea of fragrant water.

> "The ocean of the Flower Treasury Worlds is identical with the Dharma Realm, not different; adorned and extremely pure, resting peacefully in empty space."
>
> Avatamsaka Sutra
> Chapter 5

Within the flower are worlds to the number of fine motes of dust. So it's called the Flower Treasury World. That world system has twenty tiers, each containing limitless worlds. The world we live in, the Saha, is located on the thirteenth tier.

When one enlightens, one is able to see that the "defiled and pure both blend and fuse." Subject and object meld and to the exhaustion of the universe, one can hear the Flower Adornment Sutra always being spoken.

It is wisdom states such as these that keep our small minds from icing up and remind us this wrold we get so busy and worried about isn't very big at all.

At night we study these ancient and enlightened truths. But by day I still can't see it. Monk said, "May the Buddha be in each and everything you view." How does one get to see the Buddha in everything? Where do Buddhas come from? The Sutra says they come from within our own mind: when the mind is pure, the Buddha appears.

> "If there is a person who wants to see as many Buddhas as there are living beings, he will certainly get his wish. However, they come from nowhere.
>
> "One who takes the Buddha's state as his own, and concentrates his mind without rest, is one who will get to see Buddhas equal in number to his thoughts."
>
> Avatamsaka Sutra
> Chapter 24

The Buddha's bodies are not apart from all the bodies in the mundane world. To understand and know your own true self-nature, is to be a Buddha.

On Fear:

> "They have left the view of self far behind, and have no thought of self. Therefore, they have no fear of death. He well protects and guards his faculties."
>
> Avatamsaka Sutra
> Ten Grounds Chapter

A Buddhist isn't afraid others will harm him; he only fears he will harm others. Buddhists don't fear taking a loss; they only fear they won't be in time to benefit others. So they are very careful and cautious about what they do. Why? They know that whatever they put out comes back. Good returns as good; harm comes back as harm. A disciple of the Buddha is not distrustful or on his guard towards other people, rather he watches over his own door like a cat watches a mouse hole. One who guards himself needs no other protection. Without a self, what is there to fear?

Heng Sure • April 13, 1978
What's a Buddha-thought?

"Gold Wheel Dharma Lesson."

"Does anyone have a question," asks the Master, turning to look directly at me.

"Yes, Master, I do. The other day while bowing, I thought, 'When are you going to become a Buddha?'"

I answered myself, "When you only have Buddha thoughts in your head. As long as you have false-thoughts or greedy, angry, or stupid thoughts, you can't become a Buddha. When your head has only Buddha-thoughts, you are the Buddha."

(I thought this answer was eloquent and principled).

"Okay Kuo Chen, what's a Buddha-thought? Let's hear your answer?"

"Well, (stunned and blushing), it's only good thoughts…"

"I asked you what is a Buddha thought?" (pinning me down!)

"Well, I don't know, (slipping out). If I knew I would be a Buddha. Because I don't have only Buddha thoughts… I know what false thoughts are…"

"It's because you have false thoughts that you don't know. What is inexpressible, what cannot be described, is the Buddha. Anything you can put into words is still superficial. As long as you still have thoughts, you have not realized Buddhahood."

"So no-thoughts is Buddha thought?"

Wrong again. The Sutra says,

> "The ways of the Thus Come Ones, Great Immortals, are subtle, wonderful, and hard to comprehend. Not thought, they are apart from every thought."

> Avatamsaka Sutra
> Ten Grounds Chapter

"When you have no-thought, you should still go on to become free of all thoughts. If you know you have no thoughts, this is still having thoughts, still attaching to marks."

It's said,

> The path of words and language is cut off.
> The place of the mind's working is extinguished.
> Right in thoughts one is apart from thought.
> One thinks, and yet one has no thoughts.

Don't miss it! From our first step to the present moment, our constant instruction has been,

> "Do no false-thinking. Be a person of the Way with no mind."

When this work is done well, it's said that Buddhahood accomplishes itself.

Heng Chau • April 13, 1978
By practicing great giving

"The joy of giving."

Maybe it's part of growing up, maybe it's part of the bowing – maybe some of both, but today I saw that I'm selfish. Although I've been greatly given to by my parents, teachers, and friends, I arrogantly assumed that I deserved it or the world owed me this favor. It wasn't until I encountered a Good and Wise Advisor that I saw my stinginess. It stood out in contrast to his selfless giving. A Good Advisor gives away his very life, all of his good roots and virtue, to bring living beings to their highest potential – Buddhahood. He gives for the joy of giving, and never linger for a thank you.

It's said,

"Just as one lamp can disperse the darkness of a thousand years, one thought of wisdom can destroy ten thousand years of people's delusions."

I am deeply ashamed of my past ways. But to wallow in shame and guilt is not the Buddha's teaching; quickly changing toward the good is. Light and lamp, don't curse the darkness.

"Don't think of the past; it is gone and can never be recovered. Instead, think always of the future and in every thought, perfect and clear, see your own original nature."

The Sixth Patriarch Sutra

Bodhisattvas have no self. Everything they do is to benefit others. They correct their stinginess by practicing great giving, not by castigating themselves. A true disciple of the Buddha would never fight with or punish any living creature, not even himself.

"Toward all living beings he attains indestructible faith, therefore, with kind eyes he regards them all equally, and he transfers his good roots for their benefit... He accords with, cultivates and studies what the Buddhas do; he gathers in and holds all pure good roots and enters the true, real meaning. Amassing blessing and virtuous conduct, he practices great giving."

Avatamsaka Sutra
Ten Transferences Chapter

* * *

This is rugged country; hard on the hands and knees. Miles of pale, blue-green shrubs covering precipitous look-a-like mountains. The raw landscape is unrelieved by people or marks of civilization. It's great for that, too.

The solitude and harshness outside soon brings our focus of attention and awareness to the inside, on the mind. The vast and pure virgin face of the land and sea cleanses the mind and sharpens contemplation. It's all out in front, raw and real. There's no hiding from yourself here.

This A.M. in meditation, I saw the thick and endless flow of my false thoughts. Oh so many; constantly streaming from my mind! It was like the water bounding down these mountain streams and rivers. Countless drops of water fall and flow, each one different. Yet one does not know the other and they roll along mutually unaware. Like my thoughts, they come and go without purpose, without pause.

> Just as the water in a river
> Which rolls and flows, races and chases along,
> Is such that each drop of water does not know the other,
> So too are all dharma just the same.

> Avatamsaka Sutra – The Bodhisattva
> Ask for Clarification, Chapter 10

The Sutra says that all things we take for real, all that we perceive with our sense organs, are empty and without a nature. They exist only from the discriminations of the false mind. What is true and real is seen with the Dharma-eye. It's vision is not inverted. What we see with our eyes is what we have on our minds. False thinking is a temporary blindness.

Heng Sure • April 14, 1978
The dish looks suspiciously like dog food

Disciple: "Master, please explain this principle,

> Contemplate the nature of the Dharma Realm,
> it's all made from the mind alone.

Did the Master create me from his mind, or did I create the Master from my mind? Or is that really a stupid question?"

Ven. Abbot: "It's however you think it is, understand?"

Disciple: "I don't know."

Ven. Abbot: "It's however you think it is. Because if you think it's one way and someone else tells you it's another way, you aren't going to believe them. You create it yourself. No one creates it for you. However you think about it, that's how it is."

We were eating a can of Chinese Vegetarian food for lunch, a soybean product which to Heng Chau was "dried braised bean curd." That's how the label translated it. In Chinese it was different. I couldn't see English written on the other side of the can, so I was eating food with a Chinese label, which said, "red-fried vegetarian chicken, with that down-home aroma and flavor." The food was the same, but in our minds, it was different, created by the labels we read.

One dish can be as many different things as there are people to view it. For example, a platter of "Arhat" vegetables, to the ascetic, is fuel for cultivation. To the monk beside him, it is an offering by the faithful laity to be transferred into blessing and happiness. To the next monk who is working with the Five Contemplations, the plate of food is medicine which he takes in order to keep his body from suffering the sickness of hunger. To the donor, the food is a chance to plant blessings with the Sangha Jewel, the left home disciples of the Buddha. To the gourmet, the plate of food is an exciting adventure in oriental cuisine. To the newcomer to meatless eating, the dish looks suspiciously like dog food, but it tastes great.

Among these different realities, which one is more valid? Which one is true? According to the Sutra's principle, all are equally correct. "It's all made from the mind alone. You create it yourself. However you think about it, that's how it is," says the Master.

Heng Chau • April 14, 1978
There's just no way to please everybody

"Waterfall weirdos."

Heng Sure and I went to fill our water jugs at a waterfall after bowing. A low-riding, rumbling car pulled up full of gaunt, wasted-looking people. They seemed comatose or hypnotized. Long, hallow faces, dark-ringed eyes, expressionless gazes, stared at us. Finally the driver got out and walked up.

"Krishnas?"

"No. Buddhists," I answered.

"Yeah, I used to be one too. Hey, can you spare some gas?" he asked. Then he nodded over his shoulder to the people sitting in the car and said,

"I don't know who these people are, but I don't think we'll make it over the hill… Once I get to Berkeley, it'll be okay. I've got friends there… Huh? Got any spare gas, pal?"

We gave them some gas from our spare can and then went on down a narrow trail to the pool at the bottom of the fall. Purple dusk time. Three men and a dog suddenly appeared – we never heard a car or footsteps. They walked right toward us. Felt trapped and cornered. The water was at our backs; steep rocks dripping with moss on all sides. The only way out was a narrow mud-slippery slide of a footpath flanked with thick poison oak – and they had positioned themselves in front of it.

They were drunk and grinning at each other as they sized us up. The biggest one pressed up close, too close. He demanded we talk with him. He kept threatening and insisting, "You better *talk* with me!" But it was clear he had something other than just talking in mind. We had the feeling that he wanted our energy and vitality. Sounds strange, but he *was* strange – we felt like mice staring at the cat.

When we wouldn't oblige, he became red-faced, angry, and pouty.

"What's the matter," he snapped. "Why won't you *talk* to me? Am I offensive, or turning you off? Too threatening or what? I'm real disappointed you won't *talk* with me."

He said "talk" with a long drawl to make sure we got the double-entendre.

In fact I did talk to him, but he was insatiable and kept wanting more. He squatted down and tried to get us to look into his eyes face-to-face, a foot apart. He felt like an emotional whirlpool, a vacuum. There was no reasoning with him.

Fortunately, his friends were moved that we were monks and making a pilgrimage. They offered to lend a hand and carry our water jugs up the hill. But the big man sulked and stormed away.

"Goodbye," we said.

"Yeah, sure!" he yelled and gave a hostile glare.

There's just no way to please everybody. Even the Buddha couldn't make everybody happy.

We found long sticks to slip through the plastic handles of the water jugs – easier to carry up to four or six at a time that way. As we walked back to the campsite, I remembered the Master's words from our last visit,

"Try your best. No matter how people treat you, you should be good to them, even to the point of death."

In the Avatamsaka we read,

"If there is a living being who has a thought of hostility towards the Bodhisattva, the Bodhisattva views him with kind eyes as well. To the very end, he has not the slightest thought of hatred."

Avatamsaka Sutra
Ten Transferences Chapter

Heng Chau • April 15, 1978
Only the sound of changing tides

> The practices of the Tao consists in
>   subtracting day by day.
> Subtracting, and yet again subtracting.
>
> Lau Tzu

Subtraction. Outside, the road is more narrow, people fewer, towns smaller. There are less lights at night, more stillness during the day. Deer and squirrels outnumber diesel rigs; seagulls and hawks are louder than jets and police-sirens. No more rush hour roar twice daily, only the sound of the changing tides reach our ears.

Inside, the bowing and Sutra burn through our pretensions and masks. There are fewer places to hide and escape; more contentment with less "things." We feel like the click-clacking pebbles, ground and polished by the pounding surf; smaller and smaller, less edges, more solid. "Subtracting day by day." Softness overcomes hardness; weakness, the strong. Winter is taking itself away. It's spring and all things renew.

Layperson: "Well, the rainy season is over with at last. That's for sure."

Yesterday and today it rained non-stop. The winds were so strong they blew us off our feet. Nothing's for sure. The weather constantly speaks the Dharma of impermanence and non-reliance.

> "The Bodhisattva contemplates all conditioned Dharma
> as they really are. They are: impermanent, suffering, impure,
> and insecure; decaying, produced and destroyed in an instant.
> They don't come from the past or go toward the future, nor
> do they stay in the present."
>
> Avatamsaka Sutra
Ground of Emitting Light
Ten Grounds Chapter

Heng Sure • April 16, 1978
Will I be the Dharma-protector next time?

"Debts of kindness."

> Past deeds determine your present destiny.
> Present actions mold your next life.
>
> The Sutra of Cause and Effect

If I stopped to think about it, I'd wind up scratching my head all the same; instead I just use effort in cultivation, knowing some day, somehow, I will repay in full the over-flowing goodness that I've received.

This week I'm doing the finest bowing, meditating, and praying of my life. Why? Because Heng Chau traded me the Ch'an seat. It has two extra inches of head room; he gave me his *tai ji* shoes, he cooks every day, talks to the folks, drives and tunes the Plymouth. He solved my schedule snafu, pointing out the missing hour I'd overlooked, making space for extra Ch'an time.

Who wouldn't want to work hard to response to this kindness?

Will I be the Dharma-protector next time?

> All who cultivate with me assemble in one place;
> Together we will study,
> Our karmas of body, mouth, and mind the same,
> As we cultivate our practices and vows.
>
> Avatamsaka Sutra
Universal Worthy's Conduct and Vows
Chapter 40

Heng Chau • April 16, 1978
Down with some type of sickness

Overcome with some type of sickness. It came on suddenly and felt like a big one. I meditated for one hour and then took a nap. I dreamed of the Abbot and of making preparations for a long journey. We were delayed in leaving only because I figured the time wrong, not because we were actually late. We departed just when the Abbot calculated we would. A close disciple of the teacher's and an "old friend" type person pulled out a special pouch containing rare crystals. He gave me some as the Abbot watched. They tasted unusual.

When I awoke three hours later, I was better and felt rested, although weak. The illness had passed and I was able to continue making prostrations. I felt treated and cared for.

"Disciples of the Buddha, when the Bodhisattva, Mahasattva gives medicine, he uses his good roots and transfers in this way... He vows that all living beings become the Tathagata's herb (medicine) which can pluck out the poisonous arrows of all afflictions."

Avatamsaka Sutra
Ten Transferences Chapter

Heng Sure • April 17, 1978
Sugar acts on me like alcohol

"Excuses"

Made a vow to avoid sugar. Sugar acts on me like alcohol – gets me drunk, cheeks flush, spine slumps, concentration scatters. Just a little bit of sugar shows up immediately in bowing and meditation, and turns my thoughts upside-down. The vow helps, but holding it purely is as hard as reining in a galloping horse. I was a sweet tooth, and old habits have momentum.

Desire is the root of birth and death. The mind that desires sweets is the same mind that desires wealth, sex, fame, food, and sleep.

We received a bag of sweet fruit nectar. Knowing they contained sugar, corn sweetener, and glucose, I still made an excuse and swallowed a can of pear nectar, thinking,

"I don't want to make a fuss over this practice or be endlessly reading labels. If it comes to hassling tiny quantities of sugar, then I've lost concentration anyway. If the vow can keep me out of soda pop, pies and ice cream, cake, and candy, then it is a success. Fruit nectar isn't primarily a sugar-treat, so I'll drink it. The Middle Way. Amitabha."

This is my evil advisor inside acting as a defense attorney. I drank it and spent the afternoon in a dull haze, dizzy, repentant, and wishing I'd kept the vow. No more sugar! Living beings are stubborn, hard to transform. When the four elements scatter at death, will I remember this wasted afternoon and my broken promise?

Heng Chau • April 17, 1978
The Master was examining us

"I know that what I cultivate is like an illusion, like a shadow, like the moon in water, like an image in a mirror. They manifest and appear only through the union of causes and conditions. This is the way it is all the way up to and including the ultimate ground of the Tathagata."

Avatamsaka Sutra
Ten Transferences Chapter

We have two cooking pots – a 1 quart, and a 1½ quart aluminum pair that fit together. One cooks rice, the other vegetables. They were offered back at Gold Mountain before departing. Heng Sure and I were looking over the shiny new camp stove cooking set in the back of the Buddha hall. We were all excited about the idea of roughing it with mountain gear for a year or so. Pretty naive, but we didn't know what lay ahead – that we'd be living out of an old station wagon and bowing through the streets of L.A. for months.

The Master came down and asked about the details of the cooking set. "Oh? Hum. Uh huh," he said as we rapped on. I looked up and realized the Master was examining *us*, not the stove set. It was our attachments to dharmas and nice new things that was being checked out, not a couple of bright tin pots.

The pots are just dharma, tools we borrow temporarily. All dharmas are impermanent, even our Way-practices. There's not one thing that once obtained, can reveal your true nature. And so the highest state in cultivation is non-attachment. In the Avatamsaka it says,

> "A Bodhisattva's mind does not dote on the pleasures of the world, nor is it stained by attachment to what is practiced."

Dharmas are not fixed, nor can they be attached to. "The Dharma is in the human mind." It all depends on the person.

During a meditation session, a monk asked the Ch'an Master,

Monk: "There is a practice in Tibet or maybe China, where you get into a little box and there is no light, and no room to lie down. You can only sit up in lotus posture. There is only air in there. Some people go in for three years, some for their entire lives. What is the Master's view on this? Is this a good dharma?"

Master: "I've never done it. All Dharma doors have their good and bad points. It's not fixed. If people are good, then no matter what method they use, it is a good method. If the person is not good, then no matter what the method is, it is not a good one. The dharma is in the human mind. So it is said,

"When a proper person cultivates a deviant dharma, then that deviant dharma becomes proper. When a deviant person cultivates a proper dharma, then that dharma becomes deviant."

"Transformation by fire."

The Abbot told us,

"When you are working hard and the afflictions arise, you should be really patient and then suddenly it will transform, and then you have finished cooking that batch. The Sage does this (transforming) *all* of the time – the 'Dharma wheel always turns.'"

Cultivation is change. We change the bad to good, change ignorance into wisdom; affliction into Bodhi. The Chinese character for "change/transformation" is *hua* (化), and also means "to smelt." Cultivation produces a heat, an intense fire, like the ovens of a foundry. Just as the Phoenix consumes his own body at death and rises in youthful freshness from its own ashes, the cultivator puts himself through the fire of Dharma like gold smelted progressively more bright and pure.

> "Disciple of the Buddha, just as when a goldsmith well-skilled at smelting gold repeatedly puts it through the fire to make it progressively more bright and pure, subdued, compliant and accomplished, and capable of acting according to his intent, so too is the Bodhisattva also that way."
>
> Ten Grounds Chapter
> Avatamsaka Sutra

No fire, no transformation. There's an urge to cool off before the batch is baked. In the past I've opened the oven too soon and hot-tailed it to a cool Big Sur waterfall for instant relief. This is just impatience, not "waiting out the fire" as the ancients called it. Metal must be white-hot before shaping. Cultivation is the same. Besides, when I run half-baked to the waterfalls, that's when I meet the weirdos.

"Right," said the Abbot. "When you have false thoughts, troubles come."

The way to cool off is stillness, not movement. So Lao Tsu said,

> Movement overcomes cold
> But staying still overcomes heat.
> So he by his limpid calm,
> Puts right everything under heaven.

What is "limpid calm"? It's just not false thinking.

"Don't think."

I spent this A.M. bowing, trying to "figure things out." My mind took a stab at making sense of it all, attempting to fit everything under the sun into a tiny logical, black and white reality. Questions like, "Who am I?" "Where am I going to and where did I come from?" "What's the meaning of the universe, the purpose of life?" The result was a splitting headache. The subtle mysteries of this vast Dharma Realm simply cannot fit into my pea-sized discriminating mind.

While cooking lunch on the tailgate, I remembered a passage we read last evening from the Avatamsaka. I silently recited the lines and my headache went away. The solution: expand the measure of my mind to mesh with the Dharma Realm, not shrink the infinite magnitude of the universe to fit my small thoughts.

> "All worlds throughout the ten directions are just discriminations made by the thoughts of living beings. As for thought or non-thought, there is nothing which can be obtained. And in this way, he unties and penetrates all thought.
>
> Avatamsaka Sutra
> Ten Transferences Chapter

I felt the Sutra was saying, "Don't think! Use the mind that is nowhere attaching to figure things out. Use wisdom, not intellect."

Heng Chau • April 18, 1978
In any quantity, it is heavier than gravity

"Bowing Mirror."

The primary purpose of bowing is to get rid of arrogance. Arrogance is having a big view of self; seeing yourself as too important. I have not faced my own arrogance squarely, but today while bowing, it faced me and there was no way to shrug it off, no place to hide.

There's an invisible, but quite real experience when bowing, of standing in front of an all-seeing, all-knowing mirror. This bowing mirror reveals and reflects your every thought and deepest flaws. In it I saw how I have always seen myself as better than others. I felt old 'number one' was the foremost and had a monopoly on talent and blessings. My shoulders ached from lifting my head above the crowd and exalting myself over everyone else.

"Arrogance causes harm; Humility brings benefit."

Anger is the most harmful thing in the world. Where does anger come from? Pride; greed for "me." Bad temper flares up from seeing oneself as too significant, and it spreads like wildfire, until in uncontrolled rage, one does something stupid. Anger first afflicts the small world of one's own body and mind, but soon fills up the universe with foul energy and fumes of war and disasters. It all begins with a big view of self; in a word, arrogance.

As I faced the bowing mirror alone on the quiet highway, I saw my arrogance turn to anger. I bowed in shame to my teacher and Guan Yin Bodhisattva. They told me to bow to Heng Sure.

"Why Heng Sure!?" I asked. Because I'm a fresh novice and he is a Bhikshu, my senior. If it hadn't been for him, I would have never met with the chance to make a bowing pilgrimage for world peace. I owed him much. I should have bowed to him long ago. Here was a clear and near opportunity to show a change of heart, to drop some false pride and say, "I'm sorry for my ingratitude and lack of shame." So I bowed to him.

It took me a whole year to do this simple, honest act. Immediately, pounds of accumulated tension lifted off my shoulders. The self, in any quantity, is heavier than gravity. Bowing to my partner was bitter-sweet medicine. Right to the end my ego resisted, complained, and wriggled for an out. It felt so good and right. Humility feels soft and peaceful, and releases unexpected child-like energy.

> "He is reverent, respectful, and virtuous, as he cultivates the Dharma. He knows kindness, is easy to teach, and free of a bad temper. He forsakes arrogance and flattery, his heart is subdued and soft. And he progressively increases his vigor and diligence; his mind does not retreat."
>
> Avatamsaka Sutra
> Ten Grounds Chapter

* * *

"Hey my friend! My friend!" yells someone from a stopped car. It's Mike, the tow truck operator who pulled our car out of a ditch seven months ago back at Gaviota Pass. He ran a small gas station oceanside, and we became fast friends with few words. He liked the pilgrimage and felt he was making it too, in his heart, while he pumped gas and drove a tow truck. He got all cleaned up, combed and shaved one day, to come out and say goodbye and give us gas money. Now his truck was loaded down with all his belongings, including a rocking chair, balanced and roped on top.

"I quit my job. I'm headin' North for a new life." he said. "Gee, I'm really happy to see you," he twinkled, holding back some tears and grabbing my shoulders with both hands.

"You two really came far. Looks like it's been good for you; for all of us. I just had to stop – so good to see you."

Later he came back to offer some gas. "Good luck up north, Mike," I said.

"Oh, I'll see you again," he said with a knowing smile.

"I'll see you again, I know I will." He gave a big grin and a wave and drove off to a fresh beginning.

* * *

Rock slide comes crashing down. Luckily we decided to bow the other side of the road, away from the cliffs this afternoon, so we escape unharmed.

Bowed transference under two tall pine trees clinging to the side of the road. A gentle breeze, deep orange sun sinking into the sea, and light heart at day's end. Time passes swiftly when your life is full.

> "Bodhisattva's energy is strong. Their minds are pure, and they are always happy."
>
> Ten Transferences Chapter
> Avatamsaka Sutra

Heng Sure • April 19, 1978
The fantasy rolls right through

"Midnight Ch'an State."

> "The Bodhisattva in this way, understands and penetrates all states. He knows all dharmas are based on causes and conditions…
>
> Ten Transferences Chapter
> Avatamsaka Sutra

In the Plymouth on a roadside ledge above the sea, dead calm air, silent tides. Kerosene fumes from the lantern sting the eyes. Heng Chau can't find the spot, nods in lotus-posture sleep.

Rabbits in the bushes run from weasels; weasels hide from owls in the air. Passing headlights split the night, sear the brain. A tiny thought sets fire to the knees.

Hold the mind still, the fantasy rolls right through. Follow states, the play turns into pain.

"...He understands that all the mundane world is like a transformation."

Ten Transferences Chapter
Avatamsaka Sutra

Heng Chau • April 19, 1978
I don't have any plans, I wish I did

Notes on the bowing ascent of Mt. Sumeru.

"The skill of *patience*: use it 3 days and on the 4th, you can't bear it anymore. Your greed slips up, your hatred flows out, your ignorance takes over, you do upside-down things. Why do we do upside-down things? Because in the past, one thought of ignorance was done."

A young man in his early 20's from New York, stopped to watch the bowing and talk. He heard from the McCauley's in Cambria, about two monks making a pilgrimage. The McCauley's sent him on to us. Not sure why, but when we saw each other, it was as if a long-lost brother had returned. Pat was his name.

His home was a second-hand Chrysler Imperial, once the pride of Manhattan, now dented and faded and slowly touring the coast highway of California.

A road crew temporarily closed the road to clear a rockslide. Pat saw it as a chance to introduce himself without disturbing us. He was shy, honest, and wide open.

"I don't have any plans, I wish I did," said Pat softly and from his heart. We sat on the car bumper drinking tea from a thermos. A few more words passed back and forth, but the real exchange was shared wordlessly. There was just a quiet absorbing among three old friends whose paths had crossed many times without merging. Pat asked none of the usual question about the pilgrimage and our lives as monks. He seemed to know intuitively. He was content to share a few peaceful moments and watch the bowing.

"Maybe someday," he said, and bid us goodbye. Pat had a good heart and carried himself with kindness and a gentle dignity. It was a rare and genuine encounter that left us feeling softer and more humane.

Heng Sure • April 20, 1978
The real journey has now begun

> "In measureless Buddhalands in ten directions' worlds,
> going to them all, being born countless times. Never having
> a thought of fatigue, the Happy Ones walk this Path."
>
> Avatamsaka Sutra
> Ten practices Chapter

Send joy into air. Make others happy. How? Give. Cultivate the Way and plant pure causes. Give wealth, fearlessness and Dharma. Give pure deportment. Repent of past faults. Transfer good vibes to the Dharma Realm. Light up your heart to brighten the world.

"The Narrow road to the North."

While doing *tai ji quan* at sunset, I felt a door close behind us; a sensation like a curtain ringing down on the trip completed so far. The months of bowing to this very moment, were all preparation, now past history.

Heard a voice say, "You *made* it brothers. You're here. Don't worry about anything behind or ahead of you. Just do your work. The real journey has now begun."

Had a déjà vu a year ago. I envisioned this space, recognized it as a turning point. Saw it clearly before I knew it existed. Three steps, one bow, up the narrow road to the North.

Heng Chau • April 20, 1978
Jane's purifying center

The mystery person who left us fresh oranges wrapped in a silk scarf, stopped to introduce herself. Occasionally we'd catch sight of an old red VW pulling away from our parked car at the end of the day, only to find a bag of fresh food sitting on the fender. Same person. Her name is Jane. Today she offered fresh oranges and long stems of dried yerba buena, an excellent tea native to these coast hills.

Jane has turned her house into a "purifying center," for the local residents. Together they study yoga, *tai ji*, meditation, vegetarian eating, natural health, and things to make them better people. Jane was full of giving energy, and had a straight-forward, clean air about her.

"I'd like to invite you to visit our purifying center, but only if it fits in with your practice," she said.

"I want you to know what you're doing is turning a lot of people on to themselves – to looking at where they are at and cleaning up their lives."

Jane asked nothing of us. Her support was natural and effortless. Usually she simply left an offering and disappeared. She honored our practice of silence.

"I used to not talk for one day a week. It really turned me into how much I 'go out' to people – that is, seeking and leaning on others," she said. Jane has studied Buddhism from books and knew that the direction her quest for purity ultimately must lead is a pure mind. One of the four virtues of nirvana is purity, (purity, true self, permanence, and bliss). Shakyamuni Buddha was the first "purifying center." He turned his body and mind into a place of the Way (Bodhi-manda), and cultivated morality, concentration, and wisdom until he,

"Merged with empty space in substance and nature, and was cleansed of even the finest dust."

Avatamsaka Sutra

He took everything that was impure and made it pure without remainder. All karmic obstacles, ignorance, and afflictions like fine specks of dust, were swept away.

We wished Jane good luck with her center. She understood our vow not to make visits. As she walked to her car she said,

"The reason your pilgrimage is having such an influence is because you are actually going out and doing it. And 'doing it' is everything."

* * *

We decide to avoid cliff-side bowing completely. Rock slides are frequent and leave no time to scramble for safety, especially if you're down in a bow.

Seals and whales and false thoughts too many to count. Meeting genuine and unaffected people like Pat and Jane inspires me to clean my act and purify my own center. Bowing is an unsurpassed act of cleansing and returning to purity. How lucky we are for such a chance to bow all day!

> "The Bodhisattva, Mahasattva, takes his good roots that arise from repenting and clearing out all heavy karmic obstacles; his good roots that result from bowing respect to all Buddhas of the past, present, and future... and all good roots such as these that produce happiness, and he transfers them to adorn all Buddhalands."
>
> Avatamsaka Sutra
> Ten Transferences Chapter

* * *

Bowing outside, close to nature, constantly teaches us that the wonderful is found in the close at hand; that the beautiful arises from the ordinary. The magical and profound are uncovered in the simple things done sincerely, with absorption and to the ultimate.

Cultivation is an exercise in subtraction. The enlightened nature is already ours, only we don't know. Our Buddha-wisdom is covered over and obscured by too much – too much greed, too much anger, too much delusion. One doesn't acquire Bodhi or add to his wisdom-nature like a bank account. Instead, cultivators subtract, and again subtract, until all marks of self are swept away. So it's said,

> Learning consists in
>   adding to one's stock day by day.
> Cultivating the Way consists in
>   subtracting day by day.
>
> Lao Tzu

Out here on the highway, inching our way through wilderness mountains, the wealth and glow of the world seems so flavorless and empty. Before our eyes they are eaten by the earth and stolen from us by time. What greater wealth could there be than a pure, unobstructed mind; what greater contribution to mankind than a heart cleansed of all greedy selfishness!?

> Stopping the mind, ending thoughts,
>   is true riches and honor.
> Completely ending selfish greed
>   is the true field of blessings.
>
> Master Hua

Heng Sure • April 21, 1978
Like drops of water in a boundless sea

Contemplation:

Seventy years in a frail body. Two hundred years on the American continent. Five thousand years on the planet Earth. Two billion years in the Milky Way galaxy. And the Avatamsaka Sutra describes galaxies like this one as many as tiny particles of dust, all of which can fit within a single hair pore of the Buddha's body. That's old and that's big! We people just visit on this globe in space; we are no more important to the big picture than drops of water in a boundless sea. How foolish to allow our minds to get afflicted, to dwell in greedy thoughts, angry thoughts, or to hurt other beings.

The Avatamsaka exists throughout beginningless time to guide us out of the darkness into the infinite wonder of the Dharma Realm. A single thought of the purified mind contains it all!

> "...Because the Thus Come One's ability within a single hairpore to universally manifest all the worlds of the ten directions going through the kalpas of formation, dwelling, and disintegration is inconceivable."
>
> Entering the Dharma Realm
> Avatamsaka Sutra

Heng Chau • April 21, 1978
Knowing so little, it's already destroying itself

"Bowing Reflection."

Last month, sitting at the foot of the Master at Gold Wheel in L.A., we heard,

"All the troubles in the world are caused by a view of a self. The ego is as big as Mt. Sumeru, and breaking through it is as hard as breaking through Mt. Sumeru. With a mark of a self comes a view of a self. This leads to attachment to ego and then attachment to dharmas, and then you turn your back on the Bodhi-nature."

We all have the enlightened nature and put the same covering over it: the view of a self, a "me and mine." Our faults and fears, longings and attachments, are not different in kind, only in degree. Who doesn't fear being alone and dying? The fear of death is as strong as the will to live. The tiniest bugs we see as we bow, have a natural preference for life and resist dying. A mosquito will fly away as soon as you move, because it is afraid that you will kill it.

Fear, like all troubles in the world, is caused by a view of self. We do not understand who we truly are, where we come from or go to. We dread falling into emptiness, and desperately try to cling to existence. Neither brings peace of mind or deliverance.

Ignorance is not bliss, it is the root of birth and death. From dark ignorance, desire is created – desire grasping at a self, grasping for others, grasping at dharma – and there "you turn your back on the Bodhi nature," and enter a tangled net of sticky karma. Wisdom is our first business as people. If there is a purpose to life, it is to turn around and reunite with the enlightened nature.

A passing motorist stops his car, rolls down the window, and says, "Thanks pal. Your praying and living out here on the open reminded me that I got side-tracked and lost touch with the important things of life."

* * *

"Knowing without knowing."

Last night we read from the Avatamsaka,

> "Although he completely sees all dharma, yet there is nothing which is seen; everywhere he knows everything, yet there is nothing which is known."

The Bodhisattva sees things (dharmas) differently than common people. We people take dharma as real and obtainable. We believe in them. The enlightened being does not attach to dharmas. He sees everything as temporary and illusory; a fleeting mirage of causes and conditions. Although he can deeply enter and understand all dharmas, still he does not possess them, because they are all unobtainable.

Today, Phuong Kuo Wu drove out to offer lunch. Mr. Koo, an older man from Taiwan, accompanied her. Raised in a Buddhist family and culture, yet educated in Western schools, Mr. Koo had many doubts and questions about the ability of scientists and intellectuals to solve the world's problem or to understand the mysteries of life.

"I had a very erudite teacher in Asia, but somehow Buddhism is more than erudition. It goes past words and ideas to *real* wisdom. This can only be experienced directly, it can't be known just from intelligence," said Mr Koo. We all sat together on mats under a small grove of trees off the road. Mr. Koo continued,

"The Dharma is unique in this way. It is the direct experience of life's truths – the deep, eternal truths," he said.

He was happy and surprised to find so many young, educated Westerners turning to Buddhism, both as a way of life and as a more sophisticated and sensitive view of the universe. Science threatens to destroy the world.

"Quite frankly, the problem with the world today is that too many of us only believe in science. We are over-intellectualized. There is no faith or wonder for the kind of things the Dharma is involved with. Science knows only a little and already it's destroying itself."

The Great Master, the Sixth Patriarch, Hui Neng, was illiterate. His wisdom and profound understanding continue to inspire and enlighten people centuries after his death, and yet he couldn't read a single character. Once when traveling through a village in China. A Bhikshuni (Buddhist nun) asked the Master to explain a passage from the Mahaparinirvana Sutra, which she recited constantly. She held out the scroll and asked,

"What is this character?"

"Do you mean you can't read it?" he asked.

"No, I can't." she said.

"Well, I can't either!" said the Master.

"If you can't even read it, how can you know what it means?" she asked.

"The Buddha's heart, the mind Dharma, the wonderful principle of Sudden Enlightenment, has nothing to do with words. Instead, it points directly to the mind so that we can see our own nature and become Buddhas. Since the subtle meaning of all Buddhas is not based on language, it doesn't matter whether or not you can read," answered the Master.

This is the seeing without anything seen; the knowing without knowing. Heng Sure and I feel we are too smart, "over intellectualized" as Mr. Koo put it. Before cultivating the Way, without knowing, we thought we knew; without seeing, we thought we saw. Cultivation is like learning all over again from the bottom up. All this time we had been looking at things upside-down. We were rich with words but poor in wisdom. Tonight we read in the Sutra,

> All dharmas are apart from words and language,
> Their nature is empty, still, extinct, and unproduced.
> Because he wants to thoroughly and clearly
> understand this true meaning,
> The Bodhisattva first brings forth his resolve.

Ten Dwellings Chapter
Avatamsaka Sutra

Special time. The Avatamsaka really came alive for us tonight. The color, sound, and mood all felt like returning home after a long journey. We read and read into the night, translating and listening, getting all excited as it connected and brought together months of hard work.

The more we bow and meditate, the deeper and richer grows our understanding and appreciation of the Avatamsaka. I had no idea what a rare treasure was stored in this old station wagon. In the beginning, it was just another text of foreign characters to me. But now, the familiar seems foreign and what was foreign is like our homeland from the beginningless past. Who can doubt that the Dharma's coming to the West is the highest of gifts and the dream-come-true of our collective soul?! Gradually, the Sutra and the mind become one, not two. Originally, it must have been so.

It is like a sunrise glorious in the sky,
Dimming multitudes of luminaries' splendor;
Like Sumeru which spreads across the seas,
Lowering retinues of peaks' high altitudes.

Avatamsaka Preface

Heng Sure • April 22, 1978
When proper mindfulness is complete

"Mindfulness: Survival Tool"

Natives of the Great Barrier Reef, have a saying.

"When diving, be careful of the creatures and the coral. If it doesn't bite you, watch out, because it is about to sting you!"

We have learned to cultivate this way as well. Nature is harsh in Big Sur. Each step off the pavement into the underbrush requires constant, vigorous, mindfulness. Big Sur is an excellent Way-place for training and disciplining body and mind. It's said,

> "Cultivate in your mind as if walking on the edge of a deep abyss. In thought after thought, be as if fighting for your life; as if walking on thin ice. Then you can have success."

Ven. Master Hua

If the poison oak doesn't snag your precept sash, the wind blows it into the barbed wire. Concentrating on avoiding the half-inch long fire-ants, you may step on a sunbathing rattlesnake. Being mindful of deportment, Vinaya verses, and correct conduct for Bhikshu as you seek to relieve nature on the six-inch ledge of an abrupt 200 foot drop-off, takes the skill of a gymnast and the nerves of a tight-rope walker. Returning to the highway, shoes full of stinging nettles, there's not time to admire the poppies and lupine, Indian paintbrush or sea daisies. Whizzing motor-homes often cover the road shoulder as they slide through the curves. Discipline yourself.

When proper mindfulness is complete, the experience of harmony with nature is quiet, peaceful, and fine. It takes energy and full attention to do it all right, in the smallest detail, even for a moment. We wonder at the skill and strength of cultivators who never lose mindfulness in any situation, even at death when the four elements scatter.

Heng Chau • April 22, 1978
I refused to look at her again

"Like the Master Painter"

Last week on a hot day, outside and inside I lost patience and climbed back to bathe in some deep, cool, crystal pools at the foot of a small waterfall. It was delightful – too delightful. The night in a dream, I encountered a demonic obstacle in the form of a beautiful, spell-binding woman. I woke up drained of energy and scattered.

Today when I should have been bowing, I stopped to write a verse of praise for the Master's birthday. It was false thinking. Why? My motive was to flatter my teacher in hope of receiving praise and recognition, to win his approval. Thoughts like these are "off the mark" and drift wide and far from proper mindfulness. As I sat absorbed in verse writing, a car pulled over.

"Howdy brother. What's happening? This is Patti, and my name's Lou," said a tall wild-eyed looking man. He reached out his hand and said,

"Do I shake, or what's appropriate with a monk?"

"It's not fixed. Whatever feels right to you." I answered somewhat uncertain.

"Well then shake!" he said, thrusting out his hand after wiping over and back a couple times on his pants. "I'm Christian, so I guess I'll say, 'God bless.'"

There was a woman with him, but I didn't look at her as she was silent and stood to the side. Lou said he wanted to make an offering and went back to the car. The woman then moved closer and stood in front of me. I looked at her face and immediately felt my belly jump. She was the same beautiful demon woman that ensnared me in my dream the night of the waterfall bath last week. A mischievous smile came to her face when she knew I had made the connection and recognized her. I think I broke out in a sweat, and turned white on the spot.

Fortunately, Lou came striding back with a large rock in his hand,

"It's jade. Best piece I got. It's the biggest I found. Sorry it ain't much. You can rub it up and polish it, maybe carve it," he said as he rubbed it on his noise and then his jeans to make it shine. Patti kept trying to catch my eyes. But I refused to look at her again.

"It's worth maybe ten dollars if you polish it up good," declared Lou, holding the jade up to the sunlight and then handing it to me.

"Well, good luck brother, take care," said Lou shaking hands goodbye.

How could a demonic temptress experienced in a dream, suddenly manifest in front of me a week later as we bowed on the highway? In the Avatamsaka it says,

> Just as the master painter
> Cannot know his own mind,
> Still his paintings come from the mind.
> The nature of all dharmas is like this.

This encounter with Patti was a dharma, a "painting" produced from my own mind. And yet, just as the painter does not know how his paintings come from his mind, in the same way, I couldn't know how my mind painted Patti. And yet, karma is not off by hair. The fruits of retribution come from the karma one creates. The three karmas of body, mouth, and thoughts can conjure up some incredible things, and what began only as a thought in one's mind, can suddenly materialize before one's eyes as if pulled out of thin air.

Again, it's like a crafty wizard
Who stands there at the cross-roads
Conjuring up a bunch of forms and shapes.
The nature of karma is the same.

Avatamsaka Sutra
Chapter 10

Later we asked the Master about demons and how to deal with them.

"Demonic states come from a particle of desire or attachment in your mind, which unites with external conditions and manifests as a demon. The poison within unites with the poison without," he answered.

"How should we respond then when we meet up with demonic obstacles?" we asked.

"Don't move. Don't move your mind. Overcome all demons with the gung fu of patience. When karmic obstacles or demons arise, if you recognize them for what they really are, then you can ignore them. Act as if they don't exist," responded the Master.

"Is there a special method to subdue them?" we asked.

"The only defense against demons is kindness and compassion. Don't fight with them. Save them and take them across," replied the Master.

"Some demonic obstacles are really fierce," I said.

"Selfishness brings demons. If you have no desire and don't seek, then you won't be afflicted. You will be able to turn all demons," answered the Master.

A particle of desire or attachment is like a seed in the mind – sooner or later it sprouts trouble. Whether in a dream or for "real," the mind itself doesn't distinguish. The mind is neither inside nor outside. It is measureless and constantly non-dwelling; without boundaries, without time, without a place.

The mind is constantly not-dwelling.
Measureless, it is and hard to think of.
It reveals and manifest all forms
Each of which does not know the other.

Avatamsaka Sutra
Chapter 20

Heng Sure • April 23, 1978
You get splashed and the water still escapes

"One must reveal his faults, not cover up blemishes and errors. Harmful poisons and noxious weeds must be quickly gotten rid of. Expose their roots so that they can wither and dry up. When the wellspring is dry, the flow ceases."

Avatamsaka Prologue

Trying to force an end to bad habits or to conceal them is like holding your thumb over a fast-running hose: you get splashed and the water still escapes. To take charge and change the situation, shut off the water at the source. Don't dwell on the symptoms of the habit, correct the fault at its source: the false-mind of deviant views. Go for the sunlight, every day renew, repent of old mistakes. Vigorously, patiently, make room for sturdy sprouts of proper views. The Avatamsaka has a Dharma-method to counteract every affliction the mind can produce. The secret to genuine change is to cultivate according to the Dharma. Pick a method and apply the medicine to the sore spot in your thoughts. Enter

...the samadhi of the Buddha's sun appearing
in every thought.

Entering the Dharma Realm
Avatamsaka Sutra

Heng Chau • April 23, 1978
Caution – Frequent Rock slides

"Mind Slides"

After three hours of steady bowing, mindfulness wanders and the mind starts playing tricks. It wriggles and squirms, longing for the familiar and hankering after the "self and what belong to self." Like:

– Sneaking into church late to catch the last ten minutes of Sunday Mass, then rejoining my family after, outside, making it look like I was there for the entire service. Instead, I was out climbing apple trees and adventuring the alleys.

– Reading Emerson's *Essays* hidden behind the cover of "My Daily Missal" during church service and the sermon.

– Singing hymns with my mother like two drunken sailors, too small to see over the church pew.

– Father and son breakfast in the basement of St. Joe's Parochial School. Donuts, stiff suits and tie, while the professional football player talks for the Knights of Columbus.

– Small town Midwest school Christmas party at the Elks Club. Hundreds of kids singing carols at the top of their lungs until Santa Claus comes rushing in. Near pandemonium.

– Pictures of my father and uncles who wore long dresses and shoulder-length, curly hair until puberty, when they got a pair of knickers and their first hair cut. Turn of the century, Dutch-Irish. Clear rite of passage from boy to man.

– A memory of living in a palace. Spacious long rooms and corridors. Feeling of having everything, but empty and restless at heart. Wealthy with material things, but lost and looking for something true.

All these memories flashed through my mind as I stood up from a bow. A mind slide. The sign on the shoulder says, "Caution –

Frequent Rock slides." As swift and unexpectedly as a section of mountain can break loose and come tumbling down, so can the mind slide, and scatter. The road sign alerts travelers to the dangers on the road. The Avatamsaka alerts cultivators to the dangers in the mind.

> "In worlds of the ten directions he doesn't produce thoughts of grasping after and seeking the self and what belongs to self. Regarding all worlds, he does not discriminate. He does not attach to any state."
>
> Ten Transferences Chapter
> Avatamsaka Sutra

* * *

State: Every second is raw pressure, simultaneous ice and fire, joy and suffering. Cultivation is the most difficult and most wonderful thing I've ever done. "The Buddha Way is unsurpassed; I vow to attain it."

* * *

"That *tai ji* or yoga?" hollers a little man with a white beard, from his bicycle at 6 a.m.

"It's bowing."

"Yeah, I know," he says as he pulls over to talk. His name is Paul Bore, the State of California's resident highway engineer for Coast Route 1 for over fifteen years.

"I can't sit, it seems. Riding my bicycle in the early morning is my meditation. My wife is really into sitting, she jogs and exercises, and then sits in meditation. I built her a platform outside. It's great! Then she goes to work. She's a nurse," says Mr. Bore.

"We've been to Nepal, and thinking of going back. My wife wants to spend a few months in a monastery. I retire soon and I'm looking for some place to do humanitarian work that's what I like doing best."

"The Bodhisattva wants to give every peace and happiness to living beings. He wants to be a great giving host for them... He is universally mindful of living beings and constantly looks after and protects them."

Ten Transferences Chapter
Avatamsaka Sutra

We talked about the City of Ten Thousand Buddhas, Dharma Realm University, the City's hospital, schools, and monastery/convent set-up. Paul was drawn to the Bodhisattva ideal of benefiting yourself by benefiting others, and enlightening yourself by enlightening others.

"I've got a lot of skills but building road is what I do best," he said. "We've been watching you and are really interested in what you're doing. Our son lives on the land near your Way-place. It was snowing up there last week. The whole ground was covered in white, really beautiful.

As Paul peddled away on his 10-speed, I couldn't help thinking of the passage from the Sutra of Cause and Effect, which says the reward from having helped construct bridges and roads is the enjoyment of all kinds of transportation facilities that keep one from getting foot-weary.

I thought of the older man from Taiwan who told us sadly, "This is the age of science. No one believes in anything anymore." But here is Paul Bore, an engineer trained in the scientific tradition, who says, "Humanitarian work is what I like doing best." He builds roads and bridges, his wife's a nurse, and they both study Buddhism.

Actually, science is included *within* Buddhism. Science is a branch of Buddhism. For example, the Avatamsaka Sutra is a highly sophisticated and advanced treatise in physics. It contains a thorough description of the molecular arrangements and sub-atomic "fields" of the universe. As a professor of Mechanical Engineering put it,

"When I say Buddhism is science and science is just Buddhism, I enlarge both domains. Buddhism is the study of the truth of the mind – if expanded, it also covers the study of the mind as well. Science is the study of the truth of material bodies – if enlarged, its scope includes the study of the mind as well."

Professor Yu Kuo K'ung
University of Alabama

The age of science is new and relatively shortlived. Its survival is doubtful. Each day it speeds faster and faster to its own end. Without morality and virtue, nothing survives. Science knows how to create power, but not how to control it – witness the atom bomb. Recently, scientists are on the frontier of discoveries that prove and corroborate what enlightened teachers have known intuitively since time immemorial: that all is one, and that everything is made from the mind alone. These modern breakthroughs are not really new at all. As Plato said, "All learning is simply remembering."

Heng Sure • April 24, 1978
Good roots deepen

Change takes place the way nature grows trees. With each day of cultivation, good roots deepen. Branches broaden, foliage, fruit, and flowers mature in time. Before you know it, a strong tree stands tall, where once there were only twisted branches and gnarled stumps.

We are learning not to dwell on bad habits.

> When the mind is forgotten, offenses are no more.
> This is true repentance and reform.

Instead, concentrate on planting good causes and transferring the merit to all beings. Then naturally, effortlessly, diseased habits wither and give way to a forest of merit and virtue.

Heng Chau • April 24, 1978
Be a good father; and don't get angry

A man named Scott, stopped with his young son. He was distraught, almost crazy. They had camped out together overnight in the mountains and Scott took some psychedelics. He was still "tripping." He was desperate for someone to talk to and although I don't talk, except to briefly explain the pilgrimage, he was so confused and in pain, I couldn't refuse. He related family problems, how his eyes was going blind, that he didn't want his children. I told him about the five precepts and that present problems come from past offenses. "Go towards the good," I said.

"What's good? In this world, what does 'good' mean?" he asked cynically.

"Be a good father. Be patient and don't get angry. Look for the good qualities in your wife and children. Don't take drugs. Find your natural mind." I said.

* * *

Joe Marshall, the Cambria High School principal, stopped to make an offering and to wish us good luck.

"I've been following your progress. It's really impressive – especially your practice of silence. It's for peace, isn't it? That's wonderful." he said

"Is he (Heng Sure), listening to us now?" he asked, wondering if the vow of silence included not "talking" with one's ears as well.

"No, not if he's doing his job." I said.

The vow of silence is to stop talking inside with false thoughts and to be unmoved by what one hears outside, be it slander or praise. In this way, one dwells in proper concentration and can quickly progress.

"Disciples of the Buddha, what is the Bodhisattva's Dwelling in proper thought? The Bodhisattva hears ten kinds of dharmas and his mind in concentration does not move... He hears praise or slander for the Bodhisattva Dharma practices, and his mind does not move from concentration on the Buddhadharma."

Ten Dwellings Chapter
Avatamsaka Sutra

* * *

Dreams:

#1 All the waters in the world are watched over by water spirits. All the creatures who make the rivers, lakes, ponds and seas their home are protected by these spirits. If we harm and kill the living beings of the waters, the spirits get upset and angry, and floods, droughts, storms, and other disasters follow. We have to be kind to all that lives. Disasters and calamities are not accidents of nature, they are the retribution of killing and acts of destruction.

#2 I'm walking along a lake or stream. Not actively fishing, but still, holding a fishing pole with the line and lure in the water as I stroll. I caught a fish and immediately fell and spun back to lay-life and got entangled in a sticky net of emotional ties and relationships.

The next morning while bowing, a strange man stopped and asked,

"Do you eat meat?"

"No."

"How about fish?"

"No"

"No fishing even?" he exclaimed.

"No fishing." I affirmed.

"Wow! Not even a little fishing, huh?"

The Sutras say that people who hunt and fish will, in the future, undergo the retribution of insanity. "Whatever you do will come back to you," states the principle of cause and effect. People who hurt animals with a rope and net, for example, in the future will face death by hanging. In the Avatamsaka it says that the offence of taking life can cause one to be reborn in the hells as an animal or hungry ghost, and,

> "If born as a human, one undergoes two kinds of retribution: the first, is a short life, the second is much illness."
>
> Ten Grounds Chapter
> Avatamsaka Sutra

We can call it "sport and game," a "little fishing" and other euphemisms, but in the realm of cause and effect, it's all called "killing." And the retribution follows one impartially and inescapably. "This life the fisherman, next life the fish," as an old monk put it.

I've done my share of fishing. In America, fishing is a family affair, almost a religion in some places. Certainly it's as normal as summer barbecue and as patriotic as the 4th of July. And yet, as a child, when you put that worm, wriggling and writhing for its life, on a hook, inside something tilts and rings a warning bell. When you hook your first fish and pull it from the water, flapping wildly and struggling to hold on to its life, something makes you a little ashamed and sorry. Then when the hook is ripped out, half the poor fish's guts come out with it. Still alive, its gills open and close in shock. You have to hide your feelings and pretend you don't care. Otherwise, you might be called a "baby" or a "chicken" or a "sissy," who "can't take it." If fish could scream and cry, certainly few people could stand to listen while they caught their limit. I know people who become unwavering vegetarians after one visit to a slaughter-yard or meat-packing plant. They say you never get the cries out of you ears, or the smell of terror out of your nose.

When I came across these passages in the Sutra, I knew then that those feelings of pity and revulsion I smothered and tried to deny were reminding me of the truth I already knew: that fishing was killing, that killing was wrong, and that someday I'd have to pay for this offense. The Dharma is like that – it puts us back in touch with our own inherent wisdom and the truths we rush by and tune out as we "grow up."

* * *

Scott, the young father who stopped yesterday, confused and "bad tripping" on drugs, returned today much mellowed and brighter.

"I had a really good night last night because I was thinking about what we talked about. Could you tell me those five precepts again?" he asked.

"No killing, no stealing, no sexual misconduct, no false speech, and no drugs or intoxicants," I said

"Yeah. That's them. They sound so right and solid." he said.

Yesterday, Scott was full of high praise for drugs and felt they helped him get through life. He couldn't see how all his problems began when he started using drugs in Colorado. He got busted and his wife was arrested; friends were implicated, and there was revenge and much bad karma. Soon after, his home life deteriorated and difficulties arose with his children. Yesterday, high on acid, he thought he was "clear and okay," but now he knew that he was actually full of anger, speeding and disoriented. He was calling his parents "mass murderers," because his father was a career military officer, and saying he didn't know his son and wanted to get rid of him, as the little boy stood there nervously listening to every word.

Today he felt shame and remorse for his past life-style. He made an offering and asked where he could learn more about the precepts and rules for living a good life.

"If one can always hold the precepts, cultivate and study them, then one can perfect and accomplish merit and virtue. Precepts can open up the foundation for Bodhi."

Worthy Leader Chapter
Avatamsaka Sutra

* * *

Fritz, the fireman engineer from San Luis Obispo, stopped at lunch with two hinges for the tailgate of the Plymouth. The right hinge snapped months ago, and we had been using a branch stick to hold it up.

"These hinges are a rare find," said Fritz. "I've been looking for months. Your car is almost an antique, but I was finally able to find them in a salvage yard in Paso Robles."

Fritz told us about the Kern River where he grew up. "That river took many lives. It's steep, deep, and tricky. Big granite boulders get caught in whirlpools and grind holes into the river bed and rock slabs. The holes they make are like a funnel – big at the top; tight and small at the bottom. People, without thinking to check it out, go swimming or boating and get trapped in them and drown."

"All living beings get swallowed up by the waves of the great violent rivers. They enter into the flow of desire, the flow of existence, the flow of ignorance, and the flow of views. They revolve in the whirlpool of birth and death. They float and spin on the river of love. They rush over its rapids without stopping to think what they are doing and how it awakens desire, anger, and harm. And they follow along without forsaking it."

Ten Grounds Chapter
Avatamsaka Sutra

"An ancient author said, 'The earth is made to eat the flesh of men.'" I said.

"Yeah!" said Fritz. "It eats them and spits them out again; spits them out and then eats them again. That's our lot. Nobody ever got out."

"The Buddha got out."

The three of us huddled together in the Plymouth out of the rain. We do the closing meal chant and finish the dregs of green tea from a thermos. Fritz is quiet for a minute, then asks,

"Did the Buddha get out in body or spirit, or both?"

"The real body. It's called the Dharma Body." I answered.

"You mean like your *big* body, right?" says Fritz.

"Right. Your flesh body of skin and bones is like your camper truck – you stay in it for awhile, but it is not you. The Dharma body is your original Buddhanature."

"Hmm. How do you hook-up with it?" ask Fritz.

"Cultivating the Way." I said. "That's what we are doing; just beginning to look into it. It's said the Buddha cultivated until he reached the state where he 'united with empty space in substance and nature.'"

"Wow!" exclaims Fritz.

The rain stopped. Fritz fitted the new tailgate hinge and listened in while Heng Sure and I reviewed one of the Abbot's lectures from L.A. last month on recognizing one's own faults and "doing your own laundry."

* * *

We bowed into the hamlet of Gorda – a gas station, restaurant, grocery store, a few pick-up trucks, and quiet dogs. Rain and winds continue to pound in from the sea. Claire, who owns it all, came out to welcome us to "Sorta Gorda."

"We've been anticipating your arrival for some time." she said, cheerfully. The local people offered water, supplies, and camp spots for the night.

Heng Sure • April 25, 1978
With empty hands, we face King Yama

> Fish jump in the water,
> People mill around the marketplace.
> Not knowing to do good deeds,
> Willingly they create offenses.

We each arrive in the world with a certain amount of time and energy. What will we do with our karmas of body, mouth, and mind in this life? Will we cultivate merit, establish virtue, amass blessings, open wisdom? Will we create offenses, exhaust blessings, plant the seeds of the evil destinies, lose this human body?

Most of us plug into a job, tie ourselves to a mate, work like horses and cows for our children. We all seek power; some people run countries, some run motorcycles; men run the world, women run the men.

> Gold and silver piled high like mountain,
> Yet when you close your eyes, all is gone.
> With empty hands, going to see King Yama,
> With a remorseful heart, your tears begin to fall.

Attached to views of body and life, we each grab for security amid the five desires: wealth, sex, fame, food, and sleep. Yet none of these comforts survive the grave, and "with empty hands, we face King Yama," lord of the underworld. Only karma and true merit and virtue go with us at death.

When we leave this world for rebirth in another, the power of Universal Worthy's Practices and Vows will not fail us like family, friends, and possessions. If a person receives and maintains these "Kings of Vows," with a heart of profound faith, then at the moment of death, a way will appear through the darkness, to Amita Buddha's Pure Land.

"Further, when a person is on the verge of death, at the last instant of life, when all the organs scatter and he departs from his relatives; when all power and status is gone and nothing survives; when his prime ministers, great officials, inner courts and outer cities, elephants, horses, cars, and treasuries of jewels can no longer accompany him, only these kings of vows stay with him. At all times they guide him forward, and in a single split-second, he is reborn in the Land of Ultimate Bliss."

Avatamsaka Sutra
Universal Worthy's Conduct and Vows
Chapter 40

Heng Chau • April 25, 1978
You wouldn't win any beauty contest

"It is because everyone under Heaven recognizes beauty as beauty, that the idea of ugliness exists."

Lao Tzu

Roadside exchange with a man after lunch:

"What do you eat?"

"Well, today we had rice and nuts, a few vegetables, and fruit."

"You don't eat meat. Do you get enough protein that way?"

"We really don't pay attention to it. We eat what is offered. We are healthy, so whatever we need we must be getting," I said.

"Yes," he said. "You look very healthy – you wouldn't win any beauty contest, but you look healthy."

"That's great. We wouldn't want to win a beauty contest. That's how all the trouble starts."

"Ain't it the truth," he laughed, "ain't it the truth."

"Disciples of the Buddha, all living beings are equally made up of the four elements. There is no self and nothing that belongs to the self. So what is it that feels suffering and feels happiness? What is it that looks upright and pretty or ugly and crippled? ...Thus in the Dharma Realm, there is nothing beautiful and nothing evil."

Avatamsaka Sutra
Bodhisattvas Ask for Clarification Chapter

* * *

The Big Sur rains and winds pound on and on; like my mind, difficult to subdue. First it's sweating hot, then bone-chilling cold. The body is hard to tame, impossible to please. Demons, baddies, and weirdos, poison plants and rock slides teach and keep us in line. Like my mouth, the road is the source of dangers and disasters.

Patience is trying, impatience is deadly. Transforming selfish greed, anger, and stupidity, breaking through the ego, is easier said than done. Cultivation isn't easy.

"Did you think it was going to be easy?" asks a voice inside. "It's not easy to be a Bodhisattva."

"Then what *is* easy?"

"It is easy to be ghost, or to go to the hells, or to become an animal. A Bodhisattva must be able to do what others cannot do. Whatever it is mankind considers difficult, a Bodhisattva should proceed to do with ease. If you don't dare to do what is hard, you are not a Bodhisattva. Go forth with vigor, because that's what it's all about. There is no other esoteric or wonderful secret. If you can do the things other people cannot do, you are a Bodhisattva."

Tripitaka Master Hua
The Ten Dharma Realms

As if to point the way when we feel that we can't go on, the Avatamsaka tonight read,

> "Nothing can cause his mind to move or retreat. Nor does he have even a single thought of attachment. Why? Because he attaches to nothing and relies on nothing. He benefits himself by benefiting others. He is pure and fulfilled."

Ten Practices Chapter
Avatamsaka Sutra

Heng Sure • April 26, 1978
Special, above the crowd, uncommon

> The straight mind is the Way-place;
> The ordinary mind is the Way.

Spring rains washed this stretch of highway into the sea. We bow over heaps of black earth and bulldozer ruts. We bow through clouds of dust, spun by passing cars. The highway flagmen shake their heads and grin to see our slow pace everyday, crawling like snails over boulders, conduits, gravel, and dirt.

Being so close to the earth changes one's view of self, naturally, it seems. I have always valued the unique, the outstanding. In the past I enjoyed feeling myself special, above the crowd, uncommon. I recognize this deviant, arrogant view held me apart from the sense of peace and belonging I sought. Whereas, Great Compassion flows forth from identity with all beings.

> Truly recognize your own faults,
> Don't discuss the faults of others.
> Other's faults are just my own,
> Being of the same substance with everyone
> Is called Great Compassion.

Heng Chau • April 26, 1978
Demons are your good advisors

Any attachment, whether big or small, results in loss and suffering. Why? Because there is nothing to attach to, nothing that lasts. The difficulty lies in the seeking, not in what is sought. All conditioned things (dharmas), are like shadows and clouds, bubbles and echoes – they cannot be obtained; moreover, there is no one to obtain them. The self is just a word.

On our last visit to L.A., we walked into the Abbot's room upon arrival,

Abbot: "Well, what's up? How's it going?"

Monk: "I can't put down the mark of self."

Abbot: "Oh? Well bring it here. Let's have a look at it," smiling and holding out an open hand.

Monk: "Ah, well, er…"(silence)

Abbot: "Anything else?" (laughing)

> "He knows there is no self and no others, no lifespan, and no life itself. The self-nature is empty, without a doer or receiver. And right then he obtains the Liberation Gate of Emptiness which appears before him."
>
> Ten Grounds Chapter
> Avatamsaka Sutra

How can emptiness be liberation, how can nothing make one happy? Emptiness is just a way of saying there's nothing to attach to. Nothing means no obstructions, no hang-ups. Unobstructed and unattached, there is no place for suffering to stand, no place for even dust to alight. Seeing through the self and realizing it is empty is liberation.

While my teacher guides me one step ahead of myself, my practices are forever one step behind my ego. It's like trying to remove beads of oil from water with a butter knife. We keep finding new ways to make old mistakes. We are clumsy and headstrong. My teacher is patient and gets us to laugh at ourselves.

Sleep and waking states are merging. I find myself reciting and practicing in my dreams as if still out on the road. The road is full of tests and temptations, demons, and pretty women, and so are dreams. Demons don't rest or take breaks. If I do, I fall back. For example, a sleeping bag is too nice because it allows me to uncross my legs and still keep warm. This little luxury leaves the front door wide open. A blanket is better for sleeping because if I uncross my legs, my feet get cold. The chill wakes me up in time to pull my legs back into lotus position and secure the front door again. Little things count big.

Then again, it's all a test.

> "Demons are trying to test your true mind… the more you're tested, the brighter you'll get until you shine like the Autumn moon. It's like sharpening a knife – they rub you until you're sharp and bright."
>
> Ven. Abbot Hua in L.A.

How strong is your will and resolve? Are you sincere or half-hearted? Attached to success and afraid of losing face? How many times can you fall and still rouse your spirits and come back? "Demons are your good advisors. They come to help you from the opposite end," said the Master. "They test your temper and reveal your true mind."

The only thing that seems to work is nothing – no thoughts, no mind, no dwelling, no attachments. Avoid extremes; don't make plans. Hold on to an open mind. Hold on to nothing and then let nothing go, too. Subdue the body; purify the mind with morality, concentration and wisdom. Return and rely on true principles, not on conscious thought and emotions. Let it all go: stillness and emptiness is wonderful existence.

> In all countries in every direction
> He relies on nothing and dwells nowhere.
> He does not seek life itself
> Or any of the host of dharmas.
>
> Ten Transferences Chapter
> Avatamsaka Sutra

We have to use the force of false thoughts and attachments to keep us from our natural state – the Buddhanature, perfect enlightenment. If we didn't false think and everywhere grasp, we would quite spontaneously certify to the fruit of Bodhi. Cultivation of the Way is therefore called "The Great Reversal." It goes from the unnatural back to the natural; reverses the false and returns to the true. But because we have been upside-down so long, it looks like right side up to us, and for awhile, travelling the right road we feel like we're going backwards. In a sense we are, for,

> The way that goes ahead often looks as if it went back.
> In Tao, the only motion is returning.
>
> Lao Tzu

Heng Sure • April 27, 1978
Like it or not, we have to follow him

"Cheatin' in Ch'an"

Used to be as kids, when the street lights came on or when mom whistled "dinner time," we stopped the ballgames, took off our ice skates, packed away the monopoly set, and hustled home. We're not kids anymore. Cultivators take responsibility for ending their own birth and death. There's no time to play.

Ch'an meditation can resolve the matter of birth and death. When the Ghost of Impermanence whistles, if we haven't concentrated to the ultimate point, we still have to follow him, like it or not.

I've laid down a new rule in Ch'an practice: sit still until you make it through the pain gate.

Don't wriggle, don't drop your legs. Otherwise it's like drilling wood with a fire bow, drilling on and on, getting some smoke and a red glow, then quitting before the fire comes to flame. This is called cheating yourself.

> Like drilling wood to make a fire,
> If one rests before the sparks appear,
> The fire, like the effort, will disappear.
> The lazy one is also thus.
>
> The Bodhisattvas Ask for Clarification Chapter
> Avatamsaka Sutra

Heng Chau • April 27, 1978
Not kissing, bowing

Willow Creek, "Jade Beach"

A young man with sun-bleached hair, faded jeans, and bloodshot eyes walked up,

"You the guys walkin' along and kissin' the ground, right?"

"Not kissing the ground, we are bowing," I said.

He takes a swig from a pint-size can of malt liquor, and watches us bow. A bottle of cheap wine is perched on his shoulder next to an ear pierced with a gold earring.

"Boy, I don't think I could do that very long... Say, you guys don't drink do ya?" he asks offering me the beer can.

"No."

"Oh well, good luck." he says.

His eyes are glazed, his gait wobbly. Only 25 years old maybe, but he looks over the hill and already exhausted his prime. Along with a man the locals call "Indian," these two characters comb the Cape San Martin beaches for jade. They then peddle or trade for beer and wine. The area is so rich in jade its called "Jade Bridge." "Indian" has long, straight, black hair and wears a dark overcoat. He doesn't talk much. They sleep on the beaches at night or under the bridge overpass when it rains. (I went to relieve nature and accidentally stumbled onto their "home": a bottle of wine, and old pair of boots, a couple of blankets, and a big pink bottle of Pepto Bismol). During the day they sell tourists pieces of jade and immediately walk the money into Gorda's store for more wine.

We camp on the pull-offs at night atop high jade-green cliffs. Quiet and windy.

Heng Sure • April 28, 1978
Do you need a blanket?

"I'm not asking for anything."

Last month I felt I needed another blanket and a coat for late-night meditation on the cold ocean coast. I knew that seeking them was wrong. In cultivation, if your heart is sincere, what you need arrives without seeking it. I tried my best not to false-think about blankets and coats but I lost patience and wrote Heng Chau a note urging him to ask for more gear at Gold Wheel.

"If stuff comes to us I'll land it, otherwise, I'm not asking for anything."

"Good for him," I thought. "that's real backbone."

> Our job in life is to know contentment,
> Then afflictions are cast out all at once.
> Don't be fond of forms and sounds.
> Even less look for fame or benefit.
>
> Master Hua

I swallowed the urge to follow desire. At Gold Wheel I promised to "subdue myself and return to principle." Half and hour after lecture, a box full of warm jackets appeared as an offering to the

Sangha. One of the laypeople asked Heng Chau, "Do you need a blanket?"

Heng Chau • April 28, 1978
Buddhism turns the telescope around

> All in the mundane world
>   is born from conditions,
> And it's not apart from causes and conditions
>   that the Bodhisattva sees all dharmas.
>
> Ten Transferences Chapter
> Avatamsaka Sutra

The cliffs crumble and slide into the sea. The road breaks and buckles, daily needing repair to keep it from falling off the mountain. Nature speaks the Dharma of impermanence – nothing stays, everything must change. The four elements of earth, fire, wind and water, that make up our bodies, are like the four seasons, constantly going and returning. Where does spring come from and winter go to? Where do I come from and go to?

We are creatures of karma; the deeds we do and the retribution those actions bring about. Karma is a seed. The impersonal conditions of nature are like the wind. The winds blow the seeds and our lives unfold in succession. Bound by our karma as it interlaces with conditions, who of us can say we are really free?

Bodhisattvas understand cause and effect. They are not confused by karma. In the midst of all the sticky action and stained threads of cause, they float unattached, unobstructed, here, yet not here, within all dharmas, yet apart from them. It's called "still quiescence." Seeking nothing outside, clinging to nothing within, they follow in harmony with the myriad things and yet they never turn their backs on their work of benefitting living beings. What an inconceivable state! And they are always happy.

> The Bodhisattva is constantly happy
>> with dharmas of still quiescence.
> He follows in accord with them
>> and attains the ultimate state of nirvana.
> Yet he does not abandon
>> the path of living beings and
> In this way, he attains
>> subtle, wonderful wisdom.
>
> Ten Transferences Chapter
> Avatamsaka Sutra

One day life looks good and getting better. The next day things look bad and getting worse. If you find something that makes you happy, it's bound to cause sadness. Hard as you try to hold the good times, they always go flat and fade; hard as you try to shut out the bad times, they have a way of finding us all. Sometimes you get so low and weary you think you're going to die. But you don't die and no pain stays forever. Sometimes you get so high and full, you feel you'll float away or burst. But all too soon it ends like a sneeze, and you come crashing down. We move around a lot, yet never go anywhere. And in the end, we all return to the unmoving ground of level equality that sees everything the same, as if this life was just a dream or a play, nothing to take for real.

> "He vows that all beings leave all distinctions that arise from being moved from mindfulness, and enter the unmoving wisdom ground of level equality."
>
> Ten Transferences Chapter
> Avatamsaka Sutra

The world is held up by wheels. Big wheels are turned by the little wheels. The small wheels are spun around by even smaller wheels – like a giant, intricate clock. And somewhere in the center of all this turning flurry of gears and gadgets, is a single tiny wheel; the "square inch," the true mind, the Dharma wheel.

"He vows that all beings ride the wisdom vehicle and turn the proper Dharma wheel."

Ten Transferences Chapter
Avatamsaka Sutra

Cultivating the way is just learning to turn one's own Dharma wheel. It is a journey within, back to the root, returning to the source. Step by measured step we go towards the good and regain control of the smallest wheel and the first movement. It's said in Ch'an (Zen), that if you can go one step beyond that last small wheel, to disappear within the "0," then you will have ended the cycle of birth and death, and gain entry to a realm that is wonderful past words, pure and blissful beyond reckoning. They say it's the hardest thing in the world to do and the highest.

Cultivating the Way is like climbing a hundred foot pole:
Sliding down is easy, going up is hard.
On the top of the pole if you can take one step further,
Then you're free to come and go
    anywhere in the universe.

verse by Tripitaka Master Hua

Our bodies ache this A.M. from the bowing and full lotus meditation, but they ache good. To obtain what is truly worthwhile requires effort and sheer will you don't think you have until you have to find it. Then it's there. True inner growth and cleansing is accompanied by pain and pressure like a mother giving birth. Wisdom is also born of difficulty and yielding.

* * *

End of day. An offering of money wrapped around the windshield wiper. Soft ocean breeze, red disc sun sinking in the sea. A man who had been quietly watching us for a couple of days came up to introduce himself. He is an astronomer with NASA and he wanted to offer his support and to say he admired the pilgrimage.

"It's really wonderful what you are doing. Anyone who sees or hears about it is sure to be moved, I feel," he said.

"I'm an astronomer. We're going to build a huge observatory on that hill soon. Perfect skies here; we can see for a long ways."

"How far can they see now?" I asked.

"Oh, right to the edge of the universe." he answered.

"I didn't know the universe had an edge." I said

"Well, we don't know exactly, really. That's the theoretician's guessing!" he replied. "It's tantalizing! Every time we go a little further out and keep thinking we are on the verge of discovering the secrets of the universe, but then there is always something beyond, and more mystery. We haven't found it yet."

"Buddhism turns the telescope around and looks within," I said.

The astronomer smiled and nodded,

"Exactly! You know I believe that's the only way to do it. You people have the right idea. Yup, that's the only way to do it." he said.

In the Avatamsaka it says,

> The ways of the Thus Come Ones, Great Immortals,
> Are subtle, wonderful, and hard to comprehend,
> Not thought, they are apart from every thought,
> Those seeking them in seeing can't attain them.

Astronomers "seek by seeing" further and further out. Physicists "seek by seeing" smaller and smaller in; (atomic and subatomic research). Soon, maybe, they will be seeing each other as big and small, the one and the many, interpenetrate and fuse without obstruction. With a telescope, seeing the entire universe as no bigger than the tip of a single hair; with a microscope, seeing in the tip of a single hair the entire universe. An astronomer may see the furthest shining star, only to discover it's the reflected light off a microscope that someone else is using to observe this tiny atom we call the world.

Heng Sure • April 29, 1978
The Buddhist bowing computer

"Memories: April, Big Sur"

The Buddhist Bowing Computer: five stones and a bottle cap in a line.

Cultivating the 42 Hands and Eyes at sunrise and midnight, in the Plymouth.

Tai ji quan at sunrise on the cliffs.

Lunch: boiled roadside greens on a Hi-ho Cracker, mountain spring water, peanut butter, canned Chinese vegetables, and prunes.

Avatamsaka Sutra by kerosene lamp beneath full moon.

Heng Chau • April 29, 1978
Every move I make breaks the precepts

Norm and Fritz, the firemen from San Luis, stop out with car parts. They ask to borrow whatever we have of the Avatamsaka Sutra that's been translated into English in Vajra Bodhi Sea.

"Wish there were more in English," says Norm. They offer to take care of our car while we travel to Asia.

Again he reflects: "Living beings of the world do not know to repay kindness. They make enemies instead, and quarrel among themselves. They are attached to deviant views, doubts and inversions. Living beings are ignorant. They lack wisdom and minds of faith. Following bad companions, they give rise to evil wisdom. They are filled with greed, love, ignorance and many afflictions… I only want to save and liberate all beings, to cause them to be pure and forever make good their escape."

Ten Grounds Chapter
Avatamsaka Sutra

Today while bowing I had the following heart-realization and saw that I am one of those living beings the above passage describes:

"I am a fool. I am arrogant and upside-down. Every move I make breaks the precepts. The words that leave my mouth create offenses. The ones that don't leave, but remain as thought in my mind, are worse still. With body, mouth, and mind, out of greed, anger, and stupidity, I create evil karma without pause or rest. Transgressions pass in review even while asleep. I cherish my body and have a huge view of self. My merit and virtue, wisdom and blessings, daily deplete. What have I done to repay the debt of kindness to my parents and teacher? What is meaningful and honorable in simply eating, sleeping, and wearing clothes?"

"They turn and flow in birth and death and do not seek to see the Buddha. They neither follow bright guides, nor believe in regulating Masters. They are confused and commit mistakes and errors... They leave the proper Dharma far behind and dwell in deviant dharmas. They forsake the straight and level road in favor of perilous and difficult roads. They reject the Buddha's intent and embrace the will of demons."

Ten Grounds Chapter
Avatamsaka Sutra

Time and again I have been compassionately taught to shape up and go towards the good. But time and again I turn my back on enlightenment, follow bad companions, and walk dangerous and dark roads. I lock myself in a cage and then cry and wail for someone to liberate me. Once free, I turn around and walk right back into the prison. Moreover, I pride myself on this confusion and don't even know to be sorry or ashamed.

"If this evil karma had substance and form, the limits of empty space could not contain it all!"

from the Avatamsaka Repentance

If I never stopped bowing I still would be unable to erase all my offense karma. And yet...

And yet I have met a Good and Wise Advisor with deep wisdom and vast compassion. I have encountered the unsurpassed Dharma and find myself at last walking a path with true heart. Amidst all that is phoney and impermanent, I have stumbled upon something true and eternally dwelling. I'm really lucky, really happy. Things get better and brighter with every bow. The Dharma is just that way.

> "May the sun of wisdom let fall its light to melt away the frost and dew of the karma and delusion of my body and mind. May the wind of Buddhas and Bodhisattva's kindness universally shake and level my mountain of heavy obstacles. May the long flowing river of Dharma wash away the defilements of my mind... May we all be reborn in the Land of Ultimate Bliss of Amita Buddha!"
>
> from the Avatamsaka Repentance

"Why would a young American leave everything to become a monk or nun and take an Asian Master for a teacher?" asks an elderly man of us after lunch on the roadside.

Flashback: We *did* lead a charmed life. Our blessings were a horn of plenty. Everything in life went our way. We got whatever we wanted and a few extras besides. Why leave it then? Because having everything in the world is still having nothing. Inside, spiritually, we were uprooted and lost. As good as the mundane world was to us, it never satisfied the souls longing for its true home. The soul has a voice, a sound. Try to listen and you can't hear; try to shut it out and you can't silence it. No matter what we did or where we ran, a voice inside called it straight, "This is empty, false. Who are you? What are you doing? Where are you going? You are dreaming."

We tried playing it normal, we tried dropping out. We chased after more and better, bowed to the dollar, then turned our backs on the system to live in voluntary poverty on the fringe. Didn't matter. Whether successes or misfits, straights or rebels, the world stays the same – a place of suffering. No matter how you play out your share, it never comes out as paradise. That is the nature of the Saha World we live in: it is a place to pay off karmic debts. We are in this world to transcend it, not to enjoy it. "Like fish in an evaporating pond, what joy could there be in this?" "We are just passing through and our lives speed by like an evening dream's passing time." When looked at from the mind's eye, "leaving everything" is leaving nothing. Putting it all down isn't the end, it's the beginning.

That a person could end up as a monk or nun living in a pure Way-place despite having everything one could wish for in life, says something. It says that the vows and compassion of the Buddha are vast and deep; it says the Buddhadharma doesn't discriminate and equally reaches all beings, not just those who are easy to save or deserve it; and, it says nothing is fixed or fated.

Inconceivable and wonderful things still happen in the world, and anybody who has faith and sincerity can be touched by the magic and have their deepest wish come true... (end flashback).

"I mean," says the elder man as we clear the dishes from straw mats, "most people would be suspicious and distrustful of an Asian monk, yet you two have such faith in your teacher and the Dharma. Why?"

"Asian or American, what does that matter if it's the truth? The Buddha and the precepts are our teacher! Buddhism is the teaching of all living beings and points directly to the true mind. It has no country, or race, or age, or color, or language." I answer. "It belongs to everybody."

"He produces pure faith in the Buddha, the Dharma, and the Sangha. From this faith comes forth a vast, great resolve. He does not want the five desires or a king's throne. He want not wealth or success, not amusement or fame. He wants only to end for all eternity, the sufferings of living beings, and so he makes his resolution to benefit the world."

Worthy Leader Chapter
Avatamsaka Sutra

* * *

End of day a barefooted, smiling woman dressed like a colorful gypsy, walked up, checked us out as she moved dance-like around us. She said her name was Dana. Friendly, but strange. We kept silence. She folded her hands, smiled and left.

Heng Sure • April 30, 1978
And let the bowing speak

"Sorta Gorda"

Tiny community centered around a homey, natural foods restaurant, a general store, and gas pump. Mossy boulders, misty cliffs, poison oak, and empty space surround on three sides. To the West, the endless, lonely ocean. The solitudes makes Gorda an oasis of human contact. Why "Sorta Gorda"? Because it's only so big, it's sorta not there.

This silent pilgrim found it hard to miss all the same. I don't socialize but my heart is not made of wood. Bowing past Gorda I had a few false thoughts of seeking ties and sharing smiles. But vows are made to be kept. I work for everyone. Not joining in the social flow is hard for a while, but ending the suffering of birth and death is the one great matter facing us all. The Dharma door of silent contemplation suits my nature and prevent many a karmic calamity.

> All disasters emerge from the mouth,
> All illnesses enter through the mouth.

One day I'll gain control of the mind and tongue. At that time, silence and talking will be the same. Until then, I'll hold my words and wish the friends at Sorta Gorda good energy along with all beings, and let the bowing speak.

Heng Chau • April 30, 1978
Teaching and transforming in playful samadhi

The cold and rain, the heat and wind, are part of the natural world. If I see them as problems and hassles it is because I have put myself above nature. In all worlds amid the trees, rivers, grasses, stars, and countless living creatures, there is no self and nothing that belongs to a self. All is one, without beginning or end. All of the Buddha' teaching point to this truth and of all the myriad things in Nature, none do not constantly speak the Dharma.

> "Within it, all is empty: free of self and what belongs to self, devoid of knowing and awareness, with no doer and no receiver. Like grass and woods, like rocks and walls, and also like reflections. Still, living beings are unaware and do not know."
>
> Ten Grounds Chapter
> Avatamsaka Sutra

All of our false thoughts and attachments pull us away from the truth "as it truly is." But bowing on the open highway and studying the Avatamsaka Sutra has a gentle way of bringing us back, again and again, to the simple truths we drift away from.

> "They do not give rise to a thought of duality towards their own bodies and all worlds."
>
> Entering the Dharma Realm
> Avatamsaka Sutra

* * *

"Avatamsaka Reflections"

How can there be nothing? Nothing means there's nothing to attach to. All dharmas have no self and no dwelling place. It's like empty space: if you try to find it in any direction, in the past, present, or future, you will fail to get at it. However, it's not the case that empty space does not exist. And all things are this way too.

> "All dharmas are totally unobtainable. But it is not the case that all dharmas do not exist."
>
> Ten Practices Chapter
> Avatamsaka Sutra

Everything arises from our thoughts and nothing exists outside the limit of the mind. Good thoughts create good realities; bad thoughts create bad realities. No thought, it's said, is the enlightened state, and within it, the entire substance appears as clearly as an apple in your hand.

"Bodhisattvas dwell within these adornment..." Adornments are the decorations of the mind ground. They are jewels and treasures manifested from pure precepts and the fullness of merit and virtue. They emit a light, a radiance that shows in one's face and deportment. People like to look at such a person and feel peaceful and happy just to be in their presence. The light comes from samadhi power.

> "The samadhi of emitting the light of the perfection of all merit and virtue that universally illumines the world."
>
> Entering the Dharma Realm
> Avatamsaka Sutra

Wake up stiff and cold in the A.M. Raining again. Slip into soggy, rain slicks, step out into the mud.

"Are you enjoying this lovely stretch of the coast?" shouts a cheerful, passing motorist.

* * *

Sometimes we both get stiff and uptight. Everything seems to be going wrong and we spin in circles, getting more and more afflicted. A happy, relaxed face feels like an affront and soon a cloud of anger gather around our heads. Because we are so attached to ourselves, every little thing gets blown to cosmic proportions and we become immobilized – squinting, frowning, starched, and bound.

That was our sorry state when we set out on the pilgrimage the first day. Like frozen soldiers going into battle for the first and last time. The Master was with us as we nervously waited for our flight to L.A. in the San Francisco airport.

As we slowly inched our way up the crowded boarding ramp, the Master started to smile and then suddenly stepped out of line and hopped into a wheelchair. Joking and laughing, and giggling like a little kid, he wheeled and spun up and down the ramp. It broke everybody up to see an elder Venerable monk dressed in long gold robes and sash, dashing and whirling around in a wheelchair without a care in the world or the slightest embarrassment. And it melted the frigid, self-conscious hearts of these two young monks.

> The Guiding Master for living beings
> Takes each opportunity to speak the Dharma.
> Wherever he can transform someone,
> There he appears in his victorious form.
>
> Avatamsaka Sutra
> Praises in the Tushita Heaven Palace
> Chapter 24

This is called teaching and transforming in playful samadhi, using measureless expedient means. This A.M., I remembered that airport scene and teaching, in joy. A year and one hundred miles later, and the image of the Abbot grinning in a wheelchair on the airport boarding ramp still softens my heart and melts my worries. There's a kind of fear that only joy and laughter can dispel. So it's said,

> From ancient times,
>   the immortals had no other method,
> But to stay happy at all times,
>   and never get vexed.

* * * * * * * *
May 1978

Heng Sure • May 1, 1978
First injury in four hundred miles

"Thar She Blows!"

We've bowed on rough roads and railroad beds, hopped boulders and paced bike trails, all without the slightest physical injury. Concentrating on the Dharma is the secret to our survival as we walk and bow on freeways and sidewalks. Hands and knees turn to leather. We sport a distinctive "bowing callous" on our foreheads. Otherwise, the bowing has brought only benefit, and no harm to our bodies.

Until today. A false-thought appeared before my eyes and concentration fled.

"You should keep a lookout, you might see whales," someone said to us. "They migrate in the spring, you know." Whales! Ever since reading Moby Dick I have always wanted to see a real live whale. Too big for zoos, whales are a rare sight for Midwestern land-lubbers. My heart goes out to the anti-whaling heroes who risk their lives to save whales from slaughter. Now we are bowing inches from the deep blue sea and it's whale season!

Heng Chau saw whales sporting about in the cove below, yesterday. Today my false thoughts were spinning. I was half bowing, half scanning the waves to my left for great white whales.

The road shoulder was rough, full of big rocks and deep holes. Right on schedule, a huge grey whale and two sleek baby whales surfaced not two hundred yards away. Looking like express trains, they cut the waves as they went. Eyes glued to the water, I took a careless step and tumbled to the ground with a sprained ankle. First injury in four hundred miles.

"Did you see any Buddhas today, Kuo Chen?" I asked myself contemplating the instant-karma Dharma-lecture. "No, but I saw some big fish, and hooked myself good."

They have no greed for benefits or offerings,
They only delight in Buddha's Bodhi.
With one mind they seek the Buddha's wisdom,
Concentration undivided with no other thought.

Ten Grounds Chapter
Avatamsaka Sutra

Heng Chau • May 1, 1978
When are they going to do something?

"What are they doing?" asks one man to another as they watch us bow.

"I dunno," answers his friend.

"Well, when are they going to *do* something?" he demands.

"I dunno," softly answers the other man.

"I don't think they are doing *anything*!" he says, hot under the collar.

"They're doing *nothing*, I think," calmly answers his friend.

"Huh?!" says the first man.

"The Sage does nothing, yet achieves everything.

Lao Tzu

We can trace all of our problems on this trip to "doing;" meddling and interfering out of impatience and desire. When things go well, invariably it's the result of doing nothing. But there is a lot to doing nothing, because this principle doesn't simply mean turning into a stump of wood or a vegetable. Rather, it is an alert and sensitive harmonizing with people and according with conditions. Doing nothing is the art of letting things happen naturally, devoid of force or desire, without grasping and contending. To pull off "action that is actionless," one has to be empty of all greed, anger, and ignorance. The Tao and the response can intertwine in a most wonderful way, but only where there is no selfishness or big ego obstructing the magic.

> So long as I "do nothing"
>> the people will of themselves be transformed.
> So long as I love quietude,
>> the people will of themselves go straight.
> So long as I act only by inactivity,
>> the people will of themselves become prosperous.
> So long as I have no wants,
>> the people will of themselves
>> return to the "state of the uncarved block."
>
> Lao Tzu

* * *

Because he clearly sees that all things (dharma) are unobtainable, a Bodhisattva can "do nothing" yet increase the good in the world. He can cultivate the Way without harming or possessing anyone or anything. He can "do nothing, yet achieve everything." Because he is without attachment to a self, what he does naturally accords with everything and benefits everyone. He doesn't have a thought of difference between himself and the entire Dharma Realm.

> "He clearly sees how the Dharma Realm is vast, big, and peacefully set up. He understands that the entire world as well as the dharmas, are level, equal and non-dual, and he leaves all attachments behind."
>
> Ten Transferences Chapter
Avatamsaka Sutra

Heng Sure • May 2, 1978
Coming up from a bow beside a huge boulder

> "Faith is the precious raft that carries us across the flood of affliction."
>
> Water and Mirror Reflections
> Tripitaka Master Hua

Forty-mile per hour howling windstorm, bowing track as rugged and rocky as the moon. Hear a car door slam behind me. Struggle for balance against the wind each time I stand from a bow. Truly a test of patience and resolve. Heng Chau appears to the left, signals "time to meditate," his eyes squinting, his nose dripping, his cheeks cherry-red with wind-burn. We look back down the dusty track. Coming up from a bow beside a huge boulder is an elderly laywoman in a long, whipping, black robe, white basketball shoes, a wide-brimmed, yellow, ten-gallon hat, her face wearing a peaceful smile, untroubled, with deep faith in the Buddhadharma.

Heng Chau • May 2, 1978
Thoughts are just thoughts

Everything we do with our bodies, mouths, and minds, creates karma and comes back to us. Good returns as good; evil as evil. Every step we take waits for us down the road, even the steps of our thoughts. All the ideas, perceptions, impressions, daydreams, and images – pure or defiled – are coming back to me now while bowing. In reality, they never simply pass through the mind like one passes through a small town on a long journey, but they lodge in the deeper consciousness and when the time is ripe, they reappear in flawless recall.

"Oh well," someone might say, "thoughts are just thoughts. No harm in just thinking, is there?" Consider this: last night I had a terrible and troubled dream that scattered my Way-karma and left me drained. While washing dishes after lunch, I suddenly remembered that the dream was an exact replay of an improper fantasy I entertained over ten years ago. It was just a passing thought. I never acted on it and yet the retribution was precise and sharp. So the verse says,

> Even after hundreds of thousands of kalpas,
> The karma you've created is not forgotten.
> When the proper conditions combine,
> You'll still have to undergo the retribution.

No harm in false thinking? False thinking is the root cause of all the troubles and disasters in the world. The power of thought is inconceivable. As the Avatamsaka says, "All evil is born from the mind. There are no dharmas it does not create."

Last month in L.A., the Abbot said that peoples' false thoughts ruin the world and that we are unaware,

> "When everyone is selfish and self-seeking, they ruin the world. They casually and confusedly have false thoughts and they don't even know it. They don't see how it makes the world go bad."

Last night's bad dream wasn't a quirk of fate or an accident. Karma's retribution appears right in the ups and downs, joys and sorrows, benefits and losses of daily life. Sometimes we see it; sometimes we miss it. But it never misses us and is not off by a hair.

> "Therefore, on this day I have come to believe deeply in cause and effect. I give rise to deep shame and great fear, and repent. I cut off that incessant (evil) mind and bring forth the Bodhi Mind; cut off evil and cultivate good; go diligently forward in the three karmic actions (body, mouth, and mind), reform all my past errors, and rejoice compliantly in the slightest hairsbreadth of the good of sages and ordinary people."

from the Great Compassion Repentance Ceremony

* * *

What is the mind? It is what I am always looking for and can never find; it is what I try to run away from and can never leave.

> The Bodhisattva contemplates
>   the mind as not outside;
> Moreover, it cannot be gotten at inside.
> He knows the nature of the mind
>   does not exist at all;
> Self and dharmas are all left behind,
>   forever still and extinct.

Ten Transferences Chapter
Avatamsaka Sutra

Heng Sure • May 3, 1978
Use patience and accord with conditions

"Pep Talk"

Since we landed on this ridge below Mt. Mars, I've cultivated like a roller-coaster. Retreat by inches, then leap ahead; grasping at new insights, then crash. Can't find solid ground to level false thoughts inside, or to stand on outside. What to do?

> "Don't forsake what's near for what's distant. Cultivate as much as you know. Don't go reaching for the lofty, profound Dharma. If you can't control thoughts of food, clothes, and sleep, then you've got no cultivation to speak of."

Master Hua

This is rugged, empty land. Be honest. Big Sur isn't Easy street. Use patience and accord with conditions. You've been skipping meditation and gone for a nap after bowing. No wonder false thoughts abound. Quiet your noisy mind. Concentrate and hold to the unruffled Tao where there is neither high nor low, and everything is just right.

Seek the Middle Way in all things. Go on as always, return to basics. Skipping practices while seeking states puts your ladder on a tipsy edge; you're sure to fall. Better to stand firm, use effort in the mind, and not in trying to expand. Continue, and let the Dharma-magic work.

> Too fast and you'll stumble.
> Too slow and you'll fall behind.
> Not too slow, not too fast, and
> You'll arrive right on time.

Heng Chau • May 3, 1978
That harmless-looking plant

It's spring in the mountains. This stretch of the coast is particularly rich in wild edible plants and herbs. We have limited ourselves to foraging about ten species, because wild plants hunting can quickly become an obsession. Like the Chinese literary art of matching couplets. People get so taken with matching couplets that they can't eat or sleep trying to think of the matching line. The plant dharma has the same lure and challenge. Holding bowing mindfulness is our first priority. Food seems to take care of itself when we take care of bowing.

Mostly we eat "greens" – large-leaf pot herbs that are easy to identify and require little preparation. Dock, mustard, dandelion, prickly saw-thistle, sweet coltsfoot, all boil down like spinach, and grow along the road and ditches. Raw salads can be made from miner's lettuce, sourgrass, clover, fennel, and heron's bill. Mellow and plantain take some getting used to, and quickweed isn't as widely distributed as the others, but we've eaten all of them when available.

Yarrow and yerba buena make excellent clear teas; as does the red bark from manzanita, which pulls off in layers about twice a year.

The Dharma protectors who turned us on to edible plants always made a special point of cautioning us to be extremely careful in identifying and gathering wild plants and herbs. As one biologist told us, "There are two kinds of wild plant gatherers: old ones and bold ones. But there are no old, bold ones."

If in doubt about a species, it's better to be safe than sorry. We almost ate a variety of a fennel-looking plant, but we waited because we weren't positive of the identification.

When our plant man came out, he informed us that the harmless-looking plant we had in mind to eat was so poisonous that a piece one-half of your body finger could drop a full-grown cow in its tracks. The plant was not fennel, it was water hemlock, a toxic cousin of the hemlock that killed Socrates.

Plants are hotels for bugs and insects. Ants, for example, like to hang out in the base of fennel; a tiny spider-like being nests on the underside of dandelion. One has to be careful when picking and washing not to break the precept against talking life. The ancients were so careful about not killing that if they found even lice in their clothes, they would put the little bugs in a bamboo tube and keep them warm by filling and wrapping the tube with cotton. Then, for fear the bugs would starve, they would feed them with greasy food, because that's what they like to eat.

There was another teaching we picked up from the plants. A wealth of nutritious and free food, healthy herbs and medicines grew all around us, but we never knew. We were just like the Sound-Hearers who although they were right inside the Jeta Grove, face to face with the Buddha, couldn't see the Buddha's spiritual transformations, not hear the wonderful Dharma that he spoke. "They had eyes but could not see the Buddha; They had ears, but couldn't hear the perfect, sudden teaching." Why? Because they had renounced All-wisdom and were covered over by the cataract of ignorance. The Avatamsaka makes an analogy:

"It is as in the snowy mountain where there is a multitude of medicinal herbs. A good physician who goes there can distinguish all of them. Yet the hunters and herdsmen who constantly dwell on the mountain, cannot see the medicine. And this is just the same way."

Entering the Dharma Realm
Avatamsaka Sutra

The plants are like our true mind, our inherent enlightened nature. We are like the hunters and herdsmen. Although we always live among the medicinal herbs, we can't see them; we take them for useless weeds until a good physician comes along and remove our cataract of ignorance. Then we realize we already have everything we could ever wish for.

* * *

It's time to write less and bow more. How do I know? Yesterday I stopped bowing to write in my notebook. A bird flew overhead and dropped a load of shit right in the middle of my essay. That says it.

Heng Sure • May 4, 1978
Much worse than poison oak

"Poison Oak and Advertising"

Bowing reveals the contents of the mind. I've been reviewing scenes from childhood recently – never realized how the advertising messages that I read as a kid had deeply entered my mind. For instance, I used to read the cereal boxes at the breakfast table. The breakfast cereal itself has long since passed away, but the images and values I picked up from the packages are with me still.

As I stepped over a patch of poison oak this afternoon, I recalled how I was influenced by the voice of Madison Avenue. In the same way advertising once surrounded my senses, poison oak covers the landscape in Big Sur. It clings to vertical cliffsides. Incautious pedestrians can bump into a patch of shiny leaves at eye level. It grow like ivy on tree-trunks. Poison oak hides among harmless clumps of miner's lettuce and coltsfoot. Unwary salad-green gatherers can pluck a handful of unpleasant surprises.

We've adapted our habits; dodging poison oak has become as automatic as shutting out the noise-storm of advertising once was. Heng Chau and I, luckily, haven't run into oak poisoning. The bowing slowly empties the mind of the Madison Avenue poisoning I picked up before leaving home. Which is more toxic? Which is longer lasting? The infection and rash of poison oak which swells and festers, itches and runs, or the mind-poisoning of greedy desire inflamed by advertising? Ads tells us we need more, that we are imperfect until we own this product or buy that item. Sowing discontent in people's hearts creates an insatiable itch, much worse than poison oak.

> If we cease to store products that are hard to get,
>   there will be no more thieves.
> If the people never see such things as desire,
>   their hearts will remain placid and undisturbed.
>
> Lao Tzu

Heng Chau • May 4, 1978
Except for the shoes, we passed

The Avatamsaka Sutra is the richest collection of true words I've ever come across. Because it is so profound and ultimately complete, it speaks directly and with a simple, universal eloquence that anybody could read. It is so inexhaustible in meaning, poetic imagery, and music, that one can easily enter a sublime trance just listening to its lyric sounds. It's pictures and places are so far away yet so close at hand, that each reading is like a summer afternoon's daydream. One wakes up cool and softened wondering "Was it a dream, or real? Or is *this* a dream and that was real? Did I actually go to those dust-mote Buddhalands with mani jewels and redolent incense, or, but, how…? And yet I feel like I *really* did!" It's a childlike reality. Who's to say what's real and what's a dream?

> The sage at all time, sees and hears
>   no more than an infant sees and hears.

Lao Tzu

Children's eyes are more pure than adults'. The questions children ask are pure and basic, Zen-like. They ask, "Who am I? Where did I come from before I was born? What happens when you die?" They ask about the stars, the self, the nature of dharmas, and what's good and bad, right and wrong, why is this being an animal and that one crippled? These are the questions that Buddhism deals with because Buddhism is the teaching of all living beings. The Sutras have all the answers; our own minds have all the answers.

Six-white-robed, bearded, scraggly, long-haired men stopped. They had funny stained teeth and looked faded and drained. Their leader stepped out of an old, beat-up car and brought an offering of bread, fruit, and small change they had pooled. They were friendly and supportive, but also strange and pretty spaced-out.

"You don't eat meat?" he asked.

I nodded, "No."

"Good!" he said. "And no sex?"

I nodded again.

"Good!" he smiled. "And no drugs or alcohol?"

I nodded.

"Good. Yes, very good. And you don't beg or steal?"

I nodded.

"Right on brother!" he exclaimed. "Except you shouldn't wear shoes," he said, looking down at our cotton shoes, a little disappointed. Except for the shoes, I gathered we had passed.

"Wear no shoes, stay close to the earth." he counseled. He wanted to hug me, but I stepped back and indicated "no touch monks." They waved goodbye and drove off, car choking and sputtering. Smiling out the windows, all with brown-stained and chipped-off teeth and no shoes.

Heng Sure • May 5, 1978
What's new outside?

Recognized today that cultivation is for real. The present moment can't be grasped but it contains all things. My thoughts, my words, and actions make the world I experience; the relationship is direct, no one else can stand in and receive retribution for me. It's a sobering awakening, like cold water in the face; that's the new inner weather.

What's new outside? Poisonous ticks abound. Poison oak covers the ground, the bowing track, the trees, and the cliffs. The road has narrowed to a razor-edge; we stand aside like bullfighters to let cars pass as we walk. Weather changes from deep chill to sweaty hot in seconds. The rain continues. There's no flat ground off the road; the hills play tricks with our senses. The mad Big Sur wind stings the sunburn on every exposed inch of skin. Our only contact with other people for days on end are staring, curious eyes from the windows of elephantine mobile homes.

Let it go and accord in harmony with all states. Joys and afflictions both arise from a discriminating mind. What we can know and feel is false, impermanent. The only real, lasting peace come from patient cultivation of the Dharma.

Heng Chau • May 5, 1978, Friday
Cultivation is like polishing a mirror

A station wagon full of Gold Mt. Sangha stopped on their way to L.A. Little Kuo T'o (Josh), offered a fresh pineapple. Hot outside, the pineapple will cool us off. Phong Kuo Wu, Mrs. Tsai, Susan (Kuo Shan) Anderson, came to take us to Gold Wheel Temple. A surprise. We ate lunch at a waterfall. Jane from Sorta Gorda also stopped with a gypsy named Gopal and we all ate quietly together under some pine trees.

Left the car with the Hammonds in San Luis. Kuo Wu's openness and generosity broke the ice. Very impressive, the power of giving. We drank tea and the Hammonds offered a large jar of honey from their hives for the Abbot.

* * *

We arrive in time to hear the Master's lecture. The words are like cool water to a thirsty man. They speak directly to our state and feelings, frustrations and questions. The talk stresses our major shortcomings: impatience, and being true.

"The causes and condition for success in cultivation come from patience. So it's said,

If you are off an inch in the beginning,
    you'll be off a thousand miles in the end.

"What is the beginning? It's when you don't have any false thoughts. You don't have them to begin with, but then you raise them, and that's the 'off an inch.' The slightest false thought created obscures the true inside; when that tiny bit of false thought is gone, then the true appears. It appears and for ten thousand miles there's not a cloud in the sky. There is nothing inside – not a single thing. But if you have the slightest bit, then it's false. So don't have even the slightest bit, break all attachments. Don't attach to good or bad;

don't attach to existence or absence of states. Not being attached anywhere is liberation.

"When you are liberated then there are no problems, but it is not easy to get there. Liberation is hard to obtain. With a hair's breadth of attachment, you won't be liberated. Where do you start?

"Start from the place where you can't take it. Bear what you can't bear, endure what's hard to endure, yield where you can't yield, eat what you can't eat.

The 10,000 foot towers begin from the ground.

"Start with the basics, start on the ground, and bit by bit, rub away your afflictions. Cultivation is like polishing a mirror – it is covered over with dust. But you wipe it clean and then the light and reflection appears. This is easy to talk about, but difficult to do.

"From every side and all directions, all kinds of states appear that are hard to recognize. Not recognizing states, they turn you; if you recognize the states, then you turn them. To turn these states requires a mind of patience. Use the perfection of patience. You want to be patient with everything. If there is something you can't take, be patient with it, then you can pass through the gate. If you're nervous and can't take it, then you won't make it through the gate...

"Be patient, offer up your afflictions. Although it's not easy, we still have to do it. If we don't do something because it's not easy, we'll never attain the fruit. With patience you can get to the other side. Patience is a boat that carries you across to the other shore!"

Ah, true words. Hard to swallow, but good medicine. It's late; long drive. Good to see our teacher again. Time passes so fast and yet, together again, it seems we never left.

We sleep in the garage behind the temple. Feels most at home there after the Plymouth and the open highway.

Heng Chau • May 6, 1978
Because they cultivated in the past

Two new pair of pants to cover our bodies, and more Dharma to cover our hearts.

> "He vows that all beings vigorously cultivate good roots as a cover for their bodies, and forever be shaded by all Buddhas."
>
> Ten Transferences Chapter
Avatamsaka Sutra

Being away from one's teacher, bowing alone on the highway, makes these visits in L.A. that much more special and valued. Absence sets things straight and solitude puts values in order. The false and superficial fades and is quickly forgotten like the city's lights at dawn. What is true and deep shines forth like the noon sun or a harvest moon. Cultivating the Way is life's greatest joy; drawing near a Good and Wise Teacher makes it joy supreme.

> "A good teacher is a door that tends toward all-wisdom, for he enables me to enter the true and actual way.

> "A good teacher is a road that tends towards all-wisdom, for he enables me to enter the City of Nirvana.

> "A good teacher is a bridge that tends towards all-wisdom, for he takes me across treacherous and evil places.

> "A good teacher is a canopy that tends towards all-wisdom, for he enables me to produce the coolness of great kindness.

> "A good teacher is a tide that tends towards all-wisdom, for he fills me with the water of great compassion."
>
> from Entering the Dharma Realm
Flower Adornment Sutra

It's hot and bitter, cool and sweet, all at the same time. Why? Because in cultivation, the do-it-yourself style is like water – it takes the path of least resistance. Cultivating with a Good Teacher is suffering because one meets the resistance head-on. So it's said,

"The Dharma arises from difficulty."

True ease and comfort (*dz dzai*), comes after difficulty, not before or instead of. Without a Good Advisor we'd take easy street, which in the end, is the most suffering of all.

* * *

The Abbot composed a verse for the City of Ten Thousand Buddhas. This is a rough translation:

> The three-thousand worlds
>   are within a single thought.
> From the small comes forth the great,
>   and beyond is yet another heaven.
> The wind blows through Ukiah;
>   the pretty little herbs and flowers are laughing.
> Talmage's rain moistens the grass and trees
>   and makes them happy.
> Limitless joy and giving,
>   benefit living beings.
> Kindness and compassion, making vows
>   is replete with both suffering and bliss.
> The ever-changing earth and fields
>   speak the Great Dharma,
> And from this ground wells forth
>   Wonderful Enlightenment Mountain.

Note: the "herbs and flowers" refers to the students; the "grass and trees" are the old people. Ukiah transliterates as yoga, and Talmage as *da mo* (Dharma).

* * *

After lecture, people come and go from the small temple, bowing to the Buddha and paying their respects to the Master who tirelessly receives everyone. Spontaneous and lively exchanges often occur between the Abbot and disciple. Today people had money and investment on their minds. After lots of give-and-take laughter during an informal conversation around the kitchen table, the Master said,

"Virtue will bring wealth naturally. Without virtue, even if you're rich, you will lose it all. For one part of virtue, you get ten parts reward; from ten parts of virtue comes one hundred parts of reward."

"Yes, but Shih Fu," asks a disciple. "Some people are really rich and they don't cultivate at all. How is that?"

"People are doing well in this life because they cultivated in the past. So don't take what's before your eyes as real. If you do things right in this life, you'll get the reward in the next. If you are not straight, you'll get that too. Giving to the poor and to the Sangha brings wealth; stinginess and stealing bring poverty. You can't be off in the slightest," answered the Abbot.

> Everything's a test
> to see what you will do…

It's all a test. When you least expect it, the test arrives. When you feel the emotion and excitement rise, when you feel your sense organs rush and flush, when everything starts fanning and vibrating and looking desirable, then you know you're facing a test. And,

> …mistaking what's before you eyes
> you'll have to start anew.

L.A. is test time for us. We are learning when things don't get our way, to return the light and look into ourselves for the cause and blame, not outside. *Emotion*. We flunk our tests because of emotion; when things go amok it's due to emotion.

> When emotion is produced,
>   wisdom is cut off.
>
> Avatamsaka Sutra Prologue

Behind emotion, feeding and inflaming it, is desire. Bowing doesn't eliminate desire, it isolates and slows it down, allowing you to get a handle on it. But if you let up vigilance for an instant of self satisfaction, or think you have got your greedy, grasping, monkey-mind tamed, right then it can turn on you faster than a blink of an eye.

It's easy to get sucked into the easy-living, party atmosphere of a city like L.A. Coming from bowing in the isolated silence of the mountains, deep forests, and sea, where there is built-in contentment from fewness of desires, where the highway serves as a constant reminder of impermanence and non-dwelling, coming from this natural monastery into the heart of one of the world's busiest cities, is a shock. To cope, you need samadhi power and a cool, impartial eye. I'm short on both. After the pure stillness of Ventana Wilderness and going days without seeing another person, L.A. is like hitting treacherous white water rapids after miles on a lazy, meandering river – capsize!

The eyes, ears, nose, tongue, body and mind, get inundated with cornucopia of sights, sounds, smells, tastes, sensations and dharmas. Every dustmote in L.A. is hyped and vibrating to the non-stop freeway, greed-way, rhythm that says, "You can get anything you want, you can get anything you want..." If a cultivator doesn't recognize that he already has everything he needs, and if in a second of incaution or confusion forsakes the wish-fulfilling pearl within to reach for a cheap trinket or bauble outside, he experiences one of life's biggest disappointments, and

> ...mistaking what's before your eyes,
>   you'll have to <u>smelt</u> anew.

Heng Sure • May 7, 1978
He made her happy

"According with Living Beings' Hearts' Delights"

"Don't ever use force to control others. They may obey you for a time, but in their hearts they don't respect you. The only thing that works in teaching and transforming living beings is to move them by their feelings with Way-virtue. You yourself must have virtuous practices. Then you can even scold people and they will still happily listen to what you say."

Venerable Master Hua

Virtuous practices are all about making others happy, according with situations, and taking a loss. I watched an elder monk who practices selflessness, teach by example. I sat beside him at a lunch celebrating his birthday.

A laywoman insisted he take a sugary, coconut "longevity peach" as a token.

"No, I have enough food," he said.

"Take one, it's your birthday," she urged.

"Enough, really."

"If you don't, none of your disciples will either."

"Too sweet. I can't finish what I have already."

"Take one, take one."

And the monk, who does not eat sweets, smiled and swallowed the entire candied bun. He had every reason to say no and to make it stick. Instead, he subdued his personal preference and "accorded with living beings' hearts' delights." He made her happy.

"Universal Worthy's body's appearance is like empty space. He relies on and dwells within the True Nature, not in any country. According with the hearts' delight of living beings, he appears in a universal body equal in size with all things."

Universal Worthy's Samadhi
Avatamsaka Sutra

Heng Chau • May 7, 1978
Everyone's your sister

First anniversary. One year of bowing. Exactly ½ way to the City of Ten Thousand Buddhas. First day of 4th lunar month. Celebrate the Master's birthday today also.

Last night during lecture, a little boy came up and sat next to the Master.

Master: "Who do you like? Do you like your mother?"

Child: "Yes."

Master: "Do you like your teacher?"

Child: "Yes, I like my teacher, too."

Master: "Do you like your sister?"

Child: "But I don't have a sister."

Master: "*Everyone's* your sister."

This is the Buddha's level equality great compassion.

Heng Chau • May 8, 1978
How come you're driving the Buddha's car?

Phong Kuo Wu, Susan (Guo Shan) Anderson, and Kuo Yun, drive us back to San Luis Obispo. Norman fixed the car, the laypeople brought the Hammonds wontons, melons, and tea. Norman relates that when he took our car out for a test run, a boy on a bicycle stopped him and grilled him thoroughly before letting him go.

"Hey, what are *you* doing with the Buddha's car!?" demanded the boy.

Norman told him that he was a friend of the bowing monks.

"Yeah?" the boy continued, not satisfied. "Well, how come you're driving the Buddha's car?"

Norman then had to explain how we left the car with him for repairs while we went to L.A., but that we were coming back.

"Well… okay, but be careful." said the little boy.

The laypeople followed us back to Big Sur and bowed the remainder of the day. A big fox visits and quickly runs away.

* * *

This weekend, in an attempt to please my teacher, I really made an effort at trying to be humble and reverent. The Master saw right through my act and called me on it with a smile.

"Oh, now he's the Great King of Bowing, thinking: 'No one is as humble as me!'"

Ouch! True words sound harsh to the ears. Genuine humility is without the mark of humility. In the Sixth Patriarch's Sutra, it says,

> Inner humility is merit;
> outer practices of reverence, is virtue.

True merit and virtue is to be unobstructed in every thought. It is to be constantly in touch with the real, wonderful function of your original nature. That is, you cultivate but are without the thought that you are cultivating. If one thinks, "I am being humble and reverent now," one is still attaching to the mark of self and displaying pride.

A Good Knowing Advisor is like a kind and loving parent. He doesn't always give you what you want, but you always get what you need. Even if you don't immediately understand your teacher's intentions, you should always be in accord with him. In time, the wisdom behind even a harsh scolding, will reveal itself.

"The youth Good Wealth single-mindedly recollected how towards the Good Knowing Advisor, he should never be in opposition or rebellious... How he should regard the Good Knowing Advisor as a kind mother, so as to renounce and separate from all unbeneficial dharmas; how he should regard the Good Knowing Advisor as a compassionate father, so as to give rise to all good dharmas."

from Entering the Dharma Realm
Avatamsaka Sutra

Heng Sure • May 9, 1978
The Triple Jewel insurance company

"Life Insurance: A Precept Policy"

The air today is full of insects. Lady bugs are swarming. Sailing spiders with gossamer parachutes, beetles, gnats, and little bugs smaller than fine hairs, all land on our bodies with each bow. They fall beneath our clumsy limbs.

> From the break of dawn, until the close of day,
> All you living beings had best protect yourselves.
> If you should come to harm beneath me,
> I vow that you will immediately
> be reborn in the Pure Land.

Where do insects come from? They come from people who didn't believe in cause and effect. People who broke the rules and got reborn as insects; their consciousness scattered into fragments.

Could it happen to me? Absolutely – in the very next thought of evil, I can plant the seeds of suffering; I can reap the fruit of rebirth as a mountainside full of mosquitoes.

How to avoid it? The only insurance company that guarantees safety from suffering as an insect, is the Triple Jewel of the Buddha, the Dharma, the Sangha. Take refuge with the Triple Jewel, sign out a precept policy. The company pays high dividends to those who hold the rules. But if you do wrong, then you become a bad risk and coverage is cancelled.

You write your own policy in every word, thought, and deed, and karma is not at all polite when it comes time to collect.

Heng Chau • May 9, 1978
Yield and accord or they don't last

"Big Sur"

Big Sur is wild. We are in a whole new world, visibly and invisibly. The sheer force of the winds and rain, joined with the awesome power of the mountains and sea, keeps the face of Big Sur raw, clean, and natural. All traces of humankind are erased, sometimes within minutes of their making. Roads, houses, power lines and poles, footprints, cigarette butts, and tin cans are swept away or eaten by the untamed melees of the elements. One is ever-aware of impermanence, non-attachment, and the insignificance of self.

In the Big Sur, nothing stops moving or changing. If the road we travel on (the *only* road through Big Sur), wasn't repaired and maintained daily by road crews, it would disappear before we could traverse its length.

Life in Big Sur is tenacious; survival a question of vigilance, struggle, and luck. There is no one who conquers nature here. Nature is lord and everyone learns to yield and accord or they don't last. Consequently, there's a bred-in-the-bone quality of patience and tolerance among the inhabitants.

Those who stay (or *try* to stay, as nothing *stays* in Big Sur for long), share an open-mindedness and quiet introspection. Those who don't stay, don't linger. There's a feeling of always standing on a slide – staying in one place requires great effort; stopping is impossible.

Living out of the Plymouth with a different home every night, fits perfectly with conditions along the 80-mile stretch of coast. Big Sur is a good place to cultivate the Way, because the only way to feel at home is to leave home and be totally unattached.

"He dwells in that which cannot be obtained, without a stopping or relying, without doing or attaching to anything… and constantly happy, he leaves the home-life and his mind is tranquil and still."

Ten Transferences Chapter
Flower Adornment Sutra

Heng Sure • May 10, 1978
You're pushing too hard

"Pure, happy, and peaceful"
Our Wise Advisors have told us straight: we're pushing too hard. For two months now at Gold Wheel, we've heard the word: forcing the Way is not the Proper Dharma.

"You need only be pure, happy, and peaceful, and you will not lose the Way."

Sutra in Forty-Two Sections

Forcing is greed – seeking immediate results. It demonstrates a lack of faith.

"Cultivation is like polishing a mirror. Bit by bit, wipe the dust away. When not a speck of dust remains, the mirror then reflects with perfect brilliance. Our original natures are just that way.

"Don't seek to become a Buddha. Don't seek enlightenment. Don't seek wisdom. Go one step at a time towards the right road. You will certainly become a Buddha." the Master said.

As a child of the Space-Age, I have always been surrounded by abundance. I've never had to wait long or work hard to get what I wanted. Growing up in the industrial cities of the Mid-west, I was isolated from the rhythms of nature where seeds planted in the spring bear fruit at harvest time. My impatience is slowly being "taught and transformed" by the bowing pilgrimage. The new principle is PATIENCE. WORK HARD. And take it as it comes.

Heng Chau • May 10, 1978
Returning to the source

Of all the things in the world, cultivating the Way is the most natural. Quietly and unaware, we grow true and straight again. Effortlessly gliding along the soul's river, moving, yet still, still, yet moving, returning to the source. One day you wake up from a long sleep in a clear and empty room, sunlight streaming through the windows; cloudless sky for miles, not a care anywhere.

Dream last night: underneath the City of 10,000 Buddhas was an immense, unexplored nine-tiered structure (perhaps a building, or tower, or even another city). The Sangha was so busy doing Buddha's work and helping others, they had no time to investigate the nine layers. They were too active to even put on their shoes or sleep and eat, except on the run. Only a few had explored the second story (tier).

Heng Sure • May 11, 1978
Too much is the same as too little

A family of lay people stopped on their way home to Los Angeles to bring us a hot lunch. We ate on a dusty turn off, miles from anywhere, next to a six-foot hedge of poison oak.

I watched the infant daughter fuss over food. She sat with her mouth open as momma tempted her with another corn chip. I recognized myself in the child: stomping through the world with my mouth open, demanding to be fed by everyone, by anyone who will give to me, me, me. Yech! Heng Chau captured the state with a note:

The flies and ants eat your skin-bag
    before you check-out.
Thieves steal your clothes and food.
The weather turns your body
    into a weathered raisin,
And cars try to run you off the cliffs
    while you bow to end disasters.

"Cultivation isn't easy, is it?" asks the Master. We are getting a good, close look at who and where we *really* are these days. Lots of pressure on big and sneaky egos. If we don't see the false, how can we know what to put down?

The Middle Way is ultimately right. Too much is the same as too little. I recalled a proverb we heard at Gold Wheel and it turned the inner light back on.

Heaven and Earth cannot go for one day
    without agreeing.
People's hearts cannot be for one time
    without the spirit of joy.

The Middle Way says: there's no greater joy than recognizing your faults and changing.

* * *

"Amitabha Song"
¾ Time

Amitabha (say his name)
Amitabha (once again)
Amitabha (vow to be)
Born in the Western Land.

Amitabha (goin' to see)
Amitabha (goin' to meet)

Amitabha (vow to be)
Born in the Blissful Land.

Take me by the hand
To your blissful land.
No more suffering,
Amitabha saves
Everyone who sings…
(chorus)

Born in a lotus pool
With karma clean, pure, and cool,
Blessings and wisdom full.
From Bodhi we'll be irreversible…
(chorus)

Always hold his name,
By day and night the same.
When your life is through,
Amitabha comes to deliver you…
(chorus)

Three-part harmony

Amitabha
Amitabha
Amitabha
Born in the Western land.

Namo Amitabha Buddha
Namo Amitabha Buddha
Namo Amitabha Buddha
Born in the Western Land.

Namo Amitabha (2X)
Namo Amitabha (2X)
Namo Amitabha (2X)
Born in the Western Land.

Heng Chau • May 11, 1978
No town, no houses for miles

Hard work and patience returns us to the source. No mind, a pure heart, that's enough. One thought, a single desire, brings so much trouble.

* * *

A woman in a long, fine, white gown, wearing fancy shoes, and carrying a fresh, long-stemmed flower in her right hand, strolled by and smiled at us as we bowed this morning. Strange sight. We are on the boundary of Los Padres National Forest. Hot, dry, big boulders, semi-arid wilderness. There are no town, no houses for miles. She was alone and on foot. No cars, nothing passed by for at least an hour before and after she appeared.

* * *

"In thought after thought, seeking the Buddha's path above, and in every thought transforming living beings below; hearing the road to Buddhahood is long and far, yet not retreating in fear; contemplating that beings are hard to transform, yet not wearying of this work – as if climbing a ten-thousand foot mountain, determined to gain the peak. As if ascending a nine-story stupa with a will to reach the top – these resolves express the true Bodhi-mind."

from essay on the
"Exhortation to Bring Forth the Bodhi-Mind,"
by Great Master Hsing An (d. A.D. 1735)

Today, what's it like? Hot, still, and dusty. Facing the truth of no self. Want to run, but where? Want to bite through, but it's not time. Conditions aren't ripe. It's early; lots of miles to go, miles to go.

"...The woods are lovely, dark and deep, but I have promises to keep. And miles to go before I sleep, and miles to go before I sleep."

> "Stopping by Woods,"
> by Robert Frost

Heng Sure • May 12, 1978
We chose silence instead

We work to maintain a Ch'an session atmosphere: no talking, no joking, no socializing. We sacrifice courtesy for the sake of concentration. This morning, a van full of Dharma-friends from Los Angeles appeared through the mist. They had risen at 1 A.M. and had driven 8 hours to bring us hot food and good cheer. We felt the impulse to give something in return, to open up, talk, and glow. We chose silence instead. To let down would have sold out our vows.

It seemed natural to swap news, laugh, and share personal energy. But we are learning to maintain single-minded concentration through all states. It tastes bitter at first, but the Buddhadharma is sweeter by far. Holding the rules, silent, mindful, bowing the fog-bound cliffs alone, 100 miles from anywhere, is keeping the faith. Not changing, no matter what, is giving the gift of fearlessness.

"They attain the power of self-mastery and decisive views. They practice fearlessness, apart from the path of words."

> Ten Dwellings Chapter
> Avatamsaka Sutra

Heng Chau • May 12, 1978
At the extreme point

"Truly recognize your faults…"

What is at the heart of my finding fault with others. Just this: desire to be #1. "If everyone else has so many faults, then that makes me better, sets me above and apart" says the false mind. Bowing, especially bowing in silence close to nature, has a way of exposing and deflating a big view of self.

While bowing this morning, I saw how my false pride and arrogance leads me to constantly slight others so I can feel I am #1. The Master's words from last weekend's lecture hung in the Big Sur air and sank deeply into my heart;

> "Every person wants to be #1. No one wants to be #2. Even the most stupid person considers himself to be number one… While we are in the world, however, whatever we do, it's all a part of empty space, and all a portion of the Dharma Realm. Therefore, this is just an attachment on the part of people: attaching to this as number one, and that as number one. Attaching to oneself, being better than others, saying, 'I'm number one in the entire world.' Take a look. No matter who it is, everyone feels he is better than everyone else. No one really admits, 'I don't match up to other people.'… So that's the way people are. People who study Buddhism should have no self, and no number one."

During lunch I remembered a young Dharma Master's remark, "You plant the causes and wait for the results; it happens naturally." I realized I have a lot of faults, the biggest of which is looking for other's faults and avoiding my own. This bad habit amounts to constantly planting impure causes. How could they yield anything but impure results and obstructions? So it's said,

When the cause ground is not straight,
the results will be twisted.

No clouds, no breeze, no shade. The air is almost too thick and torrid to breathe. The flies and gnats crawl in and out of our eyes, mouth, nose, and ears. A fine, dry dust covers the ground, choking every pore. The shoulder is rough, sharp, broken gravel. A good day to go soft and slow and practice the perfection of patience.

A bus, full of rough men, drunk and smoking marijuana, stopped to test our temper. The dust thrown up by their bus hung in the air like talcum powder, filling our lungs, caking on our sweaty skin. The bugs buzzed and swarmed around our heads and faces. The men hooted insults and taunts, threats and obscenities, as they stood around us.

Sometimes things get so hard to take, so absurd and frustrating, that they bend into their opposite. At the extreme point, a situation can turn on itself – difficult becomes easy, intelligence changes into stupidity, pain turns into pleasure, pleasure into pain, suffering opens into joy, and obstructions push you through into a bright clearing.

Today was like that. We kept bowing, without hate or anger in our hearts. Just bearing it, wondering how far it would go before something "gave way." Waiting, bowing, watching it all from an unexpected place of peace and trust deep inside, there and yet not there.

Suddenly the men turned and left. A cool breeze came up from the sea carrying the heat and bugs away. Now everything was totally different as if we walked through a gate into another world. Patience and vigor saved the day. They are our best friends on this trip. Vigor is going on when everything goes against you; patience is not getting angry. Together they form a wall of protecting and nothing can get in to harm you.

As one, for example, establishes a wall around the city
To protect all the citizens,
Patience and vigor are the same:
They protect all Bodhisattvas.

Ten Grounds Chapter
Flower Adornment Sutra

The first words the Abbot spoke to us last week in L.A. were,

"From every side and all directions, all kinds of states appear that are hard to recognize. Not recognizing states, they turn you; if you recognize the states, then you turn them. To turn these states requires a mind of patience... if there is something you can't take, be patient with it, then you can pass through the gate. If you are nervous and can't take it, you won't make it through the gate...

"With patience you can get to the other side. Patience is a boat that carries you across to the other shore."

Could we have been patient today if this seed had not been planted in our minds by a Good Knowing Advisor a week earlier?

Heng Sure • May 13, 1978
Without seeking, I got help in cultivation

The world of the senses is limited; it can't deliver lasting joy. The lonely dive into sensual pleasure is the most empty and disappointing of human experiences.

How many of us are still trying, still carrying the torch of desire, still seeking freedom through love and pleasure? Originally we are alone and complete. We seek liberation from desire, freedom from wanting, freedom from dependency on others. In our own ways we are all cultivating as best we can towards Buddhahood. Falling-in-love is just getting lost temporarily; mistaking a dead-end for a freeway.

"How can one dry up the sea of love and desire and increase the sea of great compassion?"

Entering the Dharma Realm
Vol 2 (BTTS), Avatamsaka Sutra

* * *

Thieves hit us at Lucia. Mysteriously lost specific items, the crutches and comforts I attach to: alarm clock, eating bowls, a special sitting cushion, and extra warm clothes. Now it will be harder to rely on the bell in ch'an, harder to rely on fixed food-measures at lunch, harder to get too comfortable at night in sleep. Some major external places of reliance, stripped away in one swoop. Who was that thief?

Without seeking, I got help in cultivation. This is a rare chance to put down some personal attachments and concentrate on the source of wisdom; the self-sufficient, no-where-dwelling mind. I couldn't manage to drop these crutches myself. Some expedient, wise advisors helped me put them down.

Wrote a verse (in Chinese), to commemorate "the miracle theft," called "San Fan Shih," (三凡事), (Three Common Things). Translated, it says,

> There's never a day you don't eat your fill,
> Fail to wear clothes, and sleep all you will.
> Three common things, if you can't put them down,
> Practice for aeons, you'll not gain the Tao.

Another poem (translated from Chinese original)

> Tomorrow hasn't come, let it save itself.
> Yesterday has gone. No cause for worry.
> Today won't stay. Nowhere to be found.
> Got my heart's wish, seeking nothing.

Buddhist Text Translation Society Publication

Buddhist Text Translation Society
International Translation Institute

http://www.bttsonline.org

1777 Murchison Drive,
Burlingame, California 94010-4504 USA
Phone: (650) 692-5912 Fax: (650) 692-5056

When Buddhism first came to China from India, one of the most important tasks required for its establishment was the translation of the Buddhist scriptures from Sanskrit into Chinese. This work involved a great many people, such as the renowned monk National Master Kumarajiva (fifth century), who led an assembly of over 800 people to work on the translation of the Tripitaka (Buddhist canon) for over a decade. Because of the work of individuals such as these, nearly the entire Buddhist Tripitaka of over a thousand texts exists to the present day in Chinese.

Now the banner of the Buddha's teachings is being firmly planted in Western soil, and the same translation work is being done from Chinese into English. Since 1970, the Buddhist Text Translation Society (BTTS) has been making a paramount contribution toward this goal. Aware that the Buddhist Tripitaka is a work of such magnitude that its translation could never be entrusted to a single person, the BTTS, emulating the translation assemblies of ancient times, does not publish a work until it has passed through four committees for primary translation, revision, editing, and certification. The leaders of these committees are Bhikshus (monks) and Bhikshunis (nuns) who have devoted their lives to the study and practice of the Buddha's teachings. For this reason, all of the works of the BTTS put an emphasis on what the principles of the Buddha's teachings mean in terms of actual practice and not simply hypothetical conjecture.

The translations of canonical works by the Buddhist Text Translation Society are accompanied by extensive commentaries by the Venerable Tripitaka Master Hsuan Hua.

BTTS Publications

Buddhist Sutras. Amitabha Sutra, Dharma Flower (Lotus) Sutra, Flower Adornment (Avatamsaka) Sutra, Heart Sutra & Verses without a Stand, Shurangama Sutra, Sixth Patriarch Sutra, Sutra in Forty-two Sections, Sutra of the Past Vows of Earth Store Bodhisattva, Vajra Prajna Paramita (Diamond) Sutra.

Commentarial Literature. Buddha Root Farm, City of 10 000 Buddhas Recitation Handbook, Filiality: The Human Source, Herein Lies the Treasure-trove, Listen to Yourself Think Everything Over, Shastra on the Door to Understanding the Hundred Dharmas, Song of Enlightenment, The Ten Dharma Realms Are Not Beyond a Single Thought, Venerable Master Hua's Talks on Dharma, Venerable Master Hua's Talks on Dharma during the 1993 Trip to Taiwan, Water Mirror Reflecting Heaven.

Biographical. In Memory of the Venerable Master Hsuan Hua, Pictorial Biography of the Venerable Master Hsü Yün, Records of High Sanghans, Records of the Life of the Venerable Master Hsüan Hua, Three Steps One Bow, World Peace Gathering, News from True Cultivators, Open Your Eyes Take a Look at the World, With One Heart Bowing to the City of 10 000 Buddhas.

Children's Books. Cherishing Life, Human Roots: Buddhist Stories for Young Readers, Spider Web, Giant Turtle, Patriarch Bodhidharma.

Musics, Novels and Brochures. Songs for Awakening, Awakening, The Three Cart Patriarch, City of 10 000 Buddhas Color Brochure, Celebrisi's Journey, Lots of Time Left.

The Buddhist Monthly–Vajra Bodhi Sea is a monthly journal of orthodox Buddhism which has been published by the Dharma Realm Buddhist Association, formerly known as the Sino-American Buddhist Association, since 1970. Each issue contains the most recent translations of the Buddhist canon by the Buddhist Text Translation Society. Also included in each issue are a biography of a great Patriarch of Buddhism from the ancient past, sketches of the lives of contemporary monastics and lay-followers around the world, articles on practice, and other material. The journal is bilingual, Chinese and English.

Please visit our web-site at **www.bttsonline.org** for the latest publications and for ordering information.

Dharma Realm Buddhist Association Branches

The City of Ten Thousand Buddhas
4951 Bodhi Way, Ukiah, CA 95482 USA
Tel: (707) 462-0939   Fax: (707) 462-0949
Website: **http://www.drba.org** Email: **cttb@drba.org**

Buddhist Text Translation Society Online Catalog
Website: **http://www.bttsonline.org**

Institute for World Religions (Berkeley Buddhist Monastery)
2304 McKinley Avenue, Berkeley, CA 94703 USA
Tel: (510) 848-3440 Fax: (510) 548-4551 Email: paramita@drba.org

Dharma Realm Buddhist Books Distribution Society
11th Floor, 85 Chung-hsiao E. Road, Sec. 6, Taipei, Taiwan R.O.C.
Tel: (02) 2786-3022 Fax: (02) 2786-2674 Email: drbbds@ms1.seeder.net

The City of the Dharma Realm
1029 West Capitol Avenue, West Sacramento, CA 95691 USA
Tel: (916) 374-8268 Fax: (916) 374-8234 Email: cdrclasses@yahoo.com

Gold Mountain Monastery
800 Sacramento Street, San Francisco, CA 94108 USA
Tel: (415) 421-6117 Fax: (415) 788-6001

Gold Wheel Monastery
235 North Avenue 58, Los Angeles, CA 90042 USA
Tel: (323) 258-6668 Fax: (323) 258-3619

Gold Buddha Monastery
248 East 11th Avenue, Vancouver, B.C. V5T 2C3 Canada
Tel: (604) 709-0248 Fax: (604) 684-3754 Email: drab@gbm-online.com
Website: http://www.drba/gbm-online.com

Gold Summit Monastery
233 1st Avenue, West Seattle, WA 98119 USA
Tel: (206) 284-6690 Fax: (206) 284-6918
Website: http://www.goldsummitmonastery.org

Gold Sage Monastery
11455 Clayton Road, San Jose, CA 95127-5099 USA
Tel: (408) 923-7243 Fax: (408) 923-1064

The International Translation Institute
1777 Murchison Drive, Burlingame, CA 94010-4504 USA
Tel: (650) 692-5912 Fax: (650) 692-5056

Long Beach Monastery
3361 East Ocean Boulevard, Long Beach, CA 90803 USA
Tel: (562) 438-8902

Blessings, Prosperity, & Longevity Monastery
4140 Long Beach Boulevard, Long Beach, CA 90807 USA
Tel: (562) 595-4966

Avatamsaka Vihara
9601 Seven Locks Road, Bethesda, MD 20817-9997, USA
Tel/Fax: (301) 469-8300 Email: hwa_yean88@msn.com

Avatamsaka Monastery
1009 4th Avenue, S.W. Calgary, AB T2P OK8 Canada
Tel: (403) 234-0644 Fax: (403) 263-0537
Website: http://www.avatamsaka.ca

Dharma Realm Guanyin Sagely Monastery
161, Jalan Ampang, 50450 Kuala Lumpur, West Malaysia
Tel: (03) 2164-8055 Fax: (03) 2163-7118

Prajna Guanyin Sagely Monastery (formerly Tze Yun Tung)
Batu 5½, Jalan Sungai Besi, Salak Selatan, 57100 Kuala Lumpur, Malaysia
Tel: (03) 7982-6560 Fax: (03) 7980-1272

Lotus Vihara
136, Jalan Sekolah, 45600 Batang Berjuntai, Selangor Darul Ehsan, Malaysia
Tel: (03) 3271-9439

Source of Dharma Realm – Lot S130, 2nd Floor, Green Zone, Sungai Wang
Plaza, Jalan Bukit Bintang, 55100 Kuala Lumpur, Malaysia
Tel: (03) 2164-8055

Buddhist Lecture Hall – 31 Wong Nei Chong Road, Top Floor, Happy
Valley, Hong Kong, China
Tel: (02) 2572-7644 Fax: (2) 2572-2850

Dharma Realm Sagely Monastery – 20, Tong-hsi Shan-chuang, Hsing-lung
Village, Liu-kuei Kaohsiung County, Taiwan, R.O.C.
Tel: (07) 689-3717 Fax: (07) 689-3870

Amitabha Monastery – 7, Su-chien-hui, Chih-nan Village, Shou-feng,
Hualien County, Taiwan, R.O.C.
Tel: (07) 865-1956 Fax: (07) 865-3426

Gold Coast Dharma Realm
106 Bonogin Road, Mudgeeraba, Queensland 4213 Australia
Tel/fax: (07) 61-755-228-788 (07) 61-755-227-822

The Dharma Realm Buddhist Association

Mission

The Dharma Realm Buddhist Association (formerly the Sino-American Buddhist Association) was founded by the Venerable Master Hsuan Hua in the United States of America in 1959. Taking the Dharma Realm as its scope, the Association aims to disseminate the genuine teachings of the Buddha throughout the world. The Association is dedicated to translating the Buddhist canon, propagating the Orthodox Dharma, promoting ethical education, and bringing benefit and happiness to all beings. Its hope is that individuals, families, the society, the nation, and the entire world will, under the transforming influence of the Buddhadharma, gradually reach the state of ultimate truth and goodness.

The Founder

The Venerable Master, whose names were An Tse and To Lun, received the Dharma name Hsuan Hua and the transmission of Dharma from Venerable Master Hsu Yun in the lineage of the Wei Yang Sect. He was born in Manchuria, China, at the beginning of the century. At nineteen, he entered the monastic order and dwelt in a hut by his mother's grave to practice filial piety. He meditated, studied the teachings, ate only one meal a day, and slept sitting up. In 1948 he went to Hong Kong, where he established the Buddhist Lecture Hall and other Way-places. In 1962 he brought the Proper Dharma to the West, lecturing on several dozen Mahayana Sutras in the United States. Over the years, the Master established more than twenty monasteries of Proper Dharma under the auspices of the Dharma Realm Buddhist Association and the City of Ten Thousand Buddhas. He also founded centers for the translation of the Buddhist canon and for education to spread the influence of the Dharma in the East and West. The Master manifested the stillness in the United States in 1995. Through his lifelong, selfless dedication to teaching living beings with wisdom and compassion, he influenced countless people to change their faults and to walk upon the pure, bright path to enlightenment.

Dharma Propagation, Buddhist Text Translation, and Education

The Venerable Master Hua's three great vows after leaving the home-life were (1) to propagate the Dharma, (2) to translate the Buddhist Canon, and (3) to promote education. In order to make these vows a reality, the Venerable Master based himself on the Three Principles and the Six Guidelines. Courageously facing every hardship, he founded monasteries, schools, and centers in the West, drawing in living beings and teaching them on a vast scale. Over the years, he founded the following institutions:

The City of Ten Thousand Buddhas and Its Branches

In propagating the Proper Dharma, the Venerable Master not only trained people but also founded Way-places where the Dharma wheel could turn and living beings could be saved. He wanted to provide cultivators with pure places to practice in accord with the Buddha's regulations. Over the years, he founded many Way-places of Proper Dharma. In the United States and Canada, these include the City of Ten Thousand Buddhas; Gold Mountain Monastery; Gold Sage Monastery; Gold Wheel Monastery; Gold Summit Monastery; Gold Buddha Monastery; Avatamsaka Monastery; Long Beach Monastery; the City of the Dharma Realm; Berkeley Buddhist Monastery; Avatamsaka Hermitage; and Blessings, Prosperity, and Longevity Monastery. In Taiwan, there are the Dharma Realm Buddhist Books Distribution Association, Dharma Realm Monastery, and Amitabha Monastery. In Malaysia, there are the Prajna Guanyin Sagely Monastery (formerly Tze Yun Tung Temple), Deng Bi An Monastery, and Lotus Vihara. In Hong Kong, there are the Buddhist Lecture Hall and Cixing Monastery.

Purchased in 1974, the City of Ten Thousand Buddhas is the hub of the Dharma Realm Buddhist Association. The City is located in Talmage, Mendocino County, California, 110 miles north of San Francisco. Eighty of the 488 acres of land are in active use. The remaining acreage consists of meadows, orchards, and woods. With over seventy large buildings containing over 2,000 rooms, blessed with serenity and fresh, clean air, it is the first large Buddhist monastic community in the United States. It is also an international center for the Proper Dharma.

Although the Venerable Master Hua was the Ninth Patriarch in the Wei Yang Sect of the Chan School, the monasteries he founded emphasize all of the five main practices of Mahayana Buddhism (Chan meditation, Pure Land, esoteric, Vinaya (moral discipline), and doctrinal studies). This accords with the Buddha's words: "The Dharma is level and equal, with no high or low." At the City of Ten Thousand Buddhas, the rules of purity are rigorously observed. Residents of the City strive to regulate their own conduct and to cultivate with vigor. Taking refuge in the Proper Dharma, they lead pure and selfless lives, and attain peace in body and mind. The Sutras are expounded and the Dharma wheel is turned daily. Residents dedicate themselves wholeheartedly to making Buddhism flourish. Monks and nuns in all the monasteries take one meal a day, always wear their precept sash, and follow the Three Principles:

> Freezing, we do not scheme.
> Starving, we do not beg.
> Dying of poverty, we ask for nothing.
> According with conditions, we do not change.
> Not changing, we accord with conditions.
> We adhere firmly to our three great principles.
> We renounce our lives to do the Buddha's work.
> We take the responsibility to mold our own destinies.
> We rectify our lives to fulfill the Sanghan's role.
> Encountering specific matters,
>   we understand the principles.
> Understanding the principles,
>   we apply them in specific matters.
> We carry on the single pulse of
>   the Patriarchs' mind-transmission.

The monasteries also follow the Six Guidelines: not contending, not being greedy, not seeking, not being selfish, not pursuing personal advantage, and not lying.

International Translation Institute

The Venerable Master vowed to translate the Buddhist Canon (Tripitaka) into Western languages so that it would be widely accessible throughout the world. In 1973, he founded the International Translation Institute on Washington Street in San Francisco for the purpose of translating Buddhist scriptures into English and other languages. In 1977, the Institute was merged into Dharma Realm Buddhist University as the Institute for the Translation of Buddhist Texts. In 1991, the Venerable Master purchased a large building in Burlingame (south of San Francisco) and established the International Translation Institute there for the purpose of translating and publishing Buddhist texts. To date, in addition to publishing over one hundred volumes of Buddhist texts in Chinese, the Association has published more than one hundred volumes of English, French, Spanish, Vietnamese, and Japanese translations of Buddhist texts, as well as bilingual (Chinese and English) editions. Audio and video tapes also continue to be produced. The monthly journal Vajra Bodhi Sea, which has been in circulation for nearly thirty years, has been published in bilingual (Chinese and English) format in recent years.

In the past, the difficult and vast mission of translating the Buddhist canon in China was sponsored and supported by the emperors and kings themselves. In our time, the Venerable Master encouraged his disciples to cooperatively shoulder this heavy responsibility, producing books and audio tapes and using the medium of language to turn the wheel of Proper Dharma and do the great work of the Buddha. All those who aspire to devote themselves to this work of sages should uphold the Eight Guidelines of the International Translation Institute:

1. One must free oneself from the motives of personal fame and profit.
2. One must cultivate a respectful and sincere attitude free from arrogance and conceit.
3. One must refrain from aggrandizing one's work and denigrating that of others.
4. One must not establish oneself as the standard of correctness and suppress the work of others with one's fault-finding.
5. One must take the Buddha-mind as one's own mind.
6. One must use the wisdom of Dharma-Selecting Vision to determine true principles.
7. One must request Virtuous Elders of the ten directions to certify one's translations.
8. One must endeavor to propagate the teachings by printing Sutras, Shastra texts, and Vinaya texts when the translations are certified as being correct.

These are the Venerable Master's vows, and participants in the work of translation should strive to realize them.

Instilling Goodness Elementary School, Developing Virtue Secondary School, Dharma Realm Buddhist University

"Education is the best national defense." The Venerable Master Hua saw clearly that in order to save the world, it is essential to promote good education. If we want to save the world, we have to bring about a complete change in people's minds and guide them to cast out unwholesomeness and to pursue goodness. To this end the Master founded Instilling Goodness Elementary School in 1974, and Developing Virtue Secondary School and Dharma Realm Buddhist University in 1976.

In an education embodying the spirit of Buddhism, the elementary school teaches students to be filial to parents, the secondary school teaches students to be good citizens, and the university teaches such virtues as humaneness and righteousness. Instilling Goodness Elementary School and Developing Virtue Secondary School combine the best of contemporary and traditional methods and of Western and Eastern cultures. They emphasize moral virtue and spiritual development, and aim to guide students to become good and capable citizens who will benefit humankind. The schools offer a bilingual (Chinese/English) program where boys and girls study separately. In addition to standard academic courses, the curriculum includes ethics, meditation, Buddhist studies, and so on, giving students a foundation in virtue and guiding them to understand themselves and explore the truths of the universe. Branches of the schools (Sunday schools) have been established at branch monasteries with the aim of propagating filial piety and ethical education.

Dharma Realm Buddhist University, whose curriculum focuses on the Proper Dharma, does not merely transmit academic knowledge. It emphasizes a foundation in virtue, which expands into the study of how to help all living beings discover their inherent nature. Thus, Dharma Realm Buddhist University advocates a spirit of shared inquiry and free exchange of ideas, encouraging students to study various canonical texts and use different experiences and learning styles to tap their inherent wisdom and fathom the meanings of those texts. Students are encouraged to practice the principles they have understood and apply the Buddhadharma in their lives, thereby nurturing their wisdom and virtue. The University aims to produce outstanding individuals of high moral character who will be able to bring benefit to all sentient beings.

Sangha and Laity Training Programs

In the Dharma-ending Age, in both Eastern and Western societies there are very few monasteries that actually practice the Buddha's regulations and strictly uphold the precepts. Teachers with genuine wisdom and understanding, capable of guiding those who aspire to pursue careers in Buddhism, are very rare. The Venerable Master founded the Sangha and Laity Training Programs in 1982 with the goals of raising the caliber of the Sangha, perpetuating the Proper Dharma, providing professional training for Buddhists around the world on both practical and theoretical levels, and transmitting the wisdom of the Buddha.

The Sangha Training Program gives monastics a solid foundation in Buddhist studies and practice, training them in the practical affairs of Buddhism and Sangha management. After graduation, students will be able to assume various responsibilities related to Buddhism in monasteries, institutions, and other settings. The program emphasizes a thorough knowledge of Buddhism, understanding of the scriptures, earnest cultivation, strict observance of precepts, and the development of a virtuous character, so that students will be able to propagate the Proper Dharma and perpetuate the Buddha's wisdom. The Laity Training Program offers courses to help laypeople develop correct views, study and practice the teachings, and understand monastic regulations and ceremonies, so that they will be able to contribute their abilities in Buddhist organizations.

Let Us Go Forward Together

In this Dharma-ending Age when the world is becoming increasingly dangerous and evil, the Dharma Realm Buddhist Association, in consonance with its guiding principles, opens the doors of its monasteries and centers to those of all religions and nationalities. Anyone who is devoted to humaneness, righteousness, virtue, and the pursuit of truth, and who wishes to understand him or herself and help humankind, is welcome to come study and practice with us. May we together bring benefit and happiness to all living beings.

Verse of Transference

May the merit and virtue accrued from this work,
Adorn the Buddhas' Pure Lands,
Repaying four kinds of kindness above,
And aiding those suffering in the paths below.

May those who see and hear of this,
All bring forth the resolve for Bodhi,
And when this retribution body is over,
Be born together in the Land of Ultimate Bliss.

Dharma Protector Wei Tuo Bodhisattva